A HISTORY OF PHILOSOPHY
Volume 2
The Modern Age to Romanticism

A HISTORY
OF
PHILOSOPHY

Volume 2

The Modern Age to Romanticism

ANDERS WEDBERG

CLARENDON PRESS · OXFORD

1982

Oxford University Press, Walton Street, Oxford OX2 6DP

London Glasgow New York Toronto
Delhi Bombay Calcutta Madras Karachi
Kuala Lumpur Singapore Hong Kong Tokyo
Nairobi Dar es Salaam Cape Town
Melbourne Auckland
and associates in
Beirut Berlin Ibadan Mexico City Nicosia

Published in the United States by
Oxford University Press, New York

First published in 1959 in a Swedish edition entitled
Filosofins Historia: Nyare tiden till romantiken. New edition
(including Appendix) first published 1970

© Anders Wedberg 1959, 1970

This translation © Bergljot Wedberg 1982

British Library Cataloguing in Publication Data
Wedberg, Anders
    A history of philosophy.
    Vol. 2: The modern age to Romanticism
    1. Philosophy, Comparative
    I. Title   II. Filosofins historia. English
    109   B799
    ISBN 0-19-824640-4
        0-19-824692-7 paperback

Library of Congress Cataloging in Publication Data
Wedberg, Anders, 1913-1976.
    A history of philosophy.
    Translation of: Filosofins historia.
    Includes index.
    Contents: v. 1. Antiquity and the Middle Ages.
—v. 2. The modern age to romanticism.
    1. Philosophy—History.   I. Title.
B99.S82W413   190   81-22418
ISBN 0-19-824640-4
    0-19-824692-7 paperback

Typeset by Anne Joshua Associates, Oxford
Printed in Great Britain
at the University Press, Oxford
by Eric Buckley
Printer to the University

Note on the translation

Several people have been involved in the translation into English of the present work. The translation of volumes I and II was begun by Mr John Swaffield. Volume III was first translated by Professor David E. Johnson. In the end, however, Wedberg himself embarked on a translation and produced a version which seems to be essentially his own work. Dr Mark Platts went over the whole of this version and had several discussions of it with Wedberg in 1973. The translation as it now appears is substantially the one Wedberg left behind when he died in 1978. Some polishing has been done by Hans-Jörgen Ulfstedt (vol. I) and Torkel Franzén (vols. II and III) of the Philosophy Department, University of Stockholm, by myself, and by the staff of the Oxford University Press. The proofs were read by Torkel Franzén. Thanks are due to Professor W. H. Walsh, formerly Professor of Logic and Metaphysics in the University of Edinburgh, for his advice and assistance in the preparation of the English edition.

Dag Prawitz

Contents

Introduction

1. PROBLEMS AND TRENDS

Just as it is impossible to understand medieval philosophy apart from Christianity and the Bible, so modern philosophy is incomprehensible unless seen in relation to the growth of science. It would be a mistake however to presume that a sudden change in the intellectual climate occurred at a particular time. If philosophy was primarily a satellite of religion during the Middle Ages, in the period considered here its course was directed by the two centres of force, religion and science. From a position initially subordinate to religion, science gradually made gains and acquired an equal or superior influence.

In the fifteenth and sixteenth centuries, during the Renaissance, a number of rather bizarre thinkers appeared. They often trod the pantheist's or the mystic's path to God while at the same time anticipating later scientific and philosophical views (e.g. the infinity of the universe). One of the most interesting was Giordano Bruno, who was burned as a heretic in Rome in 1600. The many system builders of the seventeenth century, among whom Descartes, Spinoza, and Leibniz are usually given first place, each had the ambition to erect a unified philosophical doctrine which he hoped would comprise the truths of religion, the principles of morality, a metaphysical explanation of the nature of things, and the results of science. They regarded philosophy as a universal science in which the fundamental propositions of the various branches of knowledge would be derivable from evident rational principles. On the question of the relation between religion and metaphysics on the one hand and empirical science on the other, they represented a harmonizing tendency. Their conception of the position of philosophy can be illustrated, as in diagram (A).

It is interesting to compare such seventeenth-century

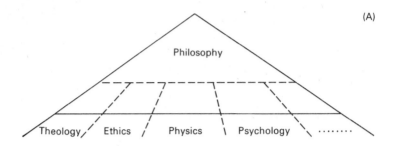

philosophers as Descartes and Leibniz with the early Greek
natural philosophers as well as with the thirteenth-century
Scholastics. With the former they had in common a uni-
versality of interests and an active preoccupation with the
natural sciences. As a legacy from the latter they had faith
in the possibility of a unified, deductive doctrinal system.

The great seventeenth-century philosophers have been
called prophets of science. There is much truth in this description. The rapid development of science and its many
technical applications filled them with an enthusiastic optimism as to the possibility of man's obtaining knowledge and
using it to improve himself and his world. Francis Bacon
was one of the first to preach this scientific gospel, which
leavened practically all of seventeenth-century philosophy.
Newton said of himself that he was like a child picking up
pebbles and shells from the shore of the ocean. Some of
the philosophers, with a *naïveté* in sharp contrast to Newton's
modesty, believed that an all-out intellectual effort could
quickly give the solution, in principle, to all the great scientifc
problems.

The mechanistic world view, which took form during the
seventeenth century, had as many adherents among physicists
as among philosophers. At that time physicist and philosopher
were often combined in the same person. This mechanistic
view will be sketched, with special emphasis on the contributions of the philosophers, in the first chapter, The Mechanistic World View in the Seventeenth and Eighteenth
Centuries.

A notable result of the intellectual labours of Descartes
and his continental followers was the revival and further

development of the ideal of a deductive science, which goes back to Plato and Aristotle. This will be discussed in the second chapter, The Revival of the Platonic–Aristotelian Ideal of Science.

The great systems on which the seventeenth-century philosophers pinned so many hopes appear to us like ruined cathedrals, where we feel wonder, respect, and alienation. In the third chapter, The Great Systems, I shall give a very brief survey of the systems of Descartes, Spinoza, and Leibniz.

The British philosophers of the empiricist tradition initiated by Locke had an attitude to contemporary science different from that of Descartes and his continental adherents. Broadly speaking, it may be said that they ceded to natural science the investigation of material reality. To philosophy they assigned the task of studying the nature of knowledge; and as they took knowledge to be given in the form of experiences of the mind ("ideas", "perceptions"), this epistemological task seemed to them to be part of the more extensive task of investigating the human mind. In pursuing this larger task, they thought they were using the same experimental methods that contemporary scientists applied in their study of nature (see the accompanying table).

	Natural Science	Philosophy
Object of Study	The material world	Mental reality (including knowledge)
Method of Study	The experimental method	

The original aim of the empiricist epistemology was to find a criterion by which it would be possible to distinguish between meaningful, well-founded assertions about reality and those that are meaningless or impossible to know. This led to two distinct questions: (i) What "ideas" can we form and express? (ii) What propositions can we know? The British empiricists' attitude to these questions, especially as formulated by Hume, will be discussed in the fourth chapter, The Empiricist Theory of Knowledge in Britain.

British empiricist psychology, which despite its experimental programme assumed an essentially impressionistic, introspective character, has been of historical importance ("the associationist psychology") but today it is of only slight independent interest. I shall therefore explain it merely to the extent necessary for an understanding of the epistemological ideas.

The epistemological reflection of the empiricists was aroused by the contrasts between experimental natural science, which had achieved so many brilliant results in such a short time, and the tradition of speculative philosophy, which seemed to have accomplished so little in 2,000 years. The systems of Plato, Aristotle, the Scholastics, and the seventeenth-century system builders were the first objects of their criticism. The targets soon changed, however: for the religious Berkeley the target became science itself, and for the atheist Hume it became religion, among other things. Some of the critical applications that the empiricists made of their basic ideas are treated in the fifth chapter, The Classical Empiricist Critique.

The contrast between the mechanistic world view and the immediate evidence of the senses gave urgency to another problem: How is the external world related to our sense perceptions? Whereas Locke adopted a mechanistic world view, Berkeley and Hume arrived at phenomenalist conclusions: the propositions of natural science describe only features of our perceptions. This line of thought is presented in the sixth chapter, Experience and the External World.

The philosophy of the Enlightenment, which played such an important political role in the eighteenth century, often contained as its principal elements the mechanistic world view, empiricist epistemology, and the revolt against authority, in about equal proportions. In a presentation which, unlike this one, would try to do justice to the cultural aspects of philosophy, the philosophy of the Enlightenment would deserve a broad treatment. I shall here, with respect, bypass it.

Towards the end of the eighteenth century, Kant's critique of reason set off a reaction against the mechanistic world view and empiricist epistemology, and indeed against the entire philosophy of the Enlightenment. Kant's conception of philosophy, as we find it in his critique of reason, has much in common with that of the British empiricists. Philosophy is the study of human reason which manifests itself in our ideas (concepts) and thoughts (judgements). But whereas the empiricists thought they were applying the experimental method of natural science to epistemology, Kant wanted to employ a special philosophical method, which he himself described by the adjective "transcendental". In actual fact, his method contains a good deal of the introspective impressionism that is found in British empiricism. It is so complex in other ways, however, that it defies all attempts to classify it in a simple manner. The accompanying table illustrates Kant's view on the relationship between science and philosophy:

	Natural Science	Psychology	Philosophy ("Critique Of Reason")
Object of Study	The Material World	Mental Reality	Mental reality ("Reason")
Method of Study	Experimental		"Transcendental"

According to empiricism, as formulated by Hume, we can never definitively verify any general propositions outside those of pure mathematics. Kant, in contrast to Hume, wished to show that certain very general propositions, which he considered to be fundamental to contemporary science, possess a validity that no future experience can ever impair. The parts of his critique of reason that are most closely concerned with this problem will be discussed in the seventh chapter, Kant on Synthetic *a priori* Judgements. When considering his argument, I shall as far as possible pare away the most abstruse and problematic of the psychological theories he presupposed.

The elements of Kant's argument which are the seeds of the reaction to the mechanistic world picture and to the Enlightenment's faith in reason are taken up in the eighth chapter: Kant's Copernican Revolution and its Aftermath. There we shall be concerned with the beginnings of the

German romantic philosophy of the nineteenth century and its many offshoots up to our own times. Although Kant had hoped to lay the philosophical foundations for natural science, his ideas led to a rift between philosophy and science.

The romantic conception of philosophy superficially had much in common with that of the seventeenth-century system builders. For the romantics, too, philosophy was a universal deductive science, but the dissimilarities outweigh the similarities. The romantic idea of deduction, which was crystallized by Hegel in his so-called dialectic method was a parody of genuine logical deduction. Whereas the seventeenth-century system builders worked in close contact with the science of their time, the German romantics of the early nineteenth century all too often tended to ignore scientific facts.

I

The Mechanistic World View in the Seventeenth and Eighteenth Centuries

2. THE NEW PHYSICS

Of all the significant events that presaged the long-portended and late-completed passage from the Middle Ages to modern times, none was as important as the birth of experimental physics during the sixteenth and seventeenth centuries. Although scientific investigation in those centuries provided valuable new insights into many different subjects, there can be no doubt that physics (understood in a wide sense of the word) was more responsible than any other science for the subsequent changes in world outlook. The factors that distinguished the method of the new physics from late medieval thought on physical problems were above all the following four:

(a) The pursuit of systematic observations and experiments;
(b) The search for measurable quantities characteristic of observable events;
(c) The search for exact, simple, and general mathematical relations between various measurable quantities;
(d) The attempt to arrange the discovered mathematical laws in deductive systems along the lines of Euclid's geometry.

Concerning (a) and (b) it should be pointed out that the development of science and of technology went hand in hand and that the possibility of observation and experiment increased rapidly with the use of the new technical devices (telescopes, microscopes, and so on). As for (c) and (d), the developments of experimental physics and of theoretical mathematics proceeded in unison; without the new algebra (Vieta, Descartes, and others), analytic geometry (Descartes, Fermat, and others), and the infinitesimal calculus (Newton,

Leibniz, and others), the new physical theories could not have been formulated.

This is not the place to give an account of the development of physics during this period. Some of the milestones were Copernicus's revival of the heliocentric hypothesis, stated already in antiquity, Kepler's discovery of the planetary laws, Stevin's invention of the parallelogram of forces, Galileo's investigations into the laws of falling bodies and his discovery of the law of inertia, Huygens's many investigations concerning, among other things, the motion of the pendulum and centrifugal force, Newton's discovery of the law of gravity and his great synthesis of earlier results in the *Philosophiae Naturalis Principia Mathematica* (1687).

Galileo–Newtonian mechanics is a mathematically formulated physical theory with a very large range of empirical applications. This theory is not identical with what may be called the mechanist world picture. The latter is a philosophical theory, undoubtedly stimulated by Newtonian mechanics but containing a series of speculative assumptions which are not theorems of this mechanics and which are difficult to state with exactness. Newton was himself only a moderate and doubtful adherent of mechanistic philosopy; but that philosophy was the prevailing opinion among the philosophers and physicists of the seventeenth and eighteenth centuries. Among the philosophers who developed, or associated themselves with, mechanistic philosophy, in one or another of its forms, may be noted the Englishman Thomas Hobbes (1588–1697), the Frenchman Pierre Gassendi (1592–1677) and René Descartes (1596–1650), the Dutchman Benedict Spinoza (1632–77), the Englishman John Locke (1632–1704), and the German Gottfried Wilhelm Leibniz (1646–1716). Spinoza and Leibniz, however, accepted mechanism only with important metaphysical reservations and additions. In the eighteenth century several of the French philosophers of the Enlightenment espoused mechanism: Voltaire (1694–1788), de la Mettrie (1709–51), Diderot (1713–84), and Holbach (1723–89) were all mechanists. The mechanist doctrine appears as a constituent (although a subordinate one) in Immanuel Kant's (1724–1804) critique of reason. Of the physicsts who embraced or sympathized with the mechanist doctrine may be mentioned the Italian Galileo Galilei (1564–1642), the Englishman Robert Boyle (1627–91), and Isaac Newton himself (1642–1726). Whereas the philosophers often considered the mechanistic system as an established truth, the physicists were usually more cautious, considering it merely as a plausible hypothesis.

Mechanism was an attitude which comprised many more or less divergent views. Without any pretensions to completeness or impartiality, I shall give an account of some of these theories in the next three sections.

3. THE CORPUSCULAR THEORY

A. *Corpuscles*

Every physical phenomenon can, according to the corpuscular theory, be explained as a phenomenon of motion, the motion of bodies. All bodies are composed of certain very small bodies, corpuscles or particles, thought of in analogy with, say, pebbles. As to whether matter ultimately consists of physically indivisible corpuscles, atoms, or whether all bodies are, in principle at least, physically divisible, opinions differed. Atomism was defended with varying degrees of conviction by many (Gassendi, Boyle, Huygens, Newton), but firmly opposed by thinkers such as Descartes and Leibniz.

It is interesting to consider why the corpuscular theory had so great an appeal for the philosophers of the seventeenth century. It was a new version of the atomism of antiquity, and the lively study of ancient philosophy naturally contributed to its popularity. An essential part of the explanation of its success must also be sought in the new physics. The theory of motion of rigid bodies was the physical discipline first and most rapidly developed. Presumably, another reason is that the corpuscular theory fulfilled a very rigorous requirement of perspicuity and conceptual simplicity. What is more easily understood than, say, a game of billiards? And how intellectually satisfying to believe that the entire physical universe is essentially similar to that well-known game!

B. *Primary and secondary qualities*

The general tendency at the time was to assume that matter can be completely described by means of the conceptual apparatus of Galileo–Newtonian mechanics. If a concept (or a quality, a property, a relation) could not be defined on the basis of this conceptual apparatus, it was felt that it had no application to the material world. In accordance with this general trend, it was thought, as it had been by the Greek Atomists, that such sensible qualities as colour, sound, taste, and odour cannot be ascribed to matter, that they exist in our subjective experience only. For the distinction between those qualities that can, and those that cannot, be ascribed to material reality, Locke gave currency to the terms "primary" and "secondary" qualities. Thus, there was an inclination to take only the conceptual apparatus of Galileo–Newtonian mechanics as primary and to treat all concepts not reducible to that basis as secondary.

Descartes went furthest in reducing the primary conceptual apparatus to a minimum. A complete description of material phenomena should be possible, he thought, merely on the basis of kinematic concepts, i.e geometric concepts, the concepts of time and position, and the concept of 'matter' or 'extended substance'. Leibniz insisted that physics must also presuppose 'force' as a primitive concept. In Newtonian mechanics the concept of 'mass' appears as still another primitive concept. (Locke and others considered 'solidity' to be a primary property of matter.)

Different thinkers advanced different reasons for the way in which they distinguished between primary and secondary qualities. The total set of reasons presented was large, and the weight of evidence was highly variable (cf. § § 24 and 25). Here, as with regard to the other components of the mechanistic philosophy, one of the deepest motives was to be found in mechanics itself; it was taken for granted that the primitive concepts that seemed to suffice for mechanics were sufficient also for a complete description of material reality.

C. *Matter and force*

In Newtonian mechanics the concepts of mass and force occur as two fundamental magnitudes logically independent of one another. The universe is seen to be a system of bodies, possessing mass and affecting each other through different kinds of forces. This view of the physical universe very soon gave rise to philosophical misgivings.

To those who base their picture of reality above all on their impressions of sight, the forces of Newtonian mechanics must appear as mysterious quantities. The empiricist Berkeley made the point that the nature of force was every bit as incomprehensible as that of divine grace, and that anyone prepared to accept Newton's dynamics ought not to have any qualms about accepting Christian theology as well.

Before the discovery of the electro-magnetic field in the nineteenth century, it was easy enough to be convinced that the forces of mechanics are merely a kind of mathematical fiction which we make use of to describe the motions of bodies in a simple way. If a body k with mass m is in a particular (spatial and temporal) relation to certain other bodies, we say that a force of magnitude f affects k. If a force of magnitude f affects k, then k receives an acceleration a satisfying the equation:

(i) $f = a \cdot m$.

Thus the force occurs as the middle term in the pair of hypothetical statements:

(ii) Given a certain configuration of mass, a certain force exists;

(iii) Given a certain force, a certain acceleration results.

If the middle term is eliminated, we arrive at the conclusion:

(iv) Given a certain configuration of mass, a certain acceleration results.

It may now be argued that the only things that "actually exist" in physical reality are configurations of mass, velocities, and accelerations, and that forces are mere mathematical fictions introduced to facilitate concise description of the relation between configurations and accelerations.

Ideas such as these appeared early in the eighteenth century. Berkeley explained in his work *De Motu* (1721) that terms such as force, gravity, and attraction, while useful in calculating motion, convey no information concerning the nature of motion and do not designate distinct qualities: they are only mathematical hypotheses. He also characterized them as "mathematical entities which have no stable essence (*stabilem essentiam*) in the nature of things (*in rerum natura*)".[1] Hume's critique of the concept of cause (cf. chapter VI) was expressly intended to apply also to the concept of force. Although he never explained in detail his view of the Newtonian concept of force, it seems likely that it went in the same direction as Berkeley's.

Alternatively, it was tempting to suppose that equation (i) contains a definition of the concept of force. Let us assume that a force is always exerted by one body upon another. In order, then, to define the concept of force we need only define the meaning of the entire statement:

(v)   The body k exerts a force f upon the body k'.

In accordance with (i), it seems that we may now assign to this expression the meaning:

(vi) f is the product of the acceleration a, which k' receives from k and the mass m of k'.

Here we presuppose as known the meaning of the statement:

(vii) k' receives the acceleration a from k.

This meaning does not have to hide any logical riddle, however. Can it not be taken to be simply:

(viii) a is the difference between the acceleration which k' would have if k were eliminated and the acceleration which k' has when k is present?

The ideas of the French mathematician d'Alembert in his *Treatise on Dynamics* (*Traité de dynamiques* 1743) may be interpreted along these lines. (Otherwise, the above formulation is essentially borrowed from a much later work, Karl Pearson's *The Grammar of Science* (1892).)

[1] *The Works of George Berkeley* (Oxford, 1901), vol. i, p. 506.

There is also a contrasting way of considering the relation between bodies and forces. It may be argued that a body manifests itself only by means of its actions and that it acts only by means of the forces it exerts. In this way we arrive at the idea of a body as being nothing but a centre of forces. This dynamic concept of matter goes back ultimately to Leibniz, according to whom the monads, the simplest building blocks of the universe, are forces. The idea appears in more explicit formulation among several later thinkers of the eighteenth century. Kant assumed that bodies are built up from elementary particles, which in turn are systems of concentric attracting and repelling forces. The Italian Boscovich (1711–87) worked out a similar but more elaborate theory.

This dynamic concept of matter is, of course, pure conjecture, without basis in experimental physics. It is, nevertheless, interesting as a step away from mechanism's originally all too solid concept of matter.

D. *Determinism*

As a piece of philosophical jargon the word "determinism" is especially imprecise. When saying that mechanistic philosophy involves a deterministic outlook, I am thinking of statements such as the following by Spinoza:

> No particular thing . . . can exist or be determined in its mode of action except by being determined as to its existence and mode of action by a cause that likewise is finite and has a determined existence. And this cause, in turn, cannot exist and be determined in its mode of action save by another cause, etc. in infinitum.[2]

His words show that he has in mind here causal chains of the type shown in diagram (B)

(B)

in which each preceding link is the cause of its successor, and which are infinite in both directions. He assumes that

[2] Spinoza, *The Ethics*, I, proposition XXVIII.

every particular or finite object is a link in some such chain. Leibniz says:

That everything occurs in a predetermined way is as certain as the fact that three times three make nine. The predetermination consists in the fact that all things are dependent on one another like the links of a chain, and that everything is going to occur as infallibly before its occurrence as it infallibly has occurred after its occurrence.

The old poets such as Homer and others have spoken of this as the golden chain that Jupiter lets hang from heaven, which will not break, however many links are added to it. And this chain consists in the sequence of causes and effects.

Each cause has its particular effect which it would bring about if it were actually acting alone. If the causes are acting in unison, a certain infallible effect or outcome arises out of their combination, in agreement with the magnitude of the forces, and this is true whether two, or ten, or one thousand, or even infinitely many, things are acting together, as is actually the case in the world. . .

From this it is apparent that everything happens in a mathematical, i.e. infallible, manner in the whole wide world, so that if someone could possess sufficient insight into the inner parts of things and enough memory and intelligence to take account of all circumstances, he would be a prophet and see the future in the present as in a mirror.[3]

Like Spinoza, Leibniz is thinking of causal chains, but his chains admit a more complex structure (see diagram (C)).

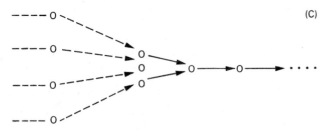

(C)

The number of causes jointly contributing to a single effect can even be infinite. In addition to this generalization of Spinoza's concept of causal chains, Leibniz's statement contains an idea that does not appear in Spinoza's, namely that the causal structure of the world makes it possible for

[3] Leibniz, *Hauptschriften zur Grundlegung der Philosophie* (Leipzig, 1903), vol. ii, pp. 129–30 (from a paper entitled 'About Fate').

a sufficiently great intelligence to predict the future. Although Spinoza does not assert the possibility of such prediction, there can hardly be any doubt that he would have been prepared to subscribe to this idea of Leibniz's. For both these philosophers, therefore, determinism comprises two assumptions, namely: (i) the world is a structure of causal chains, and (ii) it is in principle possible to predict the future. Let us look a bit more closely at assumption (ii) and try to make its import somewhat more precise.

Suppose that *S* is a "system" (for example, some sort of machine) which at different moments in time is in different states (say, the parts of the machine taking up various positions in relation to each other). There exist a number of states of the system *S* that are possible. Let us suppose further that there is a language by which we can describe this system *S*, its possible states, and its actual states at different moments of time. In this language we state rules for the behaviour of the system *S*, and we collect a number of such rules into a theory. We may say that such a theory *T* is deterministic if from *T* and a complete description of a state of *S*, one and only one complete description of every subsequent state of *S* logically follows. If, moreover, *T* is true, then from *T* and the complete, true description of a state of *S* there follows the complete, true description of each subsequent state of *S*. (These words are far from perfect as a general explanation of the notion of a deterministic theory. A formally exact and intuitively fairly adequate definition is impossible without the employment of a rather complex logical technique. Grave philosophical problems are offered by the ideas of a "law" and a "state description".)

Using this terminology, I believe that assumption (ii) above can be expressed in the form of the following postulate:

(P) The entire universe is a system for which there exists a true, deterministic theory.

The existence of the theory whose existence is asserted in (P) should, of course, be understood in such a way as to be compatible with the fact that our human intelligence is too limited to be able to formulate it or to utilize it in full for purposes of prediction.

The idea (P) was given its most clear-cut formulation by the French mathematician Laplace. In the introduction to his *Analytical Theory of Probabilities* (*Théorie analytique des probabilités*, 1812), he wrote:

Given an intelligence that could comprehend all the forces by which nature is animated and the respective situation of the beings who compose it for one instant—an intelligence sufficiently vast to submit these data to analysis—it would embrace in the same formula the movements of the greatest bodies of the universe and those of the lightest atom; for it nothing would be uncertain, and the future, like the past, would be present to its eyes. The human mind offers in the perfection it has been able to give to astronomy a feeble idea of this intelligence. . . . All these efforts in the search for truth tend to make it continually approach the vast intelligence we have just mentioned, but from which it will always remain infinitely removed.[4]

The deterministic theory advanced here by Laplace is neutral with regard to the distinction between past and future; it thus fulfils a more stringent condition than that imposed by my definition above upon a deterministic theory. In this statement Laplace points to a historically very important reason for the belief in determinism which was so characteristic a part of the mechanist philosophy. Within certain bounds, Newtonian mechanics is a deterministic theory in the given sense for our solar system; and it was believed that it should, in principle, be possible to extend this mechanics to a universal deterministic theory. In the opinion of certain historians, another cause of seventeenth-century determinism was the belief, handed down from the Middle Ages, in the orderly workings of divine providence. If God acts according to laws, and if nature is God's creation, then it is reasonable to suppose that natural events exhibit a strict regularity.

4. MATTER AND CONSCIOUSNESS

A. *Cartesian dualism*

The idea that mental phenomena have a purely material nature was first put forward by the Greek Atomists. The mechanistic view was associated with this idea in certain thinkers of the seventeenth century (e.g. in Hobbes) and more often in the eighteenth century, among the French

[4] P. S. Laplace, *A Philosophical Essay on Probabilities* (New York, 1951), p. 4.

philosophers of the Enlightenment (e.g. Holbach). This was not, however, the prevailing philosophical opinion. The Platonic concept of the soul, which was incorporated into Christian theology by St. Augustine and which dominated medieval thinking, was further sharpened by Descartes's theory of the body and the soul as two essentially different kinds of substance. This theory was to form the basis for the greater part of the seventeenth-century discussions on mind and matter.

Descartes asserts that souls are thinking but not extended substances, whereas bodies are extended but not thinking. When he speaks of bodies, he is obviously thinking, in consonance with the corpuscular theory, of solid bodies. The adjective "thinking" means for Descartes about the same thing as the more neutral adjectives "conscious", "apprehending", "perceiving", mean to us. His theory includes the following propositions:

(a) No substance is both thinking and extended;

(b) A substance is a soul if and only if it is thinking;

(c) A substance is a body if and only if it is extended.

Descartes seems to consider the following two assertions, borrowed ultimately from Plato's *Phaedo*, as corollaries of the foregoing three propositions:

(d) Every soul is simple and indivisible;

(e) Every body is compound and divisible.

Descartes's views on the possible location of the soul are not too clear. He speaks of the pineal gland of the brain as the site of the soul, and certain of his formulations give the impression that the soul actually inhabits the pineal gland. Other formulations, however, give the impression that the soul is not located anywhere in space.

This distinction between bodies and minds reappears in Spinoza in the form of a distinction between things, which are modes of the attribute of extension, and ideas, which are modes of the attribute of thinking. In Leibniz it recurs in the form of a distinction between the divisible, material things and the simple, perceiving substances, the monads. Of the British empiricists, Locke was dubious of Descartes's postulate (a), but his successor Berkeley apparently gave his allegiance to an essentially Cartesian concept of mind.

The clear-cut "dualism" introduced by the Cartesian concept of mind can be explained historically as a consequence of the new mechanics. The Cartesian notion gained its dominant position, it seems, because of the following two factors. (1) Mechanics described material events without the help of the anthropomorphic, psychological analogies found in the older, Aristotelian-Scholastic philosophy of nature. The new mechanics thus deprived matter of its "soul". (2) Under the influence of Plato's philosophy, Christian theology held the existence and immortality of the human soul to be fundamental articles of faith. From (1) and (2) a dualism such as that of Descartes's follows readily.

B. *Material and mental determinism*

What was stated above (§3 D) on determinism requires an important supplementary observation. Postulate (P) can be formulated in more detail in several different ways. If the Cartesian distinction between mind and matter is granted, then it is natural to give the postulate the following form.

Assuming the distinction between matter and consciousness to be clearly understood—which, of course, it is not—we may suppose that the distinction between a material law (a law concerning matter) and a mental law (a law concerning consciousness) is also understood. By a material theory I shall mean here a collection of material laws, and by a mental theory, a collection of mental laws. We may then say that a material theory is deterministic if, from the theory together with a complete description of one material state of the world, there follows one and only one complete description of each of its subsequent material states. Let us say that we describe a mental state of the world at a given moment when we describe the states of all the minds at that moment. Analogously, we may then say that a mental theory is deterministic if, from the theory together with a complete description of a mental state of the world, there follows one and only one complete description of each of its subsequent mental states. Using this terminology, one can substitute two more specific postulates for the general determinist postulate (P).

(P1) There exists a (possibly unknown) true deterministic material theory.

(P2) There exists a (possibly unknown) true deterministic mental theory.

It is not difficult to understand that these two postulates, (P1) and (P2), must have seemed quite plausible under the influence of the advance of natural science. Since the physical laws already established did not contain any reference to mental factors, it seemed likely that it was possible in principle to set up a theory such as that assumed in (P1). From this it was just a short step to the analogous postulate (P2). Cartesian dualism worked in the same direction. If minds and bodies are of as disparate a character as Descartes assumed, it appears difficult to understand an influence of mind on body, or of body on mind, on analogy with other, more perspicuous, cases of interaction.

Descartes himself assumed that interaction between body and mind sometimes occurs in man, and thus that man's mind sometimes influences his body. Although Descartes's own formulations are not clear enough to be interpreted with any feeling of conviction, it seems likely that he was prepared to consider this assumed influence as a counter-instance to (P1). Descartes is on his way to (P1) however, in so far as he assumes interaction only with many reservations. It does not occur in animals, which are soulless automata, and even among humans it occurs only rarely. In man as well, the body functions on the whole as an automaton. When in exceptional cases the mind does bring about a mechanical effect on the corpuscles of the brain, this effect, according to Descartes, is of a very special kind. He was aware of the principle of mechanics that the sum of the products of the masses and velocities (thought of as undirected scalar or one-dimensional magnitudes) of all the particles of an isolated system is constant. He was not aware, though, that this principle is also valid when the velocity is defined as a vectorial (directionally determined, multi-dimensional) magnitude. Here he believed that he had found a loophole through which the mind could intervene in the mechanical functioning of the brain; the mind can change the direction of motion of a particle (its vectorial velocity) though not its (scalar) velocity. Leibniz, who in contrast to Descartes knew of the law of constancy of the sum of vectorial motions, could not accept this loophole.

The so-called Occasionalists, Geulincx (1624–69) and Malebranche (1638–1715), as well as Spinoza and Leibniz, denied the possibility of interaction between mind and body. (The Occasionalists believed that when interaction seems to occur what really happens is that God adapts mental and physical events to each other.) For Spinoza and Leibniz, in any event, this denial implies an upholding of postulates (P1) and (P2), or of tenets highly similar to them.

Spinoza believed (cf. chapter III) that each material thing, each mode of the attribute of extension, is an aspect of something which from another point of view is something mental, a mode of the attribute of thought. If this is kept in mind, and if cognizance is taken of Spinoza's special terminology, it will be found that in the following statement he asserts something very much like (P1) and (P2).

As long as things are considered as modes of thought, we can explain the whole order of nature and connection between causes merely through the attribute of thought, and if they are considered as modes under the attribute of extension, the whole order of nature must be explained through this attribute.[5]

Leibniz makes the following statement, in which he denies Descartes's theory of interaction and maintains something closely resembling (P1) and (P2):

If at the time of Descartes the new law of nature which I have proved had been known, according to which not only the same total amount of force, but also its total direction remains unchanged in a system of bodies, then he would, no doubt, have arrived at my system of pre-established harmony, because he would then have seen that we must deny the mind the ability to change the directional quantity of bodies for the same reasons that we must deny it the power to change the quantity of force. Both are equally contrary to the order of things

[5] Spinoza, op. cit. II, proposition VII, n.

and to the laws of nature, and both hence equally inexplicable. Thus, according to my system, souls or vital principles change nothing in the usual course of bodies, nor do they give God any occasion to do so. The souls follow their own laws, which consist in a certain development of their perceptions in accordance with Good and Evil, whereas the bodies likewise follow their laws, i.e. the laws of motion.[6]

Leibniz says further:

Souls act according to the laws of final causes, through desire, means, and ends. Bodies act according to the laws of efficient causes or of motion. And these two realms, that of efficient and that of final causes, are in harmony with each other. . . . According to this system, bodies act as if—through an impossible fiction—there were no souls, and souls act as if there were no bodies, and both act as if the one influenced the other.[7]

As far as Leibniz is concerned, (P2) can be replaced by a still stronger postulate. By analogy with the concept of mental theory, we may frame the concept of a theory of the soul (Leibniz: the monad) S. Such a theory will speak of S, but of nothing else. A theory of S is deterministic if, from the theory together with a complete description of a state of S, there follows exactly one description of each subsequent state of S. Then, according to Leibniz's monadology, it is the case that:

(P2') For every soul (monad) S there exists a true deterministic theory of S.

C. *Conscious matter or extended consciousness*

Descartes's sharp distinction between bodies and minds was not to go undisputed. The fact that his statements about the relation of the mind to the body it inhabits were so vague permitted many very dissimilar interpretations. Did he—or did he not—mean that the mind is found "in" the pineal gland of the brain? If he did mean that it is, must we not then consider the activities of the mind to be associated with some sort of material substratum? Leibniz's theory of the perceiving monads, inspired by Descartes, could also

[6] Leibniz, op. cit., vol. ii, p. 65 (from 'On Vital Principles and Plastic Natures', 1705).
[7] Ibid., vol. ii, pp. 453–4 (from *Monadology*, § 79, published in 1714).

be construed in various ways. Many of Leibniz's statements allow of the interpretation that the monads literally have positions in physical space and that bodies are literally systems of monads, in just about the same way that an atomist regards them as systems of atoms. Other statements suggest an opposite view.

Even for those who were steeped in Descartes's ideas, it was quite natural to ask whether matter might not be able to "think", i.e. to apprehend, to be conscious, or whether minds could not have extensions in space. Locke, for example, posed this question, but left it an open problem. Several of the philosophers of the Enlightenment proposed affirmative replies to the question. The view admits, of course, of an indefinite number of variations. The ability to apprehend, to mention only one range of possible variations, may be considered as being primarily associated with (i) point entities, or (ii) the postulated smallest particles of matter, the atoms, or (iii) larger volumes, or more complex systems of material particles. I shall not go deeper into the controversies over these obscure problems, for which an *Ignorabimus* (we shall not know) will most likely hold into a very distant future. It is enough to mention that all three opinions had their apologists. Viewpoint (i) is represented by Leibniz's monadology, upon one interpretation, and it was more explicitly asserted by a number of Leibniz's successors, among them Christian Wolff. Diderot experimented at different times with (ii) as well as with (iii). A strange variant of (iii) is to be found in the work of the seventeenth-century English Platonist, Henry More. In his opinion, both souls ("spirits") and bodies are extended. What characterizes a spatial volume filled with matter is roughly the primary properties usually postulated. A spatial volume that is taken up by a soul is characterized by something he calls "essential spissitude". He believed further that a soul can expand or contract in space, and that it can take up exactly the same space as is occupied by a living organism although it need not do so.

5. SPACE AND TIME

Mechanism sees the physical universe as a system of particles in motion, i.e. particles whose position in space changes with time. In the preceding sections of this chapter I have described some of the mechanists' views of the nature of the particles. Let us now turn to how they conceived of the nature of time and space.

If today we discuss the nature of physical space (or of physical time) two questions are of necessity given a central position, namely: (i) what mathematical laws hold for, or to put it more carefully, should be used in the description of, physical space (or physical time), and (ii) what empirical criteria should we establish for the applicability of the geometric (or the chronometric) concepts. Since Euclid's geometry was the only geometrical system known in the seventeenth and eighteenth centuries, question (i) could not even arise at that time as far as space was concerned. Neither was question (ii) thought to be crucial; the geometric concepts were considered by Descartes and his successors to be the epitome of "clear and distinct ideas". One of the first to have a feeling for the problems involved was Leibniz. Nevertheless, the nature of space, like that of time, was the object of an intense debate among the thinkers who lived in the age of mechanism. In this section I shall touch very briefly on some of the more interesting features of this discussion, in particular on the question of (A) whether there exists a void, (B) whether there exists absolute space, and (C) whether there exists absolute time; and finally (D) on Leibniz's ideas about space and time as "orders".

A. *Does a void exist?*

This question was already a philosophical problem during antiquity. The ancient natural philosophers had a tendency to identify the "existent" with "filled space", and the "non-existent" with the "void". If the void is identical with the non-existent, it would seem to be obvious that the void does not exist. It appears that of all the ancient philosophers, only the Atomists (and after them the Stoics) were daring enough to reject this inference and postulate the existence of the void.[8]

Newton sided with the Atomists on this question of the void, and in the end secured victory for this view. However, the philosophers' traditional disinclination to accept the existence of the void survived long into the eighteenth century, especially on the continent. When Voltaire visited England in 1728, he wrote home that a Frenchman who travelled to England must be prepared for many surprises, among others that whereas in Paris space was everywhere filled with matter, in London there existed an absolute void. So let us consider some of the arguments that continental philosophers proposed in their battle against the void.

The following argument, which was launched by Descartes, won many adherents. Extension is an attribute of material substance (body). An attribute cannot exist other than as an attribute of a substance. A substance that has extension as an attribute is, precisely because of this fact, a material substance. Consequently there can be no extension without material substance, i.e. there can be no void.

Another argument was formulated by Leibniz. According to one of his ideas, space by its very nature is a continuously ordered manifold of elements. By this he means that each portion of space is such a manifold. If, then, there existed one cubic millimeter, say, of empty space somewhere in the universe, of what elements would it consist? The suggested answer "geometric points" is rejected by Leibniz on the ground that geometric points are nothing but "limits and modifications" of the extended. In his opinion, the elements must be some kind of "real units" or "substances"; but a space filled with substances is not a void. Leibniz thought that his monadology provided the substances required to fill every nook of space. In *A Treatise of Human Nature* Hume, too, opposed the assumption of a void. Leibniz's idea that space is an ordered manifold of elements reappears

[8]Aristotelian mechanics provided philosophers with another objection to the existence of the void. According to this theory, the velocity of a body is in direct proportion to the force acting upon it, and in inverse proportion to the resistance of the medium. As the void must be supposed to offer no resistance, any force acting in a void would give a body an infinite velocity. Since infinite velocity is impossible, the void is also impossible.

in Hume as the notion that "the idea of space or extension is nothing but the idea of visible or tangible points distributed in a certain order."[9]

B. *Does absolute space exist?*

The ancient atomist conception of an absolute space was revived by several thinkers in the seventeenth century (Gassendi, Henry More, and Isaac Barrow). Newton incorporated the concept into his mechanics, and, with the support of his authority, absolute space became an accepted part of physical theory, remaining so until the beginning of our century. Even in Newton's time, however, the assumption met with some opposition, particularly from his scientific rival, Leibniz. The latter discussed the problem in correspondence with Huygens during the year 1694, Huygens likewise dissociating himself from Newton's concept of an absolute space. Leibniz discussed the same problem more extensively in a series of polemical letters which he exchanged with Newton's friend and follower, Clarke, in the years 1715 and 1716. I shall give an account of some of the points of this discussion. Another critic of Newton's concept of an absolute space was Berkeley.

First, a few words will be appropriate to explain why the question of an absolute space interested Newton and what connection it had with mechanics. The physical description of a process of motion varies, depending upon which co-ordinate system is used in determining the positions of the bodies involved. If, for example, we take the co-ordinate system as fixed in relation to the earth, we must say that the sun circles around the earth once every twenty-four hours. If, on the contrary, we take the co-ordinate system as fixed in relation to the sun, we must say that the earth rotates about its own axis once every twenty-four hours. By a suitable choice of co-ordinate system, each body may be thought of as being either at rest or in one kind of motion or another. The law of inertia, which is Newton's first law of motion, states that a body not being acted on by an external force either remains at rest or moves

---

[9] Hume, *A Treatise of Human Nature* (ed. L. A. Selby-Bigge, 2nd edn. revised by P. H. Nidditch, Oxford, 1978), I ii 5, p. 53.

without acceleration, i.e. continues in a straight line at constant speed. If in a certain case we assume that the acting forces are already established, then clearly not all co-ordinate systems will be legitimate with respect to this. If we suppose that the body is not being acted on by external forces, and if we nevertheless choose a reference system in relation to which the body does have an acceleration, then our description of the behaviour of the body will be inconsistent with the law. Newton's second law of motion states that the sum of the external forces acting on a body is equal to the product of the mass of the body and its acceleration. If we assume that a body is being acted on by a certain external force, it follows that we cannot choose a co-ordinate system in which the body has no acceleration (for example, is at rest) without contradicting this second law. If the forces are assumed to be known, the choice of the co-ordinate system is thus limited by Newton's laws.

We may ask ourselves (i) which co-ordinate system, or (more accurately) which class of co-ordinate systems, is physically correct. Putting it still more precisely, we can ask: In a correct application of the axioms of mechanics, how is the reference system chosen? For Newton, this, let us say, physical question is linked with another, let us say, ontological question, namely: (ii) Does an absolute space exist as an independent reality, beyond observable material events? Newton was of the opinion that, for the explanation of certain phenomena of motion (rotational phenomena with centrifugal effects) we must presuppose a co-ordinate system that cannot be defined by reference to any material fixed points, which must, therefore, be an absolute space. He also defined the true, or absolute, motion, velocity, and acceleration of a body as its motion, velocity, and acceleration in relation to the absolute space itself.

The discussion between Leibniz and Clarke was essentially concerned with the ontological question, (ii). It can hardly be said to have a clear-cut meaning, but perhaps the reader will obtain some idea of the concept of an absolute space by considering the following statements, which the Newtonians believed to be correct. Infinite absolute space is everywhere uniform and unchangeable; it is only matter that changes its position in space. It is impossible to observe an absolute space directly with the senses. An absolute space could exist without the existence of any matter at all. Quite possibly the material world lies completely within a limited part of absolute space. The material world in its entirety may be moving through absolute space. Even if there were only a single body in the universe, it would be able to change position or rotate about an axis, namely in absolute space.

In opposition to these assumptions of the Newtonians, Leibniz made assumptions such as these: Space is merely matter ordered in a certain way, or a certain ordering of matter. No space can exist outside the limits of the material world. All change of position is a change of position in relation to other bodies, or, in other words, a change in the distance between bodies or points on bodies. It is meaningless to speak of a motion of the material world as a whole. If only a single body were to exist it would have no position, and it would be neither at rest nor in motion.

Leibniz's arguments against the existence of an absolute space, in Newton's sense, have the following import. Let us suppose that Newton's absolute space did exist, and that it was therefore legitimate to speak of a position in this absolute space. For each particle a there would then exist a set of three absolute position functions:

$$S_a = \langle X_a(t), Y_a(t), Z_a(t) \rangle$$

each dependent on the time t. Now the relative positions of all particles would remain the same if the position functions had instead been:

$$S'_a = \langle X_a(t) + k, Y_a(t) + l, Z_a(t) + m \rangle,$$

where k, l, and m are independent of a. Leibniz points out that this situation (which he does not state in just these terms) is in conflict with both of two very general philosophical principles which he postulates. According to the so-called Law of Sufficient Reason (*Principium rationis sufficientis*) there must be a sufficient reason, or ground, for every accidental, i.e. not necessary, fact. It is an accidental fact that the position functions are S_a rather than S'_a, and this fact must have a sufficient reason. Given the assumed uniformity of absolute space, however, it is not possible to indicate any such reason. Thus there can be no absolute space. The so-called Law of the Identity of Indiscernibles (*Principium identitatis indiscernibilium*), as Leibniz interprets it in this context, states that if there is no observable distinction between A and B, then A is the same thing as B. According to the Newtonians' own admission, there is no observable difference between a world with the position functions S_a and a world with the position functions S_a'. The distinction itself between S_a and S_a' is therefore illusory, and thus there exists no absolute space. Leibniz's law of the Identity of Indiscernibles takes on here the character of an observability principle, a "principe d'observabilité", as he says, which is reminiscent of certain ideas in modern logical empiricism. Leibniz even says that the assumption that a body undergoes a particular motion is meaningful only if the assumed fact is, at least in principle, capable of being observed, either directly or indirectly.

C. *Does absolute time exist?*

The ancient Atomists who first conceived of an absolute space did not also possess a corresponding notion of an absolute time. In the seventeenth century, however, this idea was entertained by several of the thinkers who revived the notion of an absolute space (for example, Gassendi, Barrow). Newton took over the idea and believed that it was an indispensable element of mechanics. Just as the axioms of mechanics do not hold in relation to an arbitrarily chosen co-ordinate system for the determination of position, so they do not hold in relation to an arbitrarily chosen system for the measurement of time. We may now ask: (i) In a correct application of the laws of mechanics, how should time be measured? This, let us say, physical question (i) was combined by Newton with the, let us say, ontological question (ii): Does an absolute time exist as an independent reality, beyond observable events? Newton thought that no existing material clock measures true mechanical time, and he reached the conclusion that absolute time itself is the correct clock of mechanics. The difference in time, in the absolute sense, between two events A and B is equal to the difference in time between two events C and D if the uniformly elapsing absolute time passes an equally long interval between A and B as between C and D.

The notion of an absolute time is at least as obscure as that of an absolute space. Some idea of what an absolute time is supposed to be can perhaps be grasped by considering some of the propositions maintained by the Newtonians. Infinite absolute time exists in and of itself, independently of any relation to anything material. It elapses uniformly. An absolute time could exist without the existence of any events in time. God created the material world at a particular moment. He could have done so either earlier or later than he actually did.

In his discussions with Clarke, Leibniz protests against Newton's ontology of time. His arguments are analogous to those he raised against absolute space. If an absolute time exists and if God has created the world, then he has created it at some moment t of this absolute time. In view of the uniformity of absolute time, however, it is impossible to indicate a sufficient reason as to why the world was created at t rather than at some other moment t'. By virtue of the Law of Sufficient Reason, as well as of the Law of the Identity of Indiscernibles, it is therefore necessary to reject the assumption of an absolute time.

D. *Leibniz's conception of space and time as orders*

Leibniz was in the habit of summarizing his own conception of the nature of space and time by saying that time is the order of the non-coexisting (not simultaneously existing), and that space is the order of coexisting (simultaneously existing). The meaning of these statements is not too clear, and what Leibniz meant by them seems to have changed from time to time. Even so, I believe that the basic idea in Leibniz's conception of space and time can be expressed roughly as follows.

In the world we find certain spatial relations, say S, and certain temporal relations, say T. Space is now a set of elements M_S ordered by the spatial relations S, and time is a set of elements M_T ordered by the temporal relations T.

These assertions give rise to several questions. Some of these are (i) What are the relations S and T? (ii) What are the elements of the sets M_S and M_T? (iii) What mathematical principles are assumed to hold for the relations S on the set M_S and T on M_T?

Leibniz did not provide us with an unambiguous answer to any of these questions, but he presented a number of relevant reflections. On question (ii), at least two different opinions concerning M_S are to be found in Leibniz's works: for lack of better names, these can be called the realist and the idealist conceptions. According to the realist conception, M_S is a set of real entities or substances. Leibniz at times suggests that M_S should be identified with the set of monads. In the idealist conception, the set M_S is a set of positions, these being abstractions defined by means of the following:

1. A sufficiently large system of bodies, X, Y, X . . ., forms a reference system if the bodies of this system do not change their mutual positions.

2. The body A is said to have the same position at time t as the body B has at time t', in relation to a given reference system, if A's distances at t from each of the bodies of the system are equal to B's distances at t' from the same bodies.

3. A position in relation to a given reference system is what is common to all the bodies that have the same position in relation to the system.

In this sense Leibniz says that space is "an order of positions according to which positions are distributed", and that "abstract space is the order of the positions that are considered possible."[10]

When he says that space is the order of the coexistent and time the order of the non-coexistent, he appears to be maintaining the following two assertions:

(s) For every a and b, if a and b are elements of M_S, then a is coexistent with b.
(t) For every a and b, if a and b are two distinct elements of M_T, then a is not coexistent with b.

<hr>

[10] Leibniz, op. cit., vol. i, p. 54; vol. ii, p. 401.

That all events in space are also apparently events in time is a consideration which seems to be a natural objection to (s) and (t).

With regard to question (iii), Leibniz sometimes voices the opinion that M_S as ordered by S is a three-dimensional continuum, whereas M_T as ordered by T is a linear continuum.

Leibniz's views on time and space are fragmentary and difficult to interpret; yet it is clear that they are much closer to modern ideas than Newton's are.

II

The Revival of the Platonic–Aristotelian
Ideal of Science

6. THE PHILOSOPHERS' IDEAL OF SCIENCE AND
THE METHOD OF THE PHYSICISTS

A. *Aristotelian sciences and deductive systems*

Aristotle's idea of a deductive science comprises several elements which are logically independent of each other. He makes certain purely logical demands on the construction of such a science, and he also requires a special epistemological quality of its theorems. The most important of the logical demands is that a deductive science should be based on a finite number of basic assumptions, from which its theorems are to be inferred. The most important epistemological requirements are that the basic assumptions be true and self-evident, cognitively prior to the theorems inferred, and unprovable. It is easy to see that a system of propositions can fulfil Aristotle's logical requirements without satisfying his epistemological ones. Aristotle was certainly aware of this fact, but many centuries were to pass before it became generally accepted that the setting up of systems that fulfil the logical but not the epistemological requirements can be a legitimate and fruitful scientific activity. For the sake of brevity, I introduce two technical terms here. A system of propositions will be called a "deductive system" if it satisfies Aristotle's basic logical requirement. A deductive system that, in addition, satisfies his epistemological requirements will be called an Aristotelian science. Using this terminology, one can say that it took a long time for philosophers and scientists to realize that a deductive system can have scientific value even when it is not an Aristotelian science. Despite isolated, brilliant pioneering efforts during antiquity, the first to see this fairly clearly were apparently the seventeenth-century physicists. The philosophers themselves continued to hold fast to the original Platonic–Aristotelian ideal of science.

It may be instructive to consider how a deductive system that is not an Aristotelian science can still have scientific value. A deductive system S can fail to be an Aristotelian science for one or both of the following reasons:

(i)   At least one of the basic assumptions of S is false.

(ii) At least one of the basic assumptions of S lacks self-evidence.

Aristotle and his followers thought of self-evidence as a guarantee of truth; thus from (i) follows (ii), but not the converse. A deductive system may therefore lack the Aristotelian character because (a) at least one of its basic assumptions is false, or (b) at least one of its basic assumptions, although all of them are true, is not self-evident. Let us speak of a false deductive system in case (a) and of a true but non-evident deductive system in case (b). Under what circumstances can it be of scientific value to set up and study (a) false deductive systems and (b) true but non-evident deductive systems?

The scientific interest of a body of propositions usually increases if the propositions can be arranged in a deductive system. Suppose we are dealing with a region of scientific investigation where the propositions we are inclined to assert can be arranged in such a system. Now, we have only to remember that human knowledge is fragmentary, uncertain, and tentative, in order to see why both false and non-evident deductive systems can be of scientific importance. It may happen that although the basic assumptions of a deductive system S seem reasonable to an investigator, certain theorems of S are false and S itself is thus, in my terminology, a false system. It might also happen that a theorem that can be empirically demonstrated as false comes to light only after very long and complex inferences. In order to arrive at an empirically falsifiable theorem it may thus be necessary to subject the system to a difficult and in itself interesting logical analysis. It can also happen that our search for empirical data that may confirm or refute S brings to light important facts that would have remained undiscovered had we not had S in our minds. All this may obviously be valuable activity, contributing to the advance of science. If a sound scientific instinct lies behind the choice of the system S, it is often found that, after S has been empirically falsified, it can be amended in a more or less organic way into a better system, S'. An example of what I mean by an organic relationship between theory S and a later, improved theory S' occurs when it is possible within S' to deduce the proposition, 'If A, then S', where A is a rather generally formulated condition which is fairly often fulfilled. It may happen also that though the system S is in fact false, a very long period elapses—years, decades, or even centuries—before someone succeeds in falsifying it empirically. Perhaps the empirically falsifiable theorems are logically too far removed from the basic assumptions, i.e. the necessary chains of inference are too long, or else the empirical testing is too difficult. As long as S has not been disclosed as false, it may conceivably be just as useful to us as if it were a true system. There is much that could be added here, but I shall now leave the subject of false deductive systems.

The usefulness of true, non-evident deductive systems is still easier to defend. In the empirical sciences, at best a very small portion of truth is self-evident or obvious, as the history of science so abundantly testifies. In the empirical sciences it is practically impossible to construct deductive systems with self-evident basic assumptions. Developments during this century in formal logic and in the foundations of mathematics make it seem possible that there may in this respect be essential similarities between those disciplines and the empirical sciences.

The Platonic–Aristotelian ideal of science is thus in conflict with the condition of science. As long as attention was concentrated on such fields as logic, pure mathematics, metaphysics, and theology, where contact with experience is lacking or only slight, it was possible to hold firm to the ideal. For the Scholastics influenced by Aristotle from the thirteenth century onwards this ideal seemed obligatory; but the physicists of the seventeenth century were forced to abandon it.

B. *The hypothetico-deductive method of the seventeenth-century physicists*

The hypothetico-deductive method has, in a more or less conscious manner, characterized modern natural science ever since its birth in the sixteenth and seventeenth centuries. By saying that an investigator makes use of this method, the following is usually meant:

(i) he formulates and studies deductive systems of greater or smaller scope;

(ii) he embraces a particular system only as long as the consequences deduced from it are found to hold good under empirical testing;

(iii) as long as he does embrace a system, he does not ascribe certainty to it, but merely a probability which depends essentially on the number and kind of consequences that have been found to hold good under empirical testing.

The hypothetico-deductive method was not entirely unknown to antiquity. The task, proposed to the astronomers by Plato, of "saving phenomena", by showing that the irregular movements of the planets can be explained as projections of circular motions, was in a sense a challenge to them to apply this method. Especially in the hands of the Alexandrian scientists, the method seems to have attained a certain degree of purposefulness and refinement. Through Euclid's geometry, the deductive method of the ancient mathematicians was well known to medieval philosophers from the eleventh century onwards. As mathematics played a central part in the new natural sciences, it is not surprising that the deductive method experienced a revival in the seventeenth century and that not only mathematicians but also physicists were at pains to construct their theories in the image of Euclid's. An elegant example of the deductive method in mechanics is given by Galileo in his *Discussions and Mathematical Proofs in Two New Sciences Concerning Mechanics and the Laws of Falling Bodies* (1638). The great deductive masterpiece was, of course, Newton's *Mathematical Principles of Natural Philosophy* (*Philosophiae Naturalis Principia Mathematica*).

Statements that amount to an espousal of the hypothetico-deductive method are to be found in the works of many seventeenth-century physicists. One of the clearest declarations was made by Huygens in his *Treatise on Light* (*Traité de la lumière*, 1660):

One will find here a kind of demonstration that does not create as high a degree of certainty as the geometric proof and that is actually very different from the method of proof of the mathematicians. For they prove their propositions from certain and unassailable principles, whereas here the principles are tested by means of the consequences that can be derived from them.

The nature of the subject matter does not allow any other mode of treatment. Nevertheless, it is possible to attain in this manner a probability which is only slightly less than complete certainty. This occurs when the consequences of our assumed principles are in complete agreement with observed phenomena and especially when these verifications are numerous, but to the highest degree when we frame in advance an idea of new phenomena that ought to follow from the hypotheses we use, and we thereafter find our expectations fulfilled. If in the following treatise all these criteria of probability are present together, as I believe they are, the success of my investigations is strongly corroborated and it is hardly thinkable that these things should not be almost exactly as I have described them.[1]

Newton's opinion, as it can be pieced together from various passages in his works on physics, seems in all essentials to have been the same as that of Huygens, although Newton usually expressed himself much less distinctly. In the *Opticks* (1704) he describes his method as follows.

As in mathematics, so in natural philosophy, the investigation of difficult things by the method of analysis . . . consists in making experiments and observations, and in drawing general conclusions from them by induction, and admitting of no objections against the conclusions but such as are taken from experiment, or other certain truths. For hypotheses are not to be regarded in experimental philosophy. And although the arguing from experiments and observations by induction be no demonstration of general conclusions, yet it is the best way of arguing which the nature of things admits of, and may be looked upon as so much the stronger by how much the induction is more general.

---

[1] C. Huygens, *Treatise on Light* (Chicago, 1945), pp. vi–vii.

And if no exception occur from phenomena, the conclusion may be pronounced generally. But if at any time afterward any exception shall occur from experiments, it may then begin to be pronounced with such exceptions as occur. By this way of analysis we may proceed from compounds to ingredients and from motions to the forces producing them, and in general from effects to their causes and from particular causes to more general ones, till the argument end in the most general. This is the method of analysis; and the synthesis consists in assuming the causes discovered and established as principles, and by them explaining the phenomena proceeding from them and proving the explanations.[2]

Both Huygens and Newton obviously overestimated the certainty obtained by the hypothetico-deductive method. In Newton's statement we also find a view on the role of induction and a negative attitude towards hypotheses which hardly agree with our modern understanding of the hypothetico-deductive method. Nevertheless, the idea of this method is presaged in what they say. Both Huygens and Newton obviously presuppose that all the theorems of the deductive systems that they have in mind are either true or false. In empirical science, however, it is possible to withdraw yet another step from the Platonic–Aristotelian ideal of science. One can set up and study deductive systems in which some of the theorems are mere formulas which are neither true nor false in that they do not express genuine statements about reality. Such systems can be just as useful in science as systems of the kind Huygens and Newton had in mind. The empiricist Berkeley seems to have been the first to advance this point of view. He even suggested that Newton's mechanics was a system of this more radically non-Aristotelian kind.

C. *The Platonic–Aristotelian ideal of science in seventeenth-century philosophy*

Statements defending the hypothetico-deductive method in natural science can also be found in the works of the seventeenth-century philosophers. This is true of both Descartes and Leibniz for example. Locke, the father of

---

[2] H. S. Thayer (ed.), *Newton's Philosophy of Nature* (New York, 1953), pp. 178–9.

the modern British empiricist tradition, saw clearly both
the role of induction in science and the uncertainty of the
hypotheses suggested by it. The prevailing tendency in
continental philosophy, however, was quite different. There
the Platonic–Aristotelian ideal of science in its original
unabridged form underwent an intensive revival at the
very time when it was being so deeply modified in natural
science. This revival was inaugurated by Descartes; in his
Discourse on Method (*Discours de la méthode*, 1637), the
work considered so often as ushering in a new era in philosophy, he wrote:

> Those long chains of reasoning, simple and easy as they are, of which
> geometricians make use in order to arrive at the most difficult demon-
> strations, had caused me to imagine that all those things which fall
> under the cognizance of man might very likely be mutually related
> in the same fashion.[3]

The so-called rationalist tradition, which began with
Descartes and of which Spinoza and Leibniz were the other
two most outstanding exponents, has as its most characteristic feature just this more or less unreserved adoption of
the Platonic–Aristotelian ideal of science. In §7 I shall try
to throw light upon how the nature of deductive science
was conceived within the rationalist tradition, and I shall
indicate some of the new methodological insights that
were gained. In §§8–10 I shall give an account of Leibniz's
innovating ideas on methodology, which go beyond what,
properly speaking, can be comprised under the Platonic–
Aristotelian ideal of science. This ideal was sharpened by
Leibniz into his own, the Leibnizian ideal of science.

7. THE METHODOLOGY OF THE DEDUCTIVE SCIENCES

When trying to explain the requirements he placed upon
a deductive science, Descartes was not always successful
in hitting upon the essentials. The four methodological
precepts he set forth in the *Discourse on Method* were
these:

[3] *The Philosophical Works of Descartes*, translated by E. S. Haldane and
G. R. T. Ross (Cambridge, 1967), vol. i, p. 92.

The first was to accept nothing as true which I did not clearly recognize to be so . . .

The second was to divide up each of the difficulties which I examined into as many parts as possible, and as seemed requisite in order that it might be resolved in the best manner possible . . .

The third was to carry on my reflections in due order, commencing with objects that were most simple and easy to understand, in order to rise little by little, or by degrees, to knowledge of the most complex . . .

The last was in all cases to make enumerations so complete and reviews so general that I should be certain of having omitted nothing.[4]

A conspicuous feature of these rules is that they concern not so much the deductive arrangement of a system of propositions as the best way of finding scientific truths.

Blaise Pascal (1623–62), the great mathematician, physicist, and religious thinker, held ideas on logic which were close to those of the Cartesians. In the essay, *On the Geometric Manner of Thinking* (*De l'esprit géométrique*), he formulates the deductive ideal of science of his time with unexcelled clarity. He distinguishes between the art of finding new truths and the art of proving truths already found, and states that it is in the latter of these arts that the deductive ideal is to be pursued. The mathematical method of proof is then summarized in the following eight rules:

Rules for the Definitions:

1. One should not define things that are so well known that it is impossible to find clearer expressions for their explanation.

2. One should not leave undefined those expressions that are in the least unclear or ambiguous.

3. In a definition one must only use words that are fully known or already explained.

Rules for the Axioms:

1. One should not pass over any necessary principle without asking whether it has been acknowledged, no matter how self-evident and clear it may seem.

2. One may choose for axioms only statements that are completely self-evident in themselves.

[4] Ibid., vol. i, p. 92.

Rules for the Demonstrations:

1. One must not prove anything that is so obvious that there is nothing more obvious by which to prove it.

2. One must prove every assertion that is in the slightest way unclear, and for this purpose use only very clear axioms or assertions already admitted or proved.

3. One should always mentally replace defined words by their definitions in order not to deceive oneself by the ambiguity of the expressions, which is removed by the definitions.[5]

Logic, or the Art of Thinking (*Logique ou l'art de penser*, 1662), usually called the *Logic of Port-Royal*, was written by two Jansenists, Arnauld and Nicole, who were influenced by Descartes. This work ends with a section on "method", which here means the mathematical method of proof. This section, into which the authors incorporated contributions by Descartes and Pascal, is one of the best expositions of the Descartes–Pascal version of the deductive ideal of science. Of special interest is the theory of definitions, whose author was probably Pascal and which appears in an essentially similar form in Pascal's own work, *On the Geometric Manner of Thinking*. This theory distinguishes among the following kinds of definitions:

   (i)   nominal definitions (*définitions des noms*);
   (ii) real definitions (*définitions des choses*):
         (1) real definitions properly so called,
         (2) descriptions;
   (iii) explanations of linguistic usage.

(i) *Nominal definitions.* Only these are definitions in the sense employed in statements of the mathematical method, and it is to this category that Pascal's rules are meant to apply. A definition of this kind is characterized by the following properties: 1. An arbitrarily chosen abbreviation, what we today would call the 'definiendum', is introduced in place of a longer expression, what we would call the 'definiens'. Considering nominal definitions from a slightly different point of view, it is then further maintained: 2. An arbitrarily chosen designation (definiendum) is introduced for an object, which is clearly indicated by means of the

[5] Pascal, *Œuvres* (Gallimard, 1954), p. 596.

definition (definiens). The following is given as an example of a nominal definition: "I call each number that can be divided into two equal parts an even number." According to the first point of view, the words "even number" are thus an abbreviation of the phrase "number that can be divided into two equal parts"; according to the second point of view, the words "even number" are introduced as a designation of the thing: 'number that can be divided into two equal parts'. 3. A nominal definition is completely "free": it does not run the risk of contradiction since "nothing can be more admissible than assigning any name one pleases to a thing that one has clearly indicated." A nominal definition, in other words, is not an assertion the truth of which can be debated. 4. The utility of such a definition lies in the fact that it contributes to making our speech concise and clear by "expressing with a single designation what otherwise could be said only by the use of several words".

(ii) *Real definitions.* A definition of this kind is characterized by the following properties: 1. The definiendum is already understood independently of the definition; it is accepted as a designation of a given object. 2. The definition states that the given object designated by the definiendum is identical with the object designated by the definiens. In other words, if the definiendum designates *A* and the definiens designates *B*, the definition asserts that *A* is identical with *B*. 3. The definition is not free; it has the character of a theorem which must be proved from the axioms, unless it merits being set up as an axiom itself. A real definition is therefore an assertion, the truth of which is debatable. 4. If the definition is correct then it gives an insight into an objective fact (*la vérité des choses*).

Pascal objects to a number of Aristotelian–Scholastic definitions on the ground that it is not clear whether they are intended as nominal or real definitions, and he elegantly illustrates the obscurities and pseudoproblems which arise from this unclarity.

Real definitions properly so called (ii: 1) explain the "nature" of an object by indicating its "essential attributes", whereas a description (ii: 2) gives information about an object by indicating some of its characteristic accidental properties. In modern terminology, this distinction could perhaps be expressed like this: in a real definition, properly so called, the definiens and the definiendum have the same intension; in a description they have the same extension but not the same intension.[6]

(iii) *Explanations of linguistic usage*. Definitions of this type are meant to explain "the meaning a word generally carries". Such a definition is a statement concerning linguistic usage. (Presumably it should be possible to formulate it in roughly the following way: "The expression '*A*', according to such and such usage, means *B*.") In contrast to real definitions, those of kind (iii) do not express *une vérité des choses* but merely *une vérité de l'usage*, and are said to be mainly the concern of the philologists.

This theory of definitions surpassed most of what had been written on the subject since Plato and Aristotle had first thought systematically about it—at least, as regards the literature with which I myself am acquainted. (The distinctions between the three kinds of definitions, (i)–(iii), and between the two subtypes of (ii), are extremely important. One might wish that contemporaneous and later philosophers had paid more attention to them.)

Although Descartes and his immediate followers saw in the deductive method of mathematics the ideal scientific procedure, they were indifferent to, or even opposed to, the study of formal logic. The reason for this was not that they considered formal logic to rest on theoretical error, but that they held the logical studies of the Scholastics to be scientifically barren. Mathematicians, they thought, can reason without having studied formal logic, and the philosophers who have studied it have not achieved any

[6] Two expressions are said to have the same intension if they have the same meaning. An example of this often cited is the pair of expressions, 'bachelor' and 'unmarried man'. Two expressions are said to have the same extension if they are applicable to exactly the same objects. If expressions have the same intension, they also have the same extension, but the converse does not hold. An example of two expressions that have the same extension but not the same intension is (probably) 'presently alive ruminants' and 'presently alive artiodactyl-hoofed mammals', because among animals presently alive all the ruminants are artiodactyl-hoofed mammals, and conversely. Another example is the pair, 'centaur' and 'mermaid', since, I think, neither of these expressions is applicable to anything.

worthwhile results. Oddly enough, Descartes further asserted that purely formal errors in reasoning are rare. Leibniz's evaluation of formal logic was exactly the opposite: "I hold that the discovery of the form of the syllogisms is one of the most beautiful that have been made by the human mind and also one of the most considerable. It is a sort of universal mathematics, the significance of which is not sufficiently known."[7] There were two connected reasons that led Leibniz to hold formal logic in such high esteem. One was that he endeavoured to introduce the mathematical method into regions where it had not yet been applied and that in Aristotle's syllogistic he found the first example, historically, of the application of the method outside the time-honoured domains of mathematics. The second, and much deeper, reason is allied with his ideal of science, with which we shall become acquainted in the next section.

8. LEIBNIZ'S IDEAS ON CHARACTERISTICS

Whereas the methodological rules set up by the Cartesians usually envisaged demonstrations like those in Euclid, Leibniz's ideas on methodology were inspired primarily by the symbolic language and the calculations of arithmetic and algebra. Starting from the trivial observation that human knowledge is inseparably linked with verbal expression, he went on to assert that a perfect science should fulfil certain requirements, not only with regard to the ideas involved, but also with regard to the language in which the ideas are presented. Within the symbolic language of arithmetic and algebra, it was true in Leibniz's time, and is true today to an even greater degree, that:

(1) There exist a number of formal rules of calculation such that (to a large extent) a sentence (formula) S is a logical consequence of certain sentences (formulas) $T_1 \ldots T_n$ if and only if S can be obtained from $T_1 \ldots T_n$ by the rules.

(2) For many questions of the kind, Is the sentence S a logical consequence of the sentences $T_1 \ldots T_n$?, there is a method by which correct answers can be found mechanically.

[7] C. I. Gerhardt (ed.), *Die philosophischen Schriften von Gottfried Wilhelm Leibniz* (Hildesheim, 1960), vol. v, p. 460 (from *New Essays*, completed 1704, first published 1765).

(3) For many questions of the kind, What number fulfils such and such a condition?, there is a method by which the number in question (or more accurately, a certain type of designation of the number, say a numeral), can be found mechanically.

As a result of (1), on numerous occasions it can be decided mechanically whether a given computation is correct or not. By virtue of (2) and (3), it is unnecessary for the solution of a large number of problems to rely on inventiveness; instead already known methods can be mechanically applied. It occurred to Leibniz that it should be possible to express other sciences in symbolic languages comparable to those of arithmetic and algebra, and thus to confer upon those sciences similar advantageous properties. For a given theory T, a symbolic language with the properties he had in mind was called by Leibniz a characteristic (*characteristica*) for T. With more precision in expression than can be found in Leibniz's writings, it can be stated that a symbolic language C is a characteristic, in his sense, for a theory T, if and only if the following conditions are satisfied:

(a) There exist a finite number of simple (or primitive) ideas in T such that each complex idea in T is constructed from a (finite) number of these simple ideas.

(b) There exist a number of self-evident propositions in T, the axioms, such that every other true proposition in T follows logically from these axioms.

(c) There are a finite number of simple (or primitive) symbols in C, such that every expression which appears in C is a (finite) sequence of these primitive symbols.

(d) Every meaningful expression in C is constructed in a recognizable manner from the primitive symbols according to fixed rules.

(e) Every name in C is a designation of exactly one idea in T, and every idea of T has at least one name in C.

(f) Every sentence that can be formulated in C is the expression of exactly one conceivable proposition in *T*, and every conceivable proposition in *T* can be expressed by at least one sentence which can be formulated in *C*.

(g) The sentences in *C* that express the axioms of *T* are of a recognizable form.

(h) There are a number of rules of inference such that a sentence *S* of *C* can be inferred with the help of of these rules in a finite number of steps from the sentences *U, V* . . . of *C*, if and only if the proposition of *T* expressed by *S* is a logical consequence of the propositions of *T* expressed by *U, V* . . .

Leibniz seems to have assumed also that to some extent there exist mechanical methods of solving problems which can be formulated in *C*. Exactly to what extent, in his opinion, a characteristic would provide such methods is not quite clear. An idea that frequently recurs in his discussions of the notion of a characteristic is associated with the fundamental importance he ascribes to the distinction between simple and complex ideas. He often seems to have assumed that a characteristic *C* for a theory *T* also satisfies the following condition:

(i) There is a method by means of which all questions of the following kind can be mechanically answered: Given a designation of an idea of *T* in *C*, is it the designation of a simple idea? If not, what are the designations in *C* of the simple ideas of which the first-mentioned idea is composed?

On the basis of certain assumptions Leibniz made concerning the relation between the truth of a sentence and the ideas expressed in it, (i) implies for him that:

(j) There is a method by which it can be decided mechanically whether a sentence in *C* is true or false.

Leibniz's concept of a characteristic can thus be seen to be firmly rooted both in the Platonic–Aristotelian ideal of science and in the speculations of his time about simple and complex ideas. From these sources are derived items (a), (b), (i), and (j) in the notion of a characteristic. Properties (c)–(h) are independent of these sources, however, and they anticipate the modern idea of a calculus or a formalized language. With condition (j), Leibniz may also be said to have anticipated the modern concept of a decidable calculus (cf. Vo. III, ch. VII).

Leibniz worked untiringly on creating calculi for various theories. The most remarkable of the many calculi he invented is without doubt the infinitesimal calculus. (One respect in which Leibniz's version of the infinitesimal calculus is superior to Newton's is precisely in its choice of symbolism.) An interesting suggestion for a mathematical calculus was his "geometric characteristic", which was taken up in the nineteenth century by H. Grassman in his *Geometrische Analyse, geknüpft an die von Leibniz erfundene geometrische Characteristik* (1847). Such thinkers of the eighteenth century as Gottfried Ploucquet (*Methodus Calculandi in Logicis*, 1763) and Johann Heinrich Lambert (*Neues Organon*, 1764) were inspired by, and tried to elaborate, Leibniz's logical hints. Leibniz's many logical calculi are anticipations of modern symbolic logic. He himself regarded all these calculi as mere samples of the universal characteristic (*characteristica universalis*) to which he continually returns in his works, and which at times he stated could be completed in a few years if only he could find competent collaborators. It was to remain a utopian dream, however.

Those whom we have to thank for the idea of an axiomatized theory are, in the first place, Plato and Aristotle, and in the second, the mathematicians who put the idea into practice together with those later thinkers such as Pascal who elaborated Plato's and Aristotle's original notions. The idea of a formalized theory and the first examples of such theories outside arithmetic and algebra are due primarily to Leibniz.

9. LEIBNIZ'S DISTINCTION BETWEEN ETERNAL
   AND CONTINGENT TRUTHS

In order to understand the range that Leibniz's universal characteristic was intended to possess, it is first necessary to study his distinction between eternal and contingent truths, a distinction which anyway has an independent interest.

Looking at the genealogy of the distinction, we find among its ancestors Plato's distinction between the dialectical truths about ideas and the truths—or half-truths at best, according to Plato—about the sensible world; the Stoics' distinction between necessary and contingent truths; as well as the distinction made by St. Augustine and many other medieval thinkers between truths that are eternal and unchangeable and those that are not. The distinction should also be considered against the background of ancient and medieval investigations in modal logic. Thus, Leibniz had many predecessors, and, with his wide reading in ancient and scholastic literature, he was surely well acquainted with their work. As far as I know, however, he gave the distinction a clearer form than his predecessors had done and illuminated it from several new points of view. Hume's distinction between truths about relations of ideas and truths about matters of fact is related to Leibniz's distinction. Kant's distinction between analytical and synthetic judgements was influenced by the ideas of Leibniz and Hume, and via Kant this realm of ideas has come down to modern philosophy and logic.

In a dialogue of 1677, sometimes cited as *A Dialogue on the Connection between Objects and Words*, Leibniz discusses whether the predicates true and false should properly be applied to thoughts, to things, or to words of language. His conclusion is that the predicates should be applied to words, but that the reason why an arrangement of words is true or false lies in the fact that there is a certain correspondence between the connection of the words and the connection of the objects designated by them. He thus seems to maintain that the predicates "true" and "false" are applicable to arrangements of words, to verbal sentences, interpreted in a certain manner. We may accordingly presume that his distinction between eternal and contingent truths is a distinction between two kinds of interpreted sentences that merit the attribution of truth.

Before we consider Leibniz's attempt to analyse the difference between the truths he wishes to call eternal and those he wishes to call contingent, it might be useful to look at some of his examples of the two kinds of truth:

Some of Leibniz's examples of eternal truths
   e 1. All arithmetical and geometrical principles, e.g.
       (i) $2 + 3 = 5$
       (ii) Space has three dimensions
   e 2. All logical principles, e.g.
       (i) Everything is what it is
       (ii) A proposition is either true or false
       (iii) There is a reason for every contingent truth
   e 3. "The principles of justice, goodness, and beauty"
   e 4. God exists
   e 5. Many of the theorems of the monadology (Leibniz's metaphysics).

Some of Leibniz's examples of contingent truths
   c 1. Any true proposition which asserts that one or several individual objects—other than God—exist, e.g.
       (i) I exist
       (ii) There exist bodies which exhibit an actual right angle
   c 2. Every true proposition which asserts that one or several existing individual objects—other than God—have a particular property, e.g.
       (i) Caesar decided to cross the Rubicon
       (ii) The laws of motion in mechanics.

This may perhaps be an exhaustive survey of the classes of eternal and contingent truths as Leibniz conceived of them.

Leibniz offered a series of different explanations of the concept of an eternal truth. Some of his explanations of what he means by the assertion that S is an eternal truth are:

   E 1. It is necessary that S is true.
   E 2. The negation of S involves a contradiction.
   E 3. S is true by virtue of the ideas or essences which the terms occurring in S denote.
   E 4 S holds true in all possible worlds.

A contingent truth is one that is not eternal. As immediate corollaries of the above explanations we may thus set up the following Leibnizian explications of what is meant by saying that *S* is a contingent truth:

C 1. *S* is true, but it is possible that *S* is false.
C 2. *S* is true, but the negation of *S* does not involve a contradiction.
C 3. *S* is true by virtue of "facts", not by virtue of the ideas or essences which the terms occurring in *S* denote.
C 4. *S* holds in the real world, but there is some possible world in which *S* does not hold.

As synonyms for the term 'eternal truth', Leibniz uses the phrases 'necessary truth' and 'rational truth'; as synonyms for 'contingent truth' he uses 'factual truth' and 'existential truth'.

These explanations require some comments. Concerning E 2, it is clear that the phrase "involves a contradiction" must be understood in the extended sense of "provides the logical basis for a contradiction" or "includes a contradiction among its consequences". When Leibniz suggested the explanation E 3, he obviously must have had in mind some distinction between the ideas or essences for which certain words somehow stand, and the existent things to which the same words in some other way refer. If Leibniz had developed this—which he never did—he might well have been led to something like the Stoic *lekton* theory. Explanation E 4 presupposes Leibniz's belief that our world, the real world, is but one among (infinitely) many possible worlds:

The universe is merely one selection of a certain kind of compossibles [i.e. things that are possible together] . . . And as there are various combinations of possibilities, some better than others, so are there many possible universes, since each selection of compossibles constitutes one of them.[8]

This notion can, I think, be elucidated thus: Let us assume that we have at our disposal a universal language *L* in which everything can be expressed. Let us say that a set *S* of

[8] Ibid., vol. iii, p. 573 (from a letter to Bourguet, 1714).

sentences of *L* is compossible if it is logically possible that all its sentences are simultaneously true. Let us say further that a set *S* is a maximal compossible set if *S* is a compossible set and if, for every conceivable sentence of *L*, either the sentence itself or its negation belongs to *S*. We may then think of every such maximal compossible set as a description of a possible world in Leibniz's sense.

One might ask if Leibniz's various general explanations of the concept of eternal truth are equivalent and also look for more precise formulations of them. Lack of space prevents me from entering upon such considerations here, but it should at least be noted that modern logic has supplied many concepts and points of view of relevance to those problems. One may also question the extent to which Leibniz's general explanations of the concepts fit his examples of them; but this question cannot be taken up here either. When he classifies the statement that God exists as an eternal truth (example e 4), he has in mind his own version of the ontological proof. Perhaps he would have accepted the criticisms to which the proof was later subjected, and thus might have withdrawn this example. Nowadays the principles of geometry are not usually regarded as necessary truths.

Like many earlier and later philosophers from Plato on, Leibniz distinguishes between the kind of knowledge or certainty which we obtain *a priori*, through reason or thought, and the kind we acquire *a posteriori*, through sense perception or experience. One might have expected him to equate the realm of *a priori* knowledge with eternal truth and the realm of *a posteriori* knowledge with contingent truth, but he does not do so. In his opinion, the concepts of eternal truth and *a priori* knowledge approximately coincide, it is true, and the same holds for the concepts of contingent truth and *a posteriori* knowledge; but he does not assume the coincidence to be perfect. It is sometimes possible to come to realize contingent truths *a priori*, for example certain natural laws. Leibniz mentions as one example of such *a priori* knowledge Archimedes' principle of the lever to the effect that if a lever is completely symmetric relative to its fulcrum, it remains at rest.

This principle can be seen to hold, Leibniz says, by virtue of the law of sufficient reason which is itself known to us *a priori*; there is no reason why one end of a symmetrical lever should rise rather than the other. (This example is rather strange. Leibniz seems to hold that (i) Archimedes' principle is a contingent truth, (ii) the law of sufficient reason is a necessary truth, and (iii) the principle follows logically from the law. But surely he would also be willing to admit that (iv) if *S* is a necessary truth and *T* follows logically from *S*, then *T* is likewise a necessary truth? Yet assumptions (i)–(iv) form an inconsistent combination.)

Leibniz's theory that certain contingent truths can be known *a priori* was to be transformed by Kant into a central thesis of his critique of reason, viz. the tenet that there exist synthetic *a priori* judgements. Whereas Kant saw in this presumed fact something of a mystery, to which he therefore devoted hundreds of pages of explanation, it appears that Leibniz found it no great problem. Presumably he believed that this is on a par with, and no stranger than, the fact that we can know eternal truths *a priori*. When at times he tries to explain *a priori* knowledge, he refers to man's "innate inner light".

10. LEIBNIZ'S DREAM OF A UNIVERSAL CHARACTERISTIC

Having familiarized ourselves with Leibniz's distinction between eternal and contingent truths, we can now obtain a reasonable understanding of his idea of a universal characteristic (*characteristica universalis*).

Let us suppose that in some absolute sense we can speak of the system of all eternal truths. This is a supposition which, in any event, was made by Leibniz himself. Among these eternal truths we can distinguish, on his view, between primitive eternal truths, which we know by intuition, and derivative eternal truths, of which we obtain knowledge by inference from the primitive ones. Let us now transpose these designations from the sentences to the thought contents, the propositions, that the sentences express. We assume a deductive theory *E* whose simple ideas are absolutely all simple ideas, whose complex ideas are absolutely all finitely complex ideas, whose axioms are all primitive eternal truths, and whose provable theorems are all derivative eternal truths. The universal characteristic, as Leibniz conceived it, is a symbolic language U which is (in the previously stated sense) a characteristic for this theory E. The universal characteristic is thus to have the following properties:

(a) Each name in U is a designation of exactly one idea in E, and each idea in E has at least one name in U.

(b) Each sentence that can be formulated in U expresses exactly one proposition of E, and each conceivable proposition of E is expressed by at least one sentence in U.

(c) There is a list of axioms in U, and these express exactly all the primitive eternal truths.

(d) There exist a number of rules of inference such that a sentence S of U can be inferred with the help of these rules (in a finite number of steps) from the sentences $T, V \ldots$ of U, if and only if the proposition of E expressed by S follows logically from the propositions in E expressed by $T, V \ldots$

In particular, the following holds for U:

(d′) Each derivative eternal truth is expressed by a sentence that can be deduced from the axioms of U by means of the rules of inference.

As mentioned above, Leibniz attached great importance to the distinction between simple and compound ideas and to the analysis of a compound idea into its simple components. In conformity with this view he held that the universal characteristic U should also have this property:

(e) There is a method by means of which all problems of the following type can be solved mechanically: 'Given the designation in U of an idea, is the idea simple? If not, what are the designations in U of the simple ideas of which it is composed?'

According to certain assumptions made by Leibniz, it follows from (e) that:

(f)   There is a method by which it can be mechanically decided whether a sentence in *U* expresses a truth or not.

Even by the time he wrote his work *On the Combinatory Art* (*De arte combinatoria*, 1666) at the age of twenty, Leibniz dreamed of this universal characteristic, and he described it as:

A method whereby all truths of reason would be reduced to a kind of calculus. Simultaneously, it would be a kind of universal language or universal script, but infinitely different from any that has hitherto been envisaged. Its symbols, and also its words, would guide our reason and errors—save errors of fact—would be mere errors of calculation.[9]

In this way, Plato's idea of a universal, rational science ("dialectics") was transformed by Leibniz into the idea of a formalized science of the kind described. In the light of results of modern logic, one has presumably to state that while it is possible to go a long way in the direction of Leibniz's universal characteristic, still its complete realization is in principle impossible—quite apart from the limitations of human intelligence. (I allude here to certain impossibility theorems proved in modern logic.)

[9] Ibid., vol. vii, p. 200 (from an untitled paper).

III

The Great Systems

11 THE SYSTEM OF DESCARTES

We have already become acquainted with some of Descartes's contributions to the mechanistic world picture, his ideas on the nature of mind and matter. His own version of this picture was soon seen to be untenable in the light of Newtonian mechanics. This kind of world picture has had its day, and now appears as a conjecture which is too vague, partly unverifiable, and in part even falsifiable. Nevertheless, it played an inspiring role during one of the most creative periods of scientific research. The connection between the mechanistic picture and scientific research is strikingly shown by Descartes's own twofold activity as a speculative philosopher and as a mathematician and physicist. Another of Descartes's contributions was his revival of philosophical interest in the axiomatic or deductive method.

Descartes's philosophical system is an attempt to combine a mechanistic world view and a theology of the medieval type into a unified axiomatic theory. I shall now give a summary account of its foundations and general structure.

Descartes is not prepared to accept a statement as a basic truth unless it is "impossible" for him to doubt it. As a means of finding such statements, he cultivates his famous universal doubt. He decides to reject as false anything that there is the slightest reason to doubt, in order to see whether anything is left, which it must then be impossible to doubt. As has often been pointed out, this programme is decidedly problematic; what should be done if there is reason to doubt both of two opposite opinions? However, Descartes thinks that, in accordance with this programme, he has to reject as false not only all earlier philosophical theories, but also everything he has formerly believed about the external world and his own body, and even all mathematical theorems. What finally remains is, he thinks, merely the proposition:

C 1. *Cogito* (I, Descartes, think).

In Augustine this and similar propositions (*dubito, fallor,* and so on) had already appeared as indubitable truths, resisting even the most radical scepticism, and it is probable that Descartes was influenced by the Church father. For Augustine, however, this proposition was merely one among many indubitable truths. Descartes's idea of using the statement as the foundation for a comprehensive theory was something new.

Descartes's argument to show that *C* 1 satisfies the requirement he puts on basic truths is as follows. He can imagine, he says, that there exists a malevolent demon who deceives him so thoroughly that he is led to believe in false, and only in false, propositions. In his search for basic truths, the existence of such a demon would represent the most unfavourable of all possible situations. Consider now the statement *C* 1. Suppose:

(1) I (Descartes) mistakenly believe that *C* 1 is true.

Clearly (1) cannot hold without the following also holding:

(2) I (Descartes) believe,

or, since Descartes considers belief as a form of thought:

(2′) I (Descartes) think.

Therefore, Descartes concludes, *C* 1 is an indubitable or necessary truth. The much debated question of how this argument for the indubitability of *C* 1 is to be understood must be left aside here. (I suspect that it is impossible to extract an unambiguous interpretation from Descartes's texts.)

Descartes seldom states *C* 1 alone. His usual statement is *Cogito ergo sum*; and at times he says that this whole phrase is an indubitable insight. However, if the *ergo* (therefore) is to indicate an inference, it seems more correct to look upon:

C 2. *Sum* (I, Descartes, exist)

as the first theorem deduced from *C* 1. He appears to imply, moreover, that nearly all of his philosophy can somehow be deduced from *C* 1. Next to be established are the following theorems:

C 3. The mind is a substance that thinks, and does nothing else.

C 4. God exists.

C 5. God is all-powerful and all-good.

C 6. That which I, Descartes, clearly and distinctly perceive is true.

C 7. The material world exists.

C 8. The body has extension and its determinations, and no other characteristics.

Time after time he repeats the derivation of these theorems in his writings, in very similar words and without being impressed by the forceful objections that many of his contemporaries communicated to him.

It does not take great acuteness to see that Descartes's system is wholly without logical stringency. During the course of his argument, he repeatedly introduces new premisses, taken often enough from the Scholastics, whom he so deeply despised, without any indication of their status as primitive assumptions along with C 1. In one passage[1] (in which he replies to the objections that Mersenne made against his *Meditations*), he characterizes his method as "analytic", which there seems to mean the same as heuristic. He says that he has arranged his propositions in the same order as he came upon them. He seems to think that there exists a more rigorous, "synthetic" method, namely the one that the ancient geometers used. He also sketches a synthetic demonstration of four theorems in his system, a demonstration in which he makes use of ten "definitions", seven "postulates", and ten "axioms". Quite apart from the disproportion between what he assumes and what he proves, this "synthetic" presentation appears basically to be just as arbitrary as the "analytic" one.

The success that Descartes's system was to have on the continent (but never in England) must have been due to the fact that the Aristotelian–Scholastic systems no longer appeared tenable in the light of the new findings of science,

[1] In the Reply to the Second Set of Objections (Haldane and Ross, vol. ii, pp. 48 ff.).

so that the age longed for a substitute for them. Descartes was the first to offer such a substitute, a system which appeared to do justice to theology as well as to science.

In his own writings, some of which are considered classics of French literature, his system is presented as a personal concern of great urgency. When he describes his universal doubt, his victory over this doubt, and his reconstruction of knowledge, he confesses his feelings of doubt and certainty in much the same way that Luther confessed his anxiety and method of finding peace while preaching the impossibility of salvation by deeds and its possibility through faith and divine mercy. Just like Luther, Descartes wants to guide his readers along an intellectual path similar to the one he himself has followed. This aspect of his system has also to be taken into account if his historic role is to be understood. Luther's doctrine seemed to open a private road to God and salvation, bypassing the church organizations. Analogously, Descartes's method and system appeared as an individual road to philosophical truth, bypassing the doctrinal systems sanctioned by tradition and authority. Like Luther, Descartes was to give rise to his own orthodoxy, as so often happens in history.

12. THE MOTIVES OF SPINOZA AND LEIBNIZ

During the time in which the new mechanics and the mechanistic world view evolved, two of the most original metaphysical systems ever conceived by the human mind were created, Spinoza's theory of substance and Leibniz's monadology. Spinoza's and Leibniz's theories are two different attempts to come to terms with approximately the same intellectual situation. Two decisive factors, common to Spinoza and Leibniz, are the belief in a mechanistic world view and a religious need. Each attempted in his own way to overcome the incompatibility that was felt to exist between these factors.

Spinoza's way out was this: he transferred his religious feeling from the God of the Judaic–Christian theology to the mechanistic universe itself. At the same time he left room for the mystic sense of unknown infinities by supposing that the world of physics is merely one of infinitely many aspects of one and the same divine substance.

Leibniz's course was not only different but almost dia-metrically opposite. Whereas Spinoza strove to bring his religious feeling down to the level of the mechanistic view, Leibniz tried to degrade the material world in favour of another postulated reality which better satisfied his reli-gious feeling. For Leibniz the mechanistic picture of the world is only a relative truth, a truth about subjective phe-nomena. Objective reality, the structure of which can be discovered by reasoning from abstract axioms, presents a completely different picture. It is a realm of purely spiritual beings, "monads", of which an ennobled and rarefied version of the God of the Judaic–Christian theology is president.

For both Spinoza and Leibniz there is a need for recon-ciliation with reality, for acceptance of what is. Spinoza expresses this reconciliation first and foremost by his idea that all events in the material and mental worlds are modes of the divine substance. That Peter is good means, for Spinoza, that the universe itself has the property of in-cluding this fact, and that Paul is bad means that the universe has the property of including that fact as well. Peter's good-ness along with Paul's badness, the things we call good along with those we call bad, the things that give us pleasure as well as those that cause us pain, are in this way all "modi" of the universe. Once this is realized, it is possible to love all things with the objective love that the scientist has for his subject. Leibniz's reconciliation found its formal expression in his claim that our world is the best of all possible worlds, where the bad elements contribute to the goodness of the whole. If Paul had not been bad, the world as a whole would have been worse, just as if Peter had not been good. Of everything that has already taken place, we should think that it has happened for the best. As for the future, we should resolve to act as well as possible—this being one of Leibniz's moral maxims.

It is difficult to avoid the conclusion that Spinoza's doctrine of substance has a deeper foundation in its author's personality than Leibniz's monadology has in his personality. Spinoza lived as he preached, there being no propositions in his theory that he would have doubted during his weekday

life any more than on his philosophical Sundays. Monadology does not harmonize in the same way with what we
know of Leibniz's life. In so far as Leibniz thought un-
ceasingly, and honestly respected the thoughts of others,
his theory of perceiving monads seems sincere. But how
could he, while occupied with practical projects and while
writing streams of letters to scientists, theologians, and
princesses, have truly believed that the monads have no
communication among themselves?

From a logical point of view it is interesting to observe
the part that the idea of parallelism or harmony, i.e. of
one-to-one correspondence and isomorphism, plays in both
Spinoza's and Leibniz's theories.

The attempts of Spinoza and Leibniz to give their systems
an axiomatic form and a practically universal scope were
completely in line with the ideas of Descartes. Spinoza
wanted to achieve a system which would be similar to,
but better than, that of Descartes; while Leibniz wanted
to outdo both Descartes and Spinoza, as well as the other
system builders of his time.

13. SPINOZA'S SYSTEM

A. *The theory of parallelism*

Like Descartes, Spinoza assumes an essential difference
between material things (*res*) and mental ideas or perceptions (*ideae*). We have already seen that Spinoza, like several
other seventeenth-century thinkers, postulates an immanent
material and an immanent mental determinism. Spinoza
combines this view with an assumption of his own, the so-
called theory of parallelism. He formulates it as follows:
"The order and connection of ideas is the same as the order
and connection of things." (*Ordo et connexio idearum idem
est ac ordo et connexio rerum*)[2] Spinoza is primarily thinking
here of the causal order. Less explicitly, he seems to have
extended this parallelism to hold with respect to a part–
whole relationship.[3] Summarizing in modern terminology
the official as well as the unofficial aspects of the theory
of parallelism, we have the following:

[2] Spinoza, *The Ethics*, II, proposition VII. [3] Ibid., II, proposition XV.

There is a one-to-one correspondence between ideas and things in such a way that if $i(t)$ is the idea corresponding to the thing t, then

(a) t is the cause of t, if and only if $i(t)$ is the cause of $i(t')$;

(b) t is a part of t' if and only if $i(t)$ is a part of $i(t')$.

This theory remains extremely abstract as long as no rule has been given by which we can identify the idea $i(t)$ that corresponds to a given thing t. Spinoza never presents any such rule. On searching his *Ethics* for an answer to the question of what the idea $i(t)$ is, we find three following important clues:

(c) $i(t)$ is an idea of t;

(d) $i(t)$ is "the same as" t, or "another aspect of the same entity, of which t is one aspect".

(e)   If P is a person, then $i(P$'s body$)$ is the same as P's mind.[4]

Spinoza advanced no clear reasoning in support of his theory of parallelism. It was a flight of the imagination, inspiring yet obscure. Three of its corollaries are these:

Cor. 1. All material things have a mental aspect. A thing t has the mental aspect $i(t)$.

Cor. 2. Every idea pertaining to the mental life of a person A is an idea of a phenomenon which pertains to A's body.

An idea $i(t)$, which pertains to P's mental life, is a part of P's mind, i.e. $i(P$'s body$)$, and its object t is thus a part of P's body. *Cor.* 2 raises a major difficulty for Spinoza when it comes to explaining human knowledge. To the extent that a person's knowledge occurs in the form of ideas, according to *Cor.* 2, it can be concerned, strictly speaking, only with his body.

Cor. 3. To every phenomenon t pertaining to a person's body there corresponds in his mind a (more or less distinct) idea of t.

If t is a part of P's body, then $i(t)$ is a part of $i(P$'s body$)$, i.e. P's mind.

[4] Ibid., II, proposition XIII.

A remote descendant of Spinoza's theory is the principle of psycho-physical isomorphism, which many present-day psychologists and physiologists use as a working hypothesis. The gestalt psychologist Wolfgang Köhler has formulated this principle in the following way:

Experiences can be ordered systematically, if their various kinds of nuances are put together according to their similarities. The procedure is comparable to the one by which animals are ordered in zoology and plants in botany. The processes upon which experiences depend are not directly known. But if they were known, they could also be ordered according to their similarities. Between the two systematic orders, that of experiences and that of concomitant physiological processes, various relationships may be assumed to obtain. But the relation between the two orderly systems will be simple and clear only if we postulate that both have the same form or structure *qua* systems.[5]

B. *The doctrine of substance*

The concepts of substance, attribute, and mode which the medieval Scholastics inherited from Aristotle play an important part in Spinoza's system. In his opinion there exists one and only one substance, namely the infinite universe itself. Infinite physical space is an attribute of this substance, and every material thing that exists in space is one of its modes. Just as infinite space is related to material things, so infinite thought is related to each particular, limited idea. This postulated infinite thought is another attribute of the substance, and each particular idea is one of its modes. Infinite space and infinite thought are the only two attributes of the substance that are known to us.

In addition to these two attributes, the substance also has infinitely many other attributes, unknown to us. Only an infinite number of attributes, each and every one of which, like space, is itself infinite, can adequately express the infinitude of the substance. The theory of parallelism previously stated is merely a special case of a much more general theory. What is true of the relationship between the attributes of extension and thought is also true of the relationship between any two of the infinitely many attributes.

[5] W. Köhler, *Gestalt Psychology* (1929, rev. edn. New York, 1947), p. 58.

C. *Theology and ethics*

Spinoza gives the religious name "God" to the substance-universe. His theology is interesting because it is so unlike the prevailing Christian one. It could be said that he comes to formulate his theology through application of the following scheme of inference:

The universe = God
The universe has the property E
Therefore, God has the property E.

God has no human feelings and takes no account of human feelings. He neither likes nor dislikes, neither loves nor hates, and he does not bring about things for any purpose. *Sub specie aeternitatis*, from the aspect of eternity, which is God's, there is nothing good or bad, nothing better or worse. God *is* that machine that is identical with the universe, which functions with mechanical necessity.

Like the Stoics, Spinoza contrasts the slavery under which the man ruled by his passion lives and the independence or freedom that characterizes the wise. The wise man is the one who sees that he and his fellow human beings are merely cogs in the machinery, who has freed himself from vain ambition, and who prudently strives for knowledge and peace of mind. As far as is humanly possible, the wise man considers the world from the point of view of eternity. He loves the universe, and—here Spinoza's underlying mysticism comes to the surface—this love, which a mode of God has for God, is at the same time God's own love for himself.

D. *Spinoza's axiomatic method*

Spinoza, who took over from Descartes the idea of an axiomatic philosophy, was aware of some of the shortcomings in Descartes's own application of the axiomatic method. Spinoza's earliest work, *René Descartes's Philosophical Principles, parts I and II, Proved in a Geometrical Manner* (*Renati des Cartes principiorum philosophiae, pars I et II, more geometrico demonstratae, 1663*), contains an implicit criticism of Descartes's procedure. In order to prove the Cartesian theorems, Spinoza finds it necessary to invoke far more axioms than Descartes had employed. Spinoza's *magnum opus, Ethics, Proved in Geometrical Order (Ethica ordine geometrico demonstrata*, published posthumously in 1677) demonstrates his awareness of the fact that in order to prove much, much has to be postulated without proof. In all, he makes use there of fifteen so-called axioms, eight postulates, and twenty-six fundamental definitions. Although he sought to avoid the formal errors of Descartes, his own system is logically as loose as Descartes's had been. Spinoza, too, repeatedly—and unconsciously—relies on new pre- misses which are not listed as being either axioms, postulates, or definitions. In the same way that Spinoza's entire system appeals primarily to our feelings and to our visionary con- ception of the world, so his axiomatic method appears almost like a philosophical verse form. Just as the content of a poem may find its most suitable expression in, say, the Alexandrine metre, so the axiomatic presentation seems the most adequate for Spinoza's outlook on the universe, the outlook of a Stoic and a mystic on a mechanistic world.

Spinoza's relation to the mechanistic world picture is similar to Xenophanes' relation to the oldest Greek natural philosophy. Both of them represent a sort of cosmic piety. Spinoza's contemporaries looked on his philosophy as an abominable attack on religion, a reaction to which his acute critical investigations of the Bible, set forth in the *Theologico- Political Treatise (Tractatus theologico-politicus*, 1670), contributed. Not until the close of the eighteenth century was Spinozism to find sympathizers, and then mainly in literary circles. It became a source of inspiration for the German romantic philosophy.

14. LEIBNIZ'S SYSTEM

A. *Some of the basic ideas of the monadology*

The material world, according to Leibniz, is only our im- perfect manner of comprehending a reality which in itself is constituted quite differently. This reality, which because of my imperfection I perceive, say, as a Swedish "smörgås- bord", is in itself an aggregate of purely spiritual (not very high ranking) beings, which Leibniz calls monads. The word monad (from the Greek *monas*), which is often used by the Greek philosophers (among others by Plato in his theory of

Ideas and in his arithmetical philosophy), has the same range of application as the English word "unit". It was because Leibniz thought of these spiritual beings as units that he called them monads.

We may consider the proposition that every substance is a monad or composed of monads to be the Fundamental Theorem of Monadology. The proof of this theorem—as presented for example in the *Monadology* (1714)—is the following:

We start with two postulates:

    (i)   Every substance is either simple or compound.

   (ii)   A compound substance is composed of simple substances. (This postulate derives ultimately from Zeno of Elea.)

Hence:

  (iii)   Every substance is either simple or composed of simple substances.

We now lay down two additional postulates:

  (iv)   Each material substance has a divisible extension. (The postulate may be derived from Descartes.)

   (v)   Nothing that has a divisible extension is a simple substance.

Hence:

  (vi)   No simple substance is a material substance.

At this point there comes yet another postulate borrowed from Descartes:

  (vii)   Every substance is either material or spiritual.

Hence:

 (viii)   Each simple substance is spiritual.

Consequently:

  (ix)   Each substance is either a simple spiritual substance or composed of simple spiritual substances.

If by a 'monad' we understand a 'simple spiritual substance', (ix) can also be expressed as follows:

   (x)   Each substance is either a monad or composed of monads.

Which was to be demonstrated.

To understand the importance Leibniz attributed to this fundamental proposition, one must recall the Aristotelian dichotomy between substances and universals. Anything existing in any sense is, by this dichotomy, either a substance or a universal. If the Fundamental Theorem is combined with the dichotomy, the following conclusion ensues:

(xi) Anything that exists in any way is either a monad, or composed of monads, or a universal.

Whatever this conclusion may mean, it does at least have universal application, and to that extent it is important. According to the Aristotelian dichotomy, universals cannot exist without the existence of substances, so the Fundamental Theorem, together with the Aristotelian dichotomy, guarantees that:

(xii) Monads exist.

Let us return for a moment to the smörgåsbord. As it appears to us, it is certainly not a universal in Aristotle's sense. Nor does it present itself to us as a monad or as a collection of monads. The conclusion drawn by Leibniz is the one I alluded to in my opening remarks, which can be stated thus:

(xiii) The smörgåsbord is the way in which, because of my imperfect perception, a collection of monads presents itself to me.

According to Leibniz, what has just been said about the smörgåsbord holds for the entire reality which our senses present to us. A direct consequence of what has already been stated is this:

(xiv) A monad has no extension.

Leibniz often seems to conceive of an extensionless monad as a kind of spiritual, metaphysical point. Further important ideas of the monadology include the following:

(xv) Every monad is a perceiving being.

Like his entire generation, Leibniz was deeply impressed by the Cartesian theory of mind and matter. If the monad is a spiritual substance, then, according to the Cartesian theory, it follows that the monad is perceiving (Descartes's "thinking").

(xvi)   Every monad exists at every moment of time.

Leibniz thought, as the Greek Atomists and Plato had thought before him, that only compound entities can be created and annihilated as their parts come together and disperse.

(xvii)   Every monad is perceiving at every moment of its existence.

If at any given moment a monad did not have any perceptions, then it would at that moment not be existing—just as a material thing could not exist deprived of its extension.

(xviii)   At any moment when a monad does not have conscious perceptions (*apperceptions*), it has unconscious perceptions (*petites perceptions*).

This proposition seems to be a consequence of (xvii), but Leibniz also believed that he could find direct empirical verification of it. (a) The miller, sleeping peacefully in his mill while the wheel turns, wakes up should for some reason the wheel stop. In his dreamless sleep he must therefore have unconsciously perceived the creaking of the wheel. (b) Each wave which breaks upon the beach causes a unique sound. A person listening to the waves, however, consciously hears merely an undifferentiated roar. His hearing of each sound caused by each individual wave is unconscious.

(xix)   A monad cannot be acted upon by other monads.

No kind of interaction can occur between simple substances, Leibniz thought, because simple substances can neither directly nor indirectly come in contact with each other. Contact presupposes finite extension, and monads do not have finite extension. According to (xix), what a monad perceives is independent of any external influence. Leibniz also expressed this idea in the well-known statement that the monads have no windows.[6] If what a monad perceives never depends on external influence, it must always depend exclusively on the monad itself.

---

[6] From the fact that monads are unable to touch each other, we could, of course, just as well draw a quite different conclusion. It could be said that monads do interact, and that each case of interaction between monads is therefore an instance of remote influence. Bolzano, whose metaphysics was strongly influenced by Leibniz, adopts this point of view in *The Paradoxes of the Infinite* (1851).

(xx)   A monad is in its essence a force which expresses itself in an uninterrupted stream of perceptions.

B. *The theory of the pre-established harmony*

If a monad cannot be influenced from outside, how can we explain all the mental phenomena which, according to our common sense picture of the universe, depend on external influences? How can it be that many of us see the "same" smörgåsbord, that we experience the same taste of smoked ham and aquavit? How is it that I think of Leibniz's metaphysics, am aware of myself as speaking to you about the subject and of you as giving reasonable replies, while at the same time you, *mutatis mutandis*, experience the same? If the monadology were true it seems that our entire existence would be turned into a series of incomprehensible coincidences. Leibniz was alive to this problem, and he believed that he could solve it by his theory of the pre-established harmony.

For the sake of brevity, let us use the term C-events for those coincidences that are remarkable from the point of view of the monadology, of which I have just given some examples. Unfortunately, it must be admitted that the solution to the problem of the C-events provided by the theory of the pre-established harmony throws very little light on the subject. Concerning C-events, the theory says the following:

(i)   The system of monads is so constituted by God that C-events occur.

A prominent part in Leibniz's metaphysics is played by a notion he sometimes expressed by the following words:

(a)   The nature of A mirrors the nature of B,

and sometimes by the words:

(b)   The nature of A expresses the nature of B.

By studying a mirror image we obtain knowledge about the properties of what it is an image of. There is an isomorphism between the image and its original, and once we know the rule of correspondence on which the isomorphism is based we can calculate the properties of the original from the properties of the image (and conversely). In the case of an ordinary well-made mirror, the rule of correspondence is so simple that the calculation can be performed at a glance, quite unconsciously. But when Leibniz speaks in his metaphysics of mirroring, he does not have in mind any mirrors in the literal sense. What he wishes to convey by this concrete simile is the abstract idea of isomorphism, along with the possibility this opens of calculating the properties of an original from those of the image. The phrase (b) is used by Leibniz in the same abstract sense. "In my terminology", he writes in a letter to Arnauld, "one thing expresses another when a constant and lawful connection exists between what may be said of the one and of the other. Thus, a perspectival projection expresses the projected geometrical figure."[7]

In addition to the rather uninteresting theological assertion (i), the doctrine of the pre-established harmony also contains the tenet that:

(ii) The state of each monad at each moment of time mirrors (expresses) the entire history of the entire system of monads.

Making use of Leibniz's own simile, we can say that through this assumption (ii) his universe comes to assume the character of a fantastic hall of mirrors with infinitely many mirrors, where the images are reflected back and forth in infinity.

Further, Leibniz assumes that:

(iii) Each monad mirrors the entire world of monads in a fashion characteristic of the particular monad.

No two monads mirror the world in the same way. Each monad is like a particular point of view from which the world is seen. God's majesty is reflected in the infinite number of points of view from which the world is thus being regarded.

Although the monads are not literally in space—at least, according to one of Leibniz's views, whereby space is only a subjective phenomenon—we can still arrange

[7] Leibniz, *Hauptschriften zur Grundlegung der Philosophie* (Leipzig, 1903), vol. ii, p. 233 (Leibniz to Arnauld, 9 Oct. 1687).

them in an abstract space-like order, a monad space, by taking account of "the points of view" from which they regard the universe, i.e. the ways in which they mirror or express it. In Leibniz's expositions of his theory one sometimes also catches sight of the following assumption:

(iv) The spatial order in which we perceive phenomena mirrors the order of the underlying monads in the monad space.

In our own time, Bertrand Russell was fascinated by Leibniz's metaphysics, especially the idea of a monad space, and he developed interesting variations upon the Leibnizian theme in *Our Knowledge of The External World* (1914) and *The Analysis of Mind* (1921).

C. *Another line of thought in the monadology*

The kind of demonstration sketched above under *A* was the one that Leibniz most frequently invoked. However, he sometimes employs a very different method of proof of some of the theorems of the monadology, especially in *A Discourse on Metaphysics* (1686) and in his correspondence with the Cartesian Arnauld to which this work gave rise.

As a basis for this other demonstration he takes the following assumption, borrowed from Descartes, which he presents as a self-evident axiom:

(i) A proposition is true if and only if the concept of the predicate is a part of the concept of the subject.

As regards this axiom, it should first be noted that obviously it is applicable to a given proposition only if we can pick out exactly one subject and exactly one predicate in that proposition. Presumably, Leibniz presupposed that this is the case for every proposition or, at least, that every proposition is somehow equivalent to one for which this condition is satisfied. What he means by the concept of the predicate being a part of the concept of the subject is not too clear. Probably, he would think that statements such as "All bachelors are unmarried" and its synonym, "All unmarried men are unmarried" present readily grasped examples of the intended relation between the concept of the subject (unmarried man = bachelor) and the concept of the predicate (unmarried).

In order to establish whether a proposition is true or whether it is false we have therefore to submit the subject notion to an analysis to see whether it does or does not contain the predicate notion as a part. As is well known, and as we shall see later when studying his philosophy, Kant held that such analysis of concepts is always an *a priori* business, something that can be carried out by pure thinking. Leibniz, however, avoided the conclusion that all true propositions are *a priori* truths by distinguishing between an analysis that can be carried out in a finite number of steps and one that requires an infinite sequence of intellectual operations. A human being is capable of performing a finite analysis only; God alone can carry out an infinite one. Now, only some true propositions can be shown to be true by a finite analysis: these are the so-called eternal truths, and are the only truths that are *a priori* for a human being. The so-called contingent truths can be established by analysis as true only if the analysis is continued in infinity; these truths, therefore, are not *a priori* for human beings, although they are so for God.

From (i) Leibniz infers the following:

(ii) To each substance S there corresponds (exactly) one concept C such that C applies to S and that S has P if and only if P is a part of C.

This statement goes further than (i). (i) says that any proposition, say p, is true if and only if the notion associated with the predicate of p is a part of the notion associated with the subject of p. (ii) asserts that for each substance S there is a (unique) concept C such that, whatever proposition p of the form 'S has P' we may consider, p is true if and only if P is a part of this C. The transition from (i) to (ii) is made by Leibniz as if it were self-evident. But of course it is not. A tacit premiss Leibniz may have made use of when passing from (i) to (ii) is that as long as a name, say "Caesar", is used to designate the same substance it is also associated with one and the same notion of that substance. Further, in (ii) Leibniz presupposes that any statement about a substance can somehow be reformulated into the standard form 'S has P'. The concept C which corresponds to the substance S and which is spoken of in (ii) is also designated by Leibniz by such names as "the nature", "the definition", "the essence", "the idea", or "the haecceitas" of S.

Leibniz apparently considers the following as equivalent to (ii) in some way:

(iii) If S has P, then the concept C spoken of in (ii) is the sufficient reason for S having P.

From (iii) he infers:

(iv) A substance cannot be acted upon from the outside.

When inferring this Leibniz probably reasons in something like the following way. Since the concept C is the reason why S has P, there can exist no external ground or cause of the possession of P by S.

Leibniz asserts that (ii) entails a large number of important metaphysical tenets, among them the *principium identitatis indiscernibilium*, i.e. the principle of the identity of indiscernibles:

(v) There do not exist any two substances that are exactly alike in all respects.

Here, as at so many other points, Leibniz leaves us in the dark concerning the demonstration he has in mind. Perhaps he argued as follows. If a substance S is like a substance S' in all respects, then the notion which according to (ii) applies exactly to S includes precisely the same characteristics as the notion which, likewise according to (ii), applies exactly to S'. But two notions which include exactly the same characteristics are identical. Hence, also S and S' are identical. This reconstruction of his argument, however, is only a conjecture.

D. *God and the best of all possible worlds*

It is God who, in advance, has fashioned the monads so that they present a mutual harmony. In Leibniz's conciliatory, optimistic, and perhaps socially somewhat conventional metaphysics, God assumes a prominent position. Our actual world is only one among infinitely many logically possible worlds. From among them God has selected ours and given it existence. The good Lord always selects the best, and consequently our world is the best of all possible worlds. Leibniz wrote a large work, *The Theodicy* (1710), in which he sought to refute the objections to this view which arise so readily from our experience and our moral evaluations. The evil that certain aspects of our world exhibit is necessary, he asserted, in order that the picture as a whole should be the best possible. Voltaire's *Candide* was a sarcastic reply to this argument.

At times a kind of mysticism breaks through the scholastic arguments of Leibniz as well as those of Spinoza. God's infinite perfection, says Leibniz, enables him to consider his creation from infinitely many points of view. So each monad comes to represent a divine point of view, and hence —let us draw the consequence—the mind of the other as well as that of Leibniz, the mind of the child as well as that of the grown-up, each represents such a point of view. Leibniz also likened the monads to a group of Choirs, each one of which has been assigned by God to sing in its own way a common theme.

E. *Leibniz's deductive method*

Leibniz saw the mistakes made by both his predecessors, Descartes and Spinoza, in their applications of the axiomatic method. He thought that he was avoiding those errors even while he was committing them almost as often and irreparably. Whereas both Descartes and Spinoza set forth their systems in a definite form, the restlessly versatile, universal genius, Leibniz, has given us merely various sketches of his system, jotted down on various occasions. It is difficult to determine exactly in what order and by what methods he wished to deduce his theorems. In this respect there is a great difference between the approaches in what are, perhaps, the two most exhaustive and systematic presentations of his system, *A Treatise on Metaphysics* (1686) and the *Monadology* (1714).[8] In the former, Leibniz

[8] In his *Critical exposition of the philosophy of Leibniz* (1900), Bertrand Russell maintains that the former is logically the better of the two and at the

seems to consider a certain definition of the concept of truth as the most important, if not the only, axiom for his system. In the *Monadology*, the fundamental axioms concern instead such concepts as "substance", "simple substance", "extension", "compound substance", and "spiritual substance". Like Spinoza's doctrine of substance, the theory of monads exhorts our imagination to look upon reality in an entirely new light. The deductive form in which Leibniz wished to cast his theory is of little interest.

same time the one that expresses Leibniz's true convictions, whereas the latter is logically inferior and involves a compromise with prevailing theological and philosophical opinion. It is undeniable that an age which viewed the "atheist" and "fatalist" Spinoza with dread and abhorrence might take offence at the former presentation. It is difficult, however, to see any difference between the two presentations in the matter of logical rigour.

IV

The Empiricist Theory of Knowledge
in Britain

15. INTRODUCTION

Those continental thinkers who took part in the revival of
the Platonic–Aristotelian ideal of science were only slightly
interested in the epistemological problems presented by
empirical knowledge. British philosophy, on the other hand,
had shown an empiricist bent ever since the thirteenth
century, the time of Roger Bacon and William of Ockham.
At the beginning of the seventeenth century, this tendency
was revived by Francis Bacon's (1561–1626) critique of
scholasticism and plea for induction in *Novum Organum*
(1620). Through *An Essay concerning Human Understanding*
(1690), John Locke (1632–1704) inaugurated an empiricist
tradition which has since been in continuous existence up
to our own time. It was carried on in the eighteenth century
by George Berkeley (1688–1753) and David Hume (1711–76),
by the utilitarians Jeremy Bentham (1748–1832) and John
Stuart Mill (1806–73), and in our century by Bertrand Russell
(1872–1970) and A. J. Ayer (b. 1910). In this and the two
following chapters I shall attempt to give a synoptic presentation of some of the views held by the first three great thinkers
of this tradition, Locke, Berkeley, and Hume.

Locke's work, *An Essay concerning Human Understanding*
(cited in the following as his *Essay*), introduced a number of
theories which remained basic to the thought of his two
immediate successors, even though they modified them in
various ways. The general theory of ideas and the associated
theory of meaning were two such theories. Also in this
category are Locke's views on induction and the laws of
nature, his nominalistic tendency, and his arguments for the
subjectivity of the secondary sense qualities. All these ideas
recur in Berkeley as well as in Hume. Berkeley's main epistemological works were *An Essay towards a New Theory of*

Vision (1709) (here cited as his *Theory of Vision*), *A Treatise concerning the Principles of Human Knowledge* (1710) (cited as the *Principles*), and *Three Dialogues between Hylas and Philonous* (1713) (cited as the *Dialogues*). Locke's critique of naïve realism was in these works strengthened to become a critique of the kind of critical realism which Locke himself embraced. Hume's chief epistemological works were the first book of his *A Treatise of Human Nature* (1738) (cited as his *Treatise*) and the revision of it, *An Enquiry Concerning Human Understanding* (1748) (here cited as Hume's *Enquiry*). Hume gave a sharper statement to a theory of knowledge (or verification) whose beginnings can be traced in Berkeley and Locke. Elaborating ideas uttered in passing by Berkeley, and stating them without the theology that pervades Berkeley's thought, Hume discussed induction and causality in an extremely interesting way. The community of basic philosophical outlook and philosophical interest is very strong among these three empiricists. But there is also a great diversity between them in world view, in opinions on particular points, and in temperament. Locke, the critical realist, looked upon himself as an epistemological "under-labourer" to the great new science of nature. Berkeley utilized Locke's epistemology as the foundation for his own theological "immaterialism", and rejected the "corpuscular philosophy" of his age, while Hume was a sceptic who endeavoured to show that our theoretical life is founded largely on animal habit rather than on reason. In spite of the divergences between these three great empiricists, I think that essentially correct information about many of their views can be presented in the synoptic manner I have chosen.

I take the essence of classical empiricism to consist of two theories which will be referred to here as the Empiricist Theory of Meaning and the Empiricist Theory of Knowledge, "theory of knowledge" being understood here in a particular restricted sense. The former concerns the problem of the conditions under which verbal expressions have a meaning ("stand for ideas"), so enabling them to be used in rational discourse. The latter deals with the problem of the circumstances under which a statement can be considered to be an object of knowledge. (In more modern terminology, the theories might be called the empiricists' "theory of concept formation" and their "theory of verification".)

Both theories were intended to be instruments of criticism. One aim of the Theory of Meaning was expressed as follows by Locke in the preface to his *Essay*:

> Vague and insignificant forms of speech, and abuse of language, have so long passed for mysteries of science; and hard misapplied words, with little or no meaning, have, by prescription, such a right to be mistaken for deep learning and height of speculation, that it will not be easy to persuade either those who speak or those who hear them, that they are but the covers of ignorance, and hindrance of true knowledge. To break in upon this sanctuary of vanity and ignorance will be, I suppose, some service to human understanding; though so few are apt to think they deceive or are deceived in the use of words, or that the language of the sect they are of has any faults in it which ought to be examined or corrected...[1]

What, then, was this sanctuary of vanity and ignorance that the empiricists wished to break in upon? They had in mind above all the kind of metaphysical speculation that we have met in the chapters on Plato and Aristotle, the theological philosophy of the Middle Ages, and of Spinoza and Leibniz. Thus Hume aimed penetrating criticism against such fundamental elements of seventeenth-century rationalism as the notions of substance and causation. Whereas both Locke and Berkeley were religious believers (the latter becoming a bishop), Hume was an atheist and as far as he was concerned religion and theology were included in the sanctuary.

While the purpose of the Theory of Meaning was to expose obscure or meaningless modes of expression, the aim of the Theory of Knowledge was the demarcation of knowledge from unfounded assertions. Hume stated this purpose rhetorically in the final words of the *Enquiry*:

> When we run over libraries, persuaded of these principles, what havoc must we make? If we take in our hand any volume; of divinity or school metaphysics, for instance; let us ask, *Does it contain any abstract reasoning concerning quantity and number?* No. *Does it contain*

[1] Locke, *An Essay Concerning Human Understanding* (ed. P. H. Nidditch, Oxford, 1975), p. 10, 'Epistle to the Reader'.

any experimental reasoning concerning matter of fact and existence?
No. Commit it then to the flames: for it can contain nothing but
sophistry and illusion.[2]

British empiricism is one example among many in the
history of philosophy of a school of thought that started
out with the aim of stating the principles of sound scientific
method in order to do away with vain speculation, but
came to incorporate within this statement a philosophical
theory with far-reaching speculative implications. In the
next two chapters we shall encounter some of these implications of classical British empiricism.

16. THE EMPIRICIST THEORY OF MEANING

Roughly speaking, the empiricists held verbal expressions
to be meaningful only if their meaning can be found in
experience or can be defined by means of expressions of
which this is true. They tried to express this general view
more exactly, and to justify it in the context of their theory
of ideas.

A. *The ideas of the mind*

Locke explains the word "idea", as he uses it, as meaning
"whatsoever is the object of the understanding when a man
thinks" or "whatever is meant by *phantasm, notion, species,*
or whatever it is which the mind can be employed about
in thinking".[3] As is obvious from Locke's entire philosophy,
the word "thinking" here should not be understood to refer
to a special kind of mental activity; rather, as in some of
Descartes's writings, it is used to stand for any kind of consciousness, apprehending, perceiving. To use words with
meaning and to understand the meaning of words is to
associate ideas with them. To think without words, if there
is such a thing, is likewise just to have ideas. To perceive
with one's senses is to have ideas. To see, hear, taste, smell,
or feel by touch—all these are the having of ideas of various
kinds. To have fantasies, hallucinations, etc. is likewise to
have ideas. According to Locke, to feel pain is to have an

[2] Hume, *Enquiries* (ed. L. A. Selby-Bigge, 3rd edn. revised by P. H. Nidditch,
Oxford, 1978), p. 165 (*Enquiry Concerning Understanding*, § 12, part III).
[3] Locke, op. cit., I i 8.

idea. On Hume's view, all emotions or "passions" fall under this category, too. While Locke seems at times to distinguish judgement as the separation and the joining of ideas from the mere having of ideas, Hume denies that any such distinction can be made: "conception", "judgement", and "inference", are, he says, all nothing but the conceiving, or having, of ideas. Thus, in a word, according to a tendency of thought which becomes more and more pronounced as we advance in the series Locke–Berkeley–Hume, any form of consciousness whatsoever is the having of a kind of idea.

As a matter of terminology, it should be mentioned that Locke and Berkeley use the term "idea" in an almost identical manner, while Hume prefers to employ the word "perception" in the very general sense that their "idea" carries. "Ideas" for Hume are one particular kind of perception, something to which we shall have occasion to return later.

The ideas (or perceptions) are what the mind is conscious of. When speaking of the mind's relation to its ideas, the empiricists usually employ such expressions as that the mind "perceives", "conceives of", "contemplates", "takes a view of", or (sometimes consciously as a metaphor) "sees" the ideas. In the same sense, the mind is also said to "have" them.

Frequently mentioned examples of ideas are sensible qualities such as colours ("white", "red", "black", etc.), sounds, tastes ("sweet", "bitter", etc.), odours, felt temperatures ("hot", "cold"), but also all kinds of concepts such as "metal", "gold", "justice", etc. What is present to my consciousness when I see, say, a house, is often described as a collection or combination of ideas, but it is also considered as one complex idea (perception). Since the empiricists so often discuss, or take their examples from, visual sense perception, let us try to see a little more clearly how ideas are supposed to enter into our perception of things. It is quite obvious, I think, that what the empiricists meant when talking of ideas of sight is very much the same as what Moore, Russell, and others in our century have referred to as visual "sense-data" ("sensa", "sensibles") even though the theories of the classical empiricists and those of the modern thinkers about these entities are at variance in many respects. In order to throw light on the classical empiricists' notion of an idea, I shall therefore now roughly indicate how "sense-data" may be understood. In so doing I leave Locke, Berkeley, and Hume out of sight for a moment.

It is often said that sense-data are what we *directly* perceive—here "directly" is the antithesis of "indirectly". At this moment I see a volume of Hume's works on the desk in front of me. The book is a three-dimensional object which has already been in existence for half a century and which will probably outlast me, although it may gradually change in various respects (become more worn and faded, lose pages, etc.). If we like, we may regard it as a particular part of four-dimensional space-time. In one intelligible sense of "directly see", we can say that I directly see the part of space-time that *is* the book. But this is not the sense of the expression intended here. Obviously, I do not now see the-book-in-the-year-2000 in the same way in which I now see the-book-now. It is, at most, the-book-exactly-now that I directly see, in the sense of these words that I have in mind here. The-book-exactly-now is a three-dimensional object with six plane sides, and with an interior, consisting of hundreds of printed pages. Clearly, I do not see the inside of the-book-just-now or the three planes of it that are turned away from me in the same way that I see the three planes it immediately presents to me. Going a step further, I would say that it is at most the latter three planes of the book-just-now that I directly see, in the sense relevant here. An atomic physicist would have a lot to say about the myriads of particles which, from his point of view, constitute these planes. So obviously, we have to distinguish between the planes as they look to me and the planes as they are constituted from the point of view of physics. It is only the planes of the book as they look to me that I see directly, in the sense of the words now in question. What I see directly in this sense is what is usually meant by talk of a visual sense-datum.

When Locke, Berkeley, and Hume talk of the ideas or perceptions that we are confronted with through sight, they have in mind, I think, just such visual sense-data. Both Berkeley and Hume sometimes characterize the ideas or perceptions as what is perceived "immediately". They both also discuss the question of whether, in immediately perceiving an idea or perception, we can also be said to perceive something else indirectly. In Locke, who is closer to the Aristotelian–Scholastic tradition than his successors, words are said to be signs of ideas and ideas to be signs of things. Locke's way of talking about ideas as a kind of mental sign seems to echo the medieval terminist theory of *intentiones animae*. But Locke, who is frequently inconsistent, is rather inconsistent on this point too, and often lets drop from view this theory that an idea may signify something beyond it. A characteristic part of Berkeley's and Hume's teaching is that the only way in which the mind can pass from, say, an idea or perception of sight to some object distinct therefrom is by some sort of inference, unless it is merely by a turn of the imagination. All we can properly be said to "see", they both assert, are spatial configurations of colours.

If we are to understand classical empiricism, we should attempt to generalize what has been said so far about vision to the other senses. On an occasion when we would naturally say that we hear a church bell, what we immediately hear is just a sound, this sound constituting the idea (or perception) that is auditively perceived. The church bell is either inferred or imagined. When we smell a cheese, all we then olfactorily perceive is a particular odour and that odour is the idea or perception that is sensibly given. Etc. etc.

The theory (or rather the theories) that the classical empiricists developed concerning ideas or perceptions will occupy us throughout this chapter and the two subsequent ones. Some of the properties that were, more or less explicitly, ascribed to ideas will, however, be mentioned now.

(1) According to Berkeley and Hume, ideas or perceptions are exactly as they appear to the mind. When something I see looks red or square to me, the visual datum, the idea or perception, *is* red or square.

(2) According to Berkeley and Hume, any idea we perceive *exists*. Berkeley advanced the thesis that the *esse* (the existence) of ideas is the same as their *percipi* (their being perceived). Whatever else he might have meant by this statement, he indisputably wished to assert that:

(i) An idea exists if and only if it is perceived.

Often he appears prepared to make the stronger claim that:

(ii) An idea exists at a given time if and only if it is perceived at that time.

There are many passages in Hume in which he apparently
endorses (ii) as well as (i), but in other passages he maintains
that perceptions can perfectly well exist without being perceived by any mind.

(3) Locke, Berkeley, and Hume all very frequently
employ the mode of expression that the ideas are *in* the
mind, or *in* the understanding. Berkeley occasionally explains that by saying that an idea is "in" a mind, he means
nothing more than that the idea is perceived by that mind.
But this has the character of a defensive after-thought. In
both Berkeley and Hume, this whole terminology is used
to cover a vague and comprehensive complex of thoughts
which it is hard to spell out in intelligible terms. One method
of reaching a degree of understanding as to what they meant
is to see what conclusions they thought they could draw
from the fact that ideas are in the mind. The two most important of these conclusions are that ideas cannot exist
unperceived (at times when not perceived) and that ideas
cannot be, or be parts of, or be properties of, objects in an
"external", material world. It seems that they often envisaged some such picture as that shown in diagram (D).

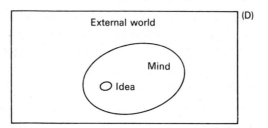

Being "in" the mind, as in this diagram, ideas clearly cannot
also be "in" the external world—even if there is such a
world.

The view that ideas are in the mind stands in a curious
opposition to other views held by the empiricists. All three,
Locke, Berkeley, and Hume, sometimes speak as if they

visualized the mind–idea realtion in this way:

$$Mind \rightarrow Idea$$

where the arrow symbolizes some "action" or "operation" that the mind (or understanding, or soul, or spirit) performs.

Hume's most considered view about the nature of the mind is that it is a contingent assembly of perceptions.

(4) Locke vacillates between the view that by means of ideas we can have knowledge of the things of which they are signs and the view that these ideas form the entire material of our knowledge. According to a line of thought predominant both in Berkeley and in Hume, the ideas or perceptions I perceive are the only objects of which I can ever gain any knowledge, and indeed, are the only object of which I can think or talk. One reason for this view is their conviction that ideas are in the mind and that the mind cannot, so to speak, reach outside itself. Another reason for this is their theory of language which we shall presently study. And still other reasons will gradually become apparent.

B. *Words and ideas*

Locke formulated a semantic principle which came to dominate British empiricist discussion in the eighteenth century: ". . . words, in their primary or immediate signification, stand for nothing but *the ideas in the mind of him that uses them* . . .".[4] Locke thus maintained:

(1) If an expression as used by a person signifies something, what it (primarily, immediately) signifies is an idea perceived by that person ("in his mind").

Besides the notion of an idea, this principle involves the notion of the following relation:

(i) Expression e (primarily, immediately) signifies x.

Regarding this relation, the Stoics had already made a distinction between the sense and the reference of an expression, and we are going to meet similar distinctions in Bolzano and in Frege in the nineteenth century. Without caring here for finer nuances we may, in the spirit of this tradition, distinguish between the following relations:

[4] Ibid., III ii 2.

(ii) Expression e has x for its sense,
(iii) Expression e refers to x.

The sense of the phrase "the planet closest to the sun" is what we grasp when we understand the phrase. What it refers to (or is a name of) is a planet. When considering Locke's semantic principle we need to ask whether he wanted to assert that ideas constitute the sense of words, or whether he wanted to say that they are what words refer to. This distinction was not entirely foreign to Locke and to Berkeley (though Hume appears to have lost sight of it). Locke often thinks about signification in terms of this schema:

Words signify *Ideas* signify *Things.*

One aspect of Locke's thought can, I think, be fairly represented by the statement:

(1a) If an expression as used by a person has a sense, then that sense is an idea perceived by that person.

This principle leaves it open what it is that expressions refer to. But Locke did not stop at the assertion (1a). He also says that words can in no way whatsoever signify anything but ideas. This position involves the assumption of the principle:

(1b) If an expression as used by a person refers to something, the thing referred to is an idea perceived by that person.

This principle is also adopted by Berkeley, although the logic of his position forces him to acknowledge that there are exceptions to it, and by Hume, to whom it seems so self-evident that he never even discusses it.

Some remarks are appropriate here so as not to give the reader an over-simplified picture.

(a) All three empiricists were inclined towards a nominalism closely akin to that of Ockham, although none of them succeeded in being consistent in this matter. According to the brand of nominalism that they, inconsistently, represent, a name such as, say, "triangle" is general, not through signifying a general or abstract idea of triangularity, but through signifying indiscriminately each particular triangle, or triangle-idea. According to this view, as Berkeley vigorously argued, a meaningful expression does not have to stand for exactly one idea: it can stand for many.

(b) Both Locke and Berkeley point out that the use of meaningful expressions is not always accompanied by corresponding ideas in him who uses them. Language can, Berkeley observes, function like the letters in algebra. However, Berkeley recommends that in philosophy one should always keep the ideas present to one's mind.

(c) Berkeley says that, besides the communication of ideas, language has other functions as well, such as to raise passions, to excite to or to deter from action, or to put the mind in a certain disposition. In modern parlance, Berkeley is insisting that language has uses other than the cognitive one.

It is a living testimony to the strength of the emotional forces steering Berkeley's thought that he did not seriously reconsider the validity of (1b), although it conflicts with the existence of words referring to spirits. With respect to such words, however, he maintained that they do, in fact, have a sense since we associate with them certain "notions", which are not, properly speaking "ideas", and he maintained further that these notions are notions of spirits. On this point, but only on this, Berkeley glimpsed a semantics of far greater sophistication than the orthodox empiricist one.

C. *The origin of ideas*

The question as to when an expression is meaningful is thus, for the empiricists, identical with the question as to when it stands for an idea or perception. On this point Locke and Hume explicitly argue in the same manner, and nothing indicates that Berkeley, in principle, disagreed. For the sake of terminological convenience, I shall now use Hume's word "perception", instead of the term "idea" used by Locke and Berkeley, to stand for the entire class of ideas. ("Idea" will now be used in the more restricted sense given to it by Hume.) The empiricists shared a presupposition which was common property in seventeenth-century philosophy:

(2) Each perception is either simple or composed of simple perceptions.

What "simple" and "compound" mean as used in the context is only very imperfectly explained by them. Locke mentions as examples of simple ideas various sense qualities such as the coldness and the hardness of a piece of ice, the whiteness of a lily and its smell, and the taste of sugar. Berkeley and Hume give similar examples.

In virtue of (2), the limits to our world of perceptions will obviously be drawn if our supply of simple perceptions and the operations by which compound ideas can be formed from these are both described. Both for Locke and for Hume, the major interest is to demarcate the supply of simple perceptions. They both assert that:

(3) All our simple perceptions are derived from "experience", "observation".

Hume thought he could make this principle more precise by employing his distinction between two kinds of perceptions which he labels "ideas" and "impressions". He explains the distinction thus:

By the term *impression*, then, I mean all our more lively perceptions, when we hear, or see, or feel, or love, or hate, or desire, or will. And impressions are distinguished from ideas, which are the less lively perceptions, of which we are conscious, when we reflect on any of those sensations or movements above mentioned.[5]

Between an idea and an impression there may obtain the relation that the former is a "copy" of the latter. When I think of, say, sunshine, my idea is, Hume would say, a copy of the impression I have when I see sunshine. Hume now restates (3) as:

(3*) If a person has a simple idea at some time, this idea is a copy of a simple impression that the same person has had at an earlier time.

The scope of our present world of perceptions is thus, in an essential respect, determined by those simple impressions that have occurred in our previous experience.

According to Locke, whose doctrine was reaffirmed by both Berkeley and Hume, we have two kinds of experience, "sensation" or external experience, and "reflection" or inner experience:

[5] Hume, op. cit., p. 18 (*Enquiry Concerning Understanding*, § 2).

Our observation, employed either about external sensible objects, or about the internal operations of our minds perceived and reflected on by ourselves, is that which supplies our understandings with all the materials of thinking. These two are the fountains of knowledge, from whence all the ideas we have, or can naturally have, do spring.[6]

Like so many of the psychological notions used in British empiricism, the notions of "sensation" and "reflection" are none too clear. The empiricists often speak as if they had in mind a picture such as is shown in diagram (E).

On the question of how compound perceptions are formed, the empiricists had hardly any well-considered views. Locke and Hume both talk of our combining, in the imagination, features we have met in previous experience into wholes which have not been so given, and which perhaps have no counterparts in reality (mythological beings, golden mountain, etc.). It seems that Locke as well as Hume supposed that:

(4)   Compound perceptions are always composed of a finite number of simple perceptions.

Combining (2), (3*), and (4), we can summarize the doctrine sketched here in the following statement:

(5)   If a person has an idea at some time, then either (i) it is simple and a copy of a simple impression that the same person has had at an earlier time, or (ii) it is composed out of a finite number of ideas for which (i) holds.

D. *To clarify the meaning of words*

Locke and Hume both express the view that to define a word is to indicate the constituents of the compound idea for which the word stands, or for which the word is, by the definition,

[6] Locke, op. cit., II i 2.

made to stand. This view, a form of what I have called the microscope theory of definition, had been taken over by them from current philosophical thought. On that view, of course, terms signifying simple ideas cannot be defined; but, as Locke and Hume point out, their significance can be shown in experience. If this theory of definition is combined with tenet (5), one finds that any meaningful expression (any signifying an idea) stands for a simple and indefinable idea which can either be shown to be a copy of a simple impression or can be defined by means of expressions for which this holds.

In the *Enquiry* Hume states the intended application of this theory:

Complex ideas may, perhaps, be well known by definition, which is nothing but an enumeration of those parts or simple ideas, that compose them. But when we have pushed up definitions to the most simple ideas, and find still some ambiguity or obscurity; what resource are we then possessed of? By what invention can we throw light upon these ideas, and render them altogether precise and determinate to our intellectual view? Produce the impressions or original sentiments, from which the ideas are copied. These impressions are all strong and sensible. They admit not of ambiguity. They are not only placed in a full light themselves, but may throw light on their correspondent ideas, which lie in obscurity.[7]

This can be interpreted both as a method for testing the meaningfulness of an expression and as a rule for the construction of a meaningful vocabulary. The method of testing is this: If you meet an expression whose meaningfulness is doubtful, start by enquiring into its definition. Concerning the terms used in defining it, ask again for definitions. And so on. Sooner or later the process of definition must come to an end. Concerning those expressions that then remain undefined, ask for the experience, the "observations" or "impressions", from which their significance can be derived. If the entire chain of requests can be satisfactorily met, the meaningfulness of the original expression has been established. If not, it must be rejected as nonsensical. The rule for the construction of a vocabulary says that one should start from undefined terms whose significance is shown in

[7] Hume, op. cit., p. 62 (*Enquiry Concerning Understanding*, §7, part I).

experience, and then define all other terms on the basis of them.

It is easy to point to the shortcomings of this empiricist theory of concept formation. We have seen how dangerously ambiguous the basic semantic principle is. Also, the entire apparatus of concepts in terms of which the theory is stated is full of vagueness and obscurity. A moment's reflection shows how difficult it is to apply all these terms, "perception", "simple", "compound", "experience", "idea", "impression", "sensation", "reflection", to the psychological realities. Even if they could be made precise in an interesting way, the objection remains that the theory is essentially an unproven dogma. How difficult it would be to establish (3) is made especially clear by consideration of Hume's version (3*). Hume himself cannot suppress a doubt concerning its universal validity.[8]

Perhaps it can be said that the rule of the construction of a meaningful vocabulary implied by the theory is more comprehensible than the theory itself. It has the character of a prescription for how to proceed in science. If we are to justify the prescription, it seems then that we must show that, if we wish to achieve such and such an aim in science, we ought to, or must, follow the prescription; and we must also show that the relevant aim is somehow desirable. The justification of this prescription must therefore be based on an enquiry into ends and means in science. The aim the empiricists had in mind was that of ensuring that the terms of one's language be correlated with determinate ideas in one's own consciousness and in the consciousness

---

[8] According to Hume, cases may occur in which the idea precedes any corresponding impression: "Suppose . . . a person to have enjoyed his sight for thirty years, and to have become perfectly acquainted with colours of all kinds except one particular shade of blue, for instance, which it never has been his fortune to meet with. Let all the different shades of that colour, except that single one, be placed before him, descending gradually from the deepest to the lightest; it is plain that he will perceive a blank, where that shade is wanting, and will be sensible that there is a greater distance in that place between the contiguous colours than in any other. Now I ask, whether it be possible for him, from his own imagination, to supply this deficiency, and raise up to himself the idea of that particular shade, though it had never been conveyed to him by his senses? I believe there are few but will be of opinion that he can . . ." (*Enquiry Concerning Understanding*, §2; p. 21 in Selby-Bigge edn.).

of one's audience. The theory of the origin of ideas is supposed to show that the recommended procedure is a means of achieving this aim. Those who do not accept the aim or are not satisfied with the psychological theory cannot, of course, feel bound by this doctrine.

In the philosophy of our own time, it is mainly the logical empiricists who have tried to formulate an empiricist theory of meaning, or of concept formation, in a manner reminiscent of the classical empiricists' attempts. Now, as in the eighteenth century, the goal has been to unmask that "sanctuary of vanity and ignorance" that nonsensical language can be.

17. THE EMPIRICIST THEORY OF KNOWLEDGE

In Locke's *Essay* the empiricist theory of knowledge that will be presented here has not yet crystallized. It is a presupposition, not quite explicitly stated, of several of Berkeley's reasonings. It is somewhat more clearly formulated in Hume's *Treatise*, but finds its most mature statement in his *Enquiry*. Here I shall above all consider the statement in the *Enquiry*.

In the *Enquiry*, Hume assumes a distinction between two kinds of truths, viz. those that assert some "relation of ideas", and those that assert some "matter of fact". If a truth expresses a relation of ideas, then, according to Hume, the negation of it involves a contradiction. If a truth states a matter of fact, its negation is free from contradiction, or is "conceivable". A matter-of-fact truth is also said to depend upon "real existence" and facts, something a truth about a relation of ideas does not depend upon. Truths about relations of ideas are, on Hume's view, found especially in arithmetic and geometry. He gives such examples as, 'Three times five is equal to half of thirty', and 'The square of the hypotenuse is equal to the sum of the squares of the two sides'. An example of a matter-of-fact truth is 'The sun will rise to-morrow'. All presumed laws of nature also belong to this category.

Like Leibniz, Hume assumes that:

(1) A truth about a relation of ideas can be discovered by "the mere operation of thought, without dependence

on what is anywhere existent in the universe",[9] i.e. either by some kind of direct intuition or by inference from intuitively grasped truths.

Hume thinks that these truths have a certainty or evidence not found in any others. He is inclined to think that only "quantity and number" belong to the province of this kind of truth.[10]

Hume further assumes that:

(2)   A truth about a matter of fact can become known only by means of experience.

[9] Hume, op. cit., p. 25 (*Enquiry Concerning Understanding*, §4, part I).

[10] Locke, like so many of his contemporaries, speaks of an "intuitive knowledge", which has the highest degree of certainty, and a "demonstrative knowledge", reached by inference from the intuitive. His inventory of intuitive knowledge in the *Essay* is somewhat unsystematic. However, he seems to include in it the following items:

   (i)   '*a* is *a*', where *a* is some idea in my consciousness (e.g., 'Blue is blue');
   (ii)   '*a* is not *b*', where *a* and *b* are two distinct ideas in my consciousness (e.g., 'Blue is not red');
   (iii) 'All *a* are *b*', where *b* is a "part" of the complex general idea *a* (e.g. 'All men are animals') or a "consequence" thereof (e.g., 'The external angle of all triangles is bigger than either of the opposite internal angles');
   (iv)   'Nothing is both *a* and *b*', where *a* and *b* are two qualities of the same kind that exclude each other (two colours, two shapes, two sizes, etc.; e.g., 'Nothing is both blue and yellow');
   (v)   'I exist';
   (vi)   Many principles in moral science;
   (vii) Many mathematical and logical truths.

Berkeley took very little explicit interest in the question of *a priori* knowledge. In his early work, the *Treatise*, Hume does not introduce the distinction between the two categories of truths, but he does operate with the notions of 'intuition' and 'demonstration' in much the same way as Locke. Besides certain qualitative judgements (concerning resemblance, contrariety, and difference in degree), we have certain knowledge, he maintains, only within arithmetic and algebra. About geometry he says that, although it "falls short of that perfect precision and certainty, which are peculiar to arithmetic and algebra, yet it excels the imperfect judgements of our senses and imagination" (*Treatise*, I iii 1). In the *Enquiry*, which is discussed in the text, Hume seems to put arithmetic, algebra, and geometry on a par. Simultaneously, he draws a sharp line between pure mathematics and mathematics "when taken into assistance of natural philosophy", or "mixed mathematics", as he calls it. The propositions of mixed mathematics, e.g., the mathematical formulas with physical significance that occur in Newton's mechanics, are not demonstrative truths: "Every part of mixed mathematics proceeds upon the supposition that certain laws are established by nature in her operations . . . the discovery of the law itself is owing merely to experience, and all the abstract reasonings in the world could never lead us one step towards the knowledge of it" (*Enquiry Concerning Understanding*, §4 part I).

At a given moment, say t, of a person's life, there are certain propositions of whose truth he has an immediate certainty through "the present testimony of our senses" and "the records of our memory".[11] Let us call these propositions the person's "t-propositions". Hume thus assumes:

(3) At any moment t, a human being has an immediate and certain experiential guarantee for the truth of all his t-propositions, and only of them.

The significance of (3) depends upon what Hume assumes the t-propositions to be. He apparently vacillates between two standpoints. According to one, sense experience directly informs me of such facts as that one billiard ball hits another. We may call this Hume's *objectivist view* concerning immediate experiential knowledge, and express it thus:

(4a) The t-propositions include propositions about events in the physical world.

But according to another view of Hume's, which we may call his *subjectivist view*, the senses and memory give us immediate knowledge only about perceptions *in* our own mind:

(4b) The t-propositions of a person are concerned only with his own perceptions.

This subjectivist view is obviously in line with the general theory of ideas that we have previously considered.

Hume further assumes that:

(5) If at a time t, a person knows a truth about a matter of fact which is not a t-proposition, then his knowledge must admit justification by an inference from t-propositions.

All inferences in which we go beyond the evidence of our senses and memory rest, according to Hume, on the assumption of some relations between cause and effect. What he really wants to say, it appears, is that all such inferences are "analogical" or, as we would say today, inductive. The kinds of induction uppermost in Hume's mind are the time-honoured ones, already discussed in antiquity:

[11] Hume, op. cit., p. 26 (*Enquiry Concerning Understanding*, §4, part I).

$$(\mathrm{P_n}) \begin{cases} a_1, \text{ which is } A, \text{ is } B \\ a_2, \text{ which is } A, \text{ is } B \\ \underline{ a_n, \text{ which is } A, \text{ is } B} \\ \text{All } A \text{ are } B, \end{cases}$$

and:

$$(\mathrm{P_n})$$
$$\underline{a_{n+1} \text{ is } A,}$$
$$a_{n+1} \text{ is } B,$$

where $a_1 \ldots a_n(a_{n+1})$ are all the As known to the person making the inference, and where he does not know that a_{n+1} is not B. These analogies have no demonstrative force, a point on which the Stoics and the Sceptics of antiquity had already insisted. One of Hume's more striking reflections runs as follows: "Nothing so like as eggs; yet no one, on account of this appearing similarity, expects the same taste and relish in all of them."[12] Hume's position implies the assumption that:

> (6) All inferences in which we infer propositions about matters of fact that go beyond the t-propositions are analogical (inductive), and give no certain guarantee of the truth of their conclusions.

Locke, Berkeley, and Hume all agreed that "laws of nature" are propositions arrived at by analogical reasoning from experience, and they all maintained the following:

> (7) We can never have certain knowledge of the truth of a "law of nature".

Locke and Berkeley both warned of the danger of placing too much confidence in the hypotheses of the physics of their time. Locke urged that:

we take care that the name of *principles* deceive us not, nor impose on us, by making us receive that for an unquestionable truth, which is really at best but a very doubtful conjecture; such are most (I had almost said all) of the hypotheses in natural philosophy.[13]

[12] Ibid., p. 36 (§4, part II).   [13] Locke, op. cit., IV xii 13.

Likewise Berkeley questioned, for example, whether it might not be rash to suppose that Newton's hypothesis of gravitation holds throughout the universe.

In our own century, the logical empiricists have put forward claims related to, and inspired by, these classical empiricist views. In logical empiricism, as in classical British empiricism, the critical purpose has been to the fore. However, views of this kind have also acted as liberating forces in the history of thought. The person imbued with them dares to reckon with the possibility that even what seem to be the most well-established and fundamental theorems of his science may need to be replaced by others. By contrast, in Kant's philosophy we shall meet with a scientific attitude of quite a different kind. In the eighteenth century, as well as much later, the opposition between the open-mindedness of empiricism and a prioristic dogmatism was especially acute with regard to the mechanics of Newton. Some of the ingredients of this mechanics were canonized by Kant as synthetic *a priori* truths. But even if Newton was not a consistent empiricist—we may think, e.g., of his doctine of absolute space and time—still it is obvious that he was much closer to the empiricist standpoint than to that of Kant. In the *Opticks* he states the following about conclusions reached by empirical induction (I quote these words once more):

And although the arguing from experiments and observations by induction be no demonstration of general conclusions, yet is is the best way of arguing which the nature of things admit of, and may be looked upon as so much the stronger by how much the induction is more general. And if no exception occur from phenomena, the conclusion may be pronounced generally. But if at any time afterward any exception shall occur from experiments, it may then begin to be pronounced with such exceptions as occur.[14]

This is, by the way, a perfect description of the fate that has befallen Newton's mechanics in our century; experiments have revealed certain exceptions, and physicists now put the theory forward in a modified form so as to allow for these.

This positive evaluation of the empiricist theory of knowledge is concerned with a general tendency of the theory. Against the details of the theory, which I have tried to

[14]Thayer (ed.), *Newton's Philosophy of Nature*, p. 178.

condense into theses (1)–(7), much justified criticism can be levelled. In the next section, we shall see also that the very purpose of the theory is not easy to discern.

18. WHAT IS THE PURPOSE OF THE EMPIRICIST THEORY OF KNOWLEDGE?

In spite of the apparent simplicity of the theory, it is, in fact, rather difficult to grasp what it is really about. How would one set about testing its correctness? Should one investigate the psychology of human beings (and, possibly, also that of animals)? Or should one study the history of science? Or undertake some logical enquiry? Hume's presentation in the *Enquiry* gives no clear answer to these essential questions, and Locke and Berkeley are equally uninformative. I think it interesting to consider the following four questions:

(i) *To what extent is the theory concerned with the psychological mechanisms by which we reach our convictions about matters of fact?*

When reading Hume one often receives the impression that it is a theory of just this kind that he intends to present. He often argues as if we always begin by scrutinizing the testimony of our senses and the records of our memory (cf. thesis (3)), and then make analogical (inductive) inferences by means of some innate analogy mechanism (cf. theses (5) and (6)). Hume thinks that his theory about the human understanding is confirmed by a study of the behaviour of animals, and, accordingly, in both the *Treatise* and the *Enquiry*, he devotes a chapter to "the reason of animals". But he also makes many statements seemingly forbidding us to interpret him as just a student of human and animal psychology.

(ii) *To what extent is the theory a suggestive confession?*

There are many kinds of feeling that one may give vent to or confess. One can express sorrow or joy, love or hate, anxiety or peace; and this is what poets are wont to do. But one can also express less romantic, but no less real, theoretical feelings, such as certainty and doubt in their many nuances. There is a great deal of so-called epistemology that it is difficult to interpret as being other than confessions or expresssions of the epistemologist's own feelings of these kinds. The empiricist theory of knowledge seems at least in part to be of this character. Hume himself held clearly apart from each other his sceptical state of mind when he philosophized and the non-sceptical state in which he found himself when not philosophizing. In part, his theory is, I think, a statement of the certainties and uncertainties he experienced while in the former state, and an attempt to induce such feelings in his readers as well. But this interpretation, too, can hardly be more than a partial truth.

(iii) *To what extent is the theory a definition of '(empirical) knowledge', or a set of corollaries of such a definition?*

Theses (3)–(5) could perhaps be construed as an attempt at framing a kind of recursive definition of the concept of "empirical knowledge"; and theses (6) and (7) could perhaps be looked upon as corollaries of that definition. I think that there is some justification for such a point of view, although no direct evidence for it can be gathered from the words of Hume.

(iv) *To what extent is the theory a methodological recommendation?*

We saw in §16 that the sibling of the present theory, the empiricist theory of meaning, contains a methodological recommendation. If the present theory is interpreted analogously, it would say something like this: "If a proposition *P* is about a relation of ideas, accept *P* if and only if *P* either is intuitively self-evident or you have demonstrated it on the basis of intuitively self-evident propositions about relations of ideas. If *P* is about a matter of fact, accept *P* unhesitatingly only if *P* is directly verified by the testimony of your senses and the records of your memory. If *P* is about a matter of fact but is not verifiable in this way, accept *P* only with the degree of conviction that an analogical inference can justify." This interpretation—which, by the way, is not so far from interpretation (ii)—no doubt catches one aspect of the theory.

Questions of these kinds are relevant with regard to very many epistemological theories, and they are practically always left unanswered by the authors of the theories. We shall meet a luminous exception in Bolzano, who resolutely settled for the view that the aim of epistemology is the description of the ways in which we reach our true convictions.

19. HUME'S DOUBT ABOUT INDUCTION

When discussing induction, or "analogy", in the *Principles*, Berkeley remarks that:

> by a diligent observation of the phenomena within our view, we may *discover the general laws of nature, and from them deduce the other phenomena*, I do not say *demonstrate*; for all deductions of that kind depend on a supposition that the Author of nature always operates uniformly, and in a constant observance of these rules we take for principles: *which we cannot evidently know.*[15]

Hume's critique of induction can be seen as an elaboration of the non-theological kernel of this remark.

We have already seen that the inductive inferences that Hume considers are not of a binding nature. In his language:

(1)   Inductive inferences are not "demonstrative".

Hume apparently thinks that, when making such inferences, we implicitly assume an extra premiss, a premiss which he formulates in a number of ways, supposed by him to be equivalent:

> The future will be conformable to the past.

> The course of nature continues always uniformly the same.

> Instances, of which we have had no experience, must resemble those, of which we have had experience.[16]

Let us refer to these and similar formulations of Hume's as the *Principle of Uniformity*. Although Hume, as we shall see, finds that there is no way of proving this principle, and although he makes some very sceptical statements concerning it, I think it is quite clear that, at least on one level of his thinking, Hume believes:

[15]Berkeley, *A Treatise Concerning the Principles of Human Knowledge*, §107.
[16]Hume, op. cit., p. 35 (*Enquiry Concerning Understanding*, §4, part II); *A Treatise of Human Nature*, I iii 6 (p. 89 in Selby-Bigge edn.).

(2)   The Principle of Uniformity is true.

Hume does not specify the effect that the introduction of this extra premiss has, on his view, upon an inductive inference. He speaks of it in terms such as that all inductive inferences "suppose" it "as their foundation"; that they are all "founded" upon it; and that if "there be any suspicion" that it fails to hold, "all experience becomes useless, and can give rise to no inference or conclusion".[17] Sayings such as these suggest that Hume entertains the following beliefs:

(3)   In all our inductive inferences we tacitly employ the Principle of Uniformity as an extra premiss.

(4)   If P is the set of true premisses and C the true conclusion of an inductive inference, then the inference from P and the Principle of Uniformity to C is demonstrative.

(5)   Employing the Principle of Uniformity as an extra premiss is the only way of rendering inductions demonstrative.

My formulation of (4) stands in need of some explanatory comment. Since, in (4), we have made the supposition that the propositions in the set P are true, we must also suppose that C is true: from true P and a true Principle of Uniformity only true conclusions can be inferred demonstratively. It would also seem unreasonable to allow for false premisses in (4): Hume could not have meant that any fanciful argument of the same form as inductions actually proceeding from experience could be rendered demonstrative by means of the Principle of Uniformity.

Before looking at Hume's next move, it may be of interest to observe how strange the belief (4) is. The inductions we make from true premisses are of two sorts, those in which our conjecture happens to be correct and those where it happens to be incorrect. The two sorts are impossible to distinguish in advance. If (4) were true, however, we should have such a means of distinguishing between them, viz. by enquiring as to whether or not they are rendered demonstrative by the addition of the Principle of Uniformity. A

[17] Hume, *Enquiries*, pp. 37–8 (*Enquiry Concerning Understanding*, §4, part II).

less sophisticated argument against (4) is that the Principle of Uniformity does not seem, in any of its (many) formulations in Hume, to render the service that is expected of it: it simply does not transform any induction (of which it is not itself the conclusion) into a demonstrative inference.

On Hume's view, then, our inductions would constitute demonstrative inferences from given knowledge to new knowledge, provided that the Principle of Uniformity were itself known to be true. But is it? Hume observes:

(6)   The Principle of Uniformity is itself a general statement about matters of fact.

By the empiricist theory of knowledge therefore:

(7)   If the Principle of Uniformity is known, it must be known by induction.

But here we run into a difficulty: "To endeavour ... the proof of this last supposition [the Principle of Uniformity] by probable arguments, or arguments regarding existence, must be evidently going in a circle, and taking that for granted, which is the very point in question."[18] What Hume observes is this:

(8)   If an induction whose conclusion is the Principle of Uniformity is rendered demonstrative by the addition of that Principle as an extra premiss, this induction becomes an obviously circular argument.

The conclusion Hume draws is that empirical induction is not "founded on reasoning, or any process of the understanding";[19] in a word, that it altogether lacks rational justification. Induction is a mere habit which we share with animals and which is explicable in terms of the association of ideas. A plausible reconstruction of Hume's reasoning here seems to be this:

(9)   Only if an inference is demonstrative is it a "rational" way of enlarging our knowledge or our beliefs.

Hence, by (5), (7), and (8):

[18]Ibid., pp. 35–6.   [19]Ibid., p. 32.

(10) The Principle of Uniformity cannot be "rationally" inferred from previous knowledge.

Hence, by (1), (4), and (5):

(11) No inductive inference is a rational inference from rationally known premises.

What Hume was looking for, and what he failed to find, was, we now see, some proposition O such that (i) O would be known to be true without the aid of induction, and (ii) if O were added to the true premises P of an empirical induction with the true conclusion C, the inference from P and O to C would be demonstrative. In our discussion of proposition (4) above, we have seen that it would be exceedingly strange if such a proposition O could be found.

Although Hume speaks of inductions as probable, and although he did pay some attention, especially in the *Treatise*, to the notion of probability, strangely enough this notion plays hardly any role in his discussion of the problem of induction.

The problem of justifying induction has often been called "Hume's problem". A study of the literature on this problem shows it to be a complex of many interrelated questions.

20. A PSYCHOLOGICAL CONTRADICTION IN BRITISH EMPIRICISM

The upholders of the Platonic–Aristotelian ideal of science, the so-called rationalists, have an interesting feature in common with the British empiricists, namely, the quest for certainty. This concern finds many expressions in the reasoning of the empiricists. Some points where it comes to the surface are these: (i) *The foundation of empirical knowledge, according to Hume*. Here I am thinking of Hume's view that I have certain knowledge at t of what I have called my t-propositions. (ii) *Hume's discussion of induction*. For Hume, a rational argument is one where the conclusion demonstratively follows from the premises: Only those inferences from experience the truth of whose conclusions is absolutely guaranteed by experience are counted as rational by Hume. (iii) *Berkeley's and Hume's discussion of the external world*. In chapter VI I shall discuss some of the empiricists' thoughts on the theme of our experience and the external world. In particular I am referring here to §28, especially to the explanation of what Berkeley requires of an adequate interpretation of what I call *m*-propositions, viz. propositions about the material world that are acceptable to common sense. As will be seen in §30, Berkeley's demands have been endorsed by many later empiricists. An adequate interpretation, in the sense of one satisfying these constraints, must make it possible to know *m*-propositions with certainty, where "certainty" has often been taken in an esoteric and utopian sense.

The quest for certainty which is found in the empiricists is the result of an unwillingness to believe at all in what does not appear absolutely certain. The attitude is one of 'all or nothing': one wishes either to believe without reservations or not to believe in any manner whatsoever. Side by side with this quest for certainty, there also exists in the empiricists a contrary attitude which can be expressed in these words: the reasons for opinions vary in strength, and I ought, in each case, to let the degree of my belief correspond to the strength of the reasons. "A wise man", says Hume, "proportions his belief to the evidence."[20] One of the fundamental tenets of classical empiricism is simply that the major part of our "knowledge" is, and must be, merely probable.

This unconscious psychological conflict has been passed down from the eighteenth-century empiricists to many modern representatives of empiricism. It is, for example, as noticeable in Bertrand Russell as in David Hume.

---

[20]Ibid., p. 110 (*Enquiry Concerning Understanding*, §10, part I).

V

The Classical Empiricist Critique

21. A SURVEY OF THE EMPIRICIST CRITIQUE

The two theories that, in different versions, were fundamental to the thought of Locke, Berkeley, and Hume—the
Empiricist Theory of Meaning and the Empiricist Theory
of Knowledge—were, as we have noted, designed as instruments of criticism. Some of the principal targets of this
empiricist critique will be now surveyed.

Locke on innate ideas. Locke begins his *Essay* with a
refutation of the doctrine that man is born with certain
"innate" principles or ideas. If this doctrine is meant to
assert that these principles or ideas are already "stamped
upon the mind" at birth, it is simply false. That a truth
is imprinted on the soul can hardly mean anything but
its being perceived by the soul. The so-called innate principles and ideas ought, then, to be known by newborn
infants, which they are not. If the doctrine asserts only
that men come to know these principles by the use of their
reason, "all the certain truths that reason ever teaches us"
will be innate.[1] The doctrine of innate ideas had many
advocates in the seventeenth century, foremost among
whom was Descartes. The notions classified as innate were
usually such as were thought to be of an especially fundamental philosophical, theological, or moral importance—
notions such as God and substance, along with basic logical,
mathematical, and moral propositions. The theory had its
ultimate historical source in Plato's doctrine of recollection.
It appeared to Locke that the rebuttal of this theory was
a necessary preparation for the statement of his empiricism.

Abstract ideas. In the previous chapter it was observed
that Locke, Berkeley, and Hume were all inclined towards
a nominalistic view of general words (such as 'white', 'man',
'triangle'), but that none of them succeeded in being a

[1] Locke, *An Essay Concerning Human Understanding*, I ii 9.

consistent nominalist. What is new in their nominalism in comparison with Ockham's nominalism is, above all, the theories they proposed about the mental mechanism whereby such general words are made to signify indifferently a large number of particulars. These theories were formulated within the framework of their theory of ideas.

Causation. Locke subscribed to the scholastic view that a cause produces the effect by its activity. Berkeley found no such activity in the sensible world. All things in it are entirely "passive". What are believed to be laws of causation, are, he maintains, merely general rules in conformity with which certain phenomena are "signs" of the occurrence of others. The active "power" that causes the phenomena and governs the course of nature resides in God. Hume devoted a substantial part of the *Treatise* and several chapters of the *Enquiry* to an analysis of the notions of causation and physical necessity. The view he arrives at is very similar to Berkeley's except that for Hume no God retains a causative power in the world. In the next section we shall undertake a closer study of Hume's analysis of causation.

Hume on mind–body interaction. In passing Hume swept all the arguments against interaction between mind and body under the table. If causation is merely "constant conjunction" of phenomena, the problem of interaction is transferred from the speculative to the empirical level. On Hume's view, our everyday experience attests the existence of constant conjunctions between mental and bodily phenomena.

Free will. The mechanistic world view, with its accompanying determinism, was often thought to exclude the possibility of man's freedom or free will. Spinoza, for instance, declared: "No absolute or free will exists. The human mind is determined to one thing or another by some cause which in turn is determined by another, this again by another, and so on in infinity."[2] In the second book of the *Treatise*, "Of the passions", Hume apparently agrees with Spinoza. In the *Enquiry*, however, Hume argues that his earlier view was the result of a deficient analysis of what is meant by "liberty". If man's free will were irreconcilable with

[2] Spinoza, *The Ethics*, II, proposition XLVIII.

determinism, freedom would be the same as chance, as the absence of a cause. It is generally acknowledged that chance, in this sense, does not exist. What we can mean by liberty when discussing whether man is free or not is only:

a power of acting or not acting, according to the determinations of the will; that is, if we choose to remain at rest, we may; if we choose to move, we also may. Now this hypothetical liberty is universally allowed to belong to every one who is not a prisoner and in chains. Here, then, is no subject of dispute.[3]

Freedom, in this hypothetical sense, is the opposite, not of necessity, but of compulsion. That a man, or his will, is hypothetically free means that he is in a situation such that his volitions (within reasonable limits) bring about corresponding actions. He is not free, in this sense, when he is under some external compulsion. That his volitions are themselves the necessary effects of certain causes— which determinism, or the doctrine of "necessity" asserts— does not cancel out this hypothetical liberty. In short, Hume maintains in his *Enquiry* that the belief in the incompatibility of freedom and determinism arises from the confusion of two distinct pairs of opposites:

Chance—Necessity
Liberty—Compulsion.

In the rather categorical form in which Hume presents this analysis of liberty, it can hardly be correct. For, like most expressions of everyday language, expressions such as "freedom", "man's freedom", "the freedom of the will", etc. no doubt have many distinct connotations. Hume's analysis at most applies to one particular use of some such expression; and Hume has hardly identified that use with sufficient accuracy.

Besides presenting a thesis about the meaning of words, Hume's argument also involves a moral position. He thinks that an action has a moral aspect if and only if it is done freely in the sense he has defined. Thus, he also maintains that the truth of determinism does not deprive our actions of their moral aspect.

[3] Hume, *Enquiries*, p. 95 (*Enquiry Concerning Human Understanding*, §8, part I).

Substance. The notion of substance was as important to the seventeenth-century rationalists as that of causation, and it became the target of an intense critique from Berkeley, and in even more radical form, from Hume. Locke accepted a notion of substance which he acknowledged to be "obscure and relative".

The idea we have, to which we give the general name of substance, being nothing but the supposed but unknown support of those qualities we find existing, which we imagine cannot subsist *sine re substante*, without something to support them, we call that support *substantia*; which, according to the true import of the word, is, in plain *English, standing under,* or *upholding.*[4]

Given, say, a spherical solid ball of such and such size and made of gold, the view Locke describes implies that there is some, otherwise unknown, entity which 'supports' and 'unites' the enumerated characteristics—the spherical form, the solidity, the size, and the properties of gold. All we know of the ball is, Locke says, the combination of its qualities.[5] As far as sensible things are concerned, Berkeley rejected Locke's unknown substances and asserted sensible things to be nothing but the collections of their qualities. Hume generalized this view to all supposed substances.

The two kinds of substance which Descartes had put at the centre of seventeenth-century discussion were the material extended substances, bodies, and the mental thinking substances, minds. Locke accepted material substances, but was hesitant as to whether spirits are a distinct kind of substance. In chapter VI we shall consider Berkeley's attempt to show that material substances do not exist. Hume repeats several of Berkeley's arguments without, however, stating an equally unambiguous conclusion.

Personal identity and mental substance. Locke discusses at length the problem of personal identity: In what sense is, say, I-1930 the same person as I-1972? He finds that the identity is not an identity of mental substance (if such there be) but an identity of "consciousness", by which he means, it seems, a measure of continuity in the mental life. If two

---

[4] Locke, op. cit., II xxii 2.   [5] Cf. ibid., II xxxi 6–10.

consciousnesses lacking all communication with each other inhabited the same body, one always by day, the other by night, we would consider the day man and the night man to be two distinct persons.

Berkeley does not explicitly consider this problem of personal identity, even though it had been of such interest to Locke. Had it caught Berkeley's attention, he would doubtless have settled for the solution rejected by Locke, namely that personal identity consists in the identity of the perceiving substance; it is this substance that I denote, on his view, by my use of the word "I":

But besides all that endless variety of ideas or objects of knowledge, there is likewise something which knows or perceives them . . . and exercises divers operations, as willing, imagining, remembering about them. This perceiving, active being is what I call *mind, spirit, soul,* or *myself.* By which words I do not denote any one of my ideas, but a thing entirely distinct from them, *wherein they exist,* or, which is the same thing, whereby they are perceived; for the existence of an idea consists in being perceived.[6]

Mind as conceived of by Berkeley, has a certain similarity to the atom of modern physics, the spirit corresponding to the nucleus and the ideas to the exchangeable electrons.

In the *Treatise,* Hume took up the question Locke had originally posed, being dissatisfied with Locke's solution of it. After a lengthy discussion, Hume finally dismisses the whole problem as "grammatical" rather than "philosophical" in nature.[7] However, for reasons more radical than those adduced by Locke, he denies that personal identity is identity of a mental substance.

As we have seen, Berkeley was already aware of the objection to his theory of mental substance which is based on the empiricist theory of meaning: namely, if words such as "spirit" or "I" stand for entities distinct from ideas, then they are meaningless. Berkeley thought he could escape this objection by his theory of 'notions'. However, the belief in mental substances had none of the attraction for Hume that it had for the theologian Berkeley, and he refused to follow Berkeley's way out. According to Hume, talk of

[6] Berkeley, *A Treatise Concerning the Principles of Human Knowledge*, §2.
[7] Hume, *A Treatise of Human Nature*, I iv 6 (p. 262).

mental substances is nonsensical. He stated his own view of the mind in words such as these:

> the true idea of the human mind, is to consider it as a system of differ-ent perceptions or different existences, which are link'd together by the relations of cause and effect, and mutually produce, destroy, influence, and modify each other. . . . One thought chases another, and draws after it a third, by which it is expelled in its turn. In this respect, I cannot compare the soul more properly to any thing than to a republic or commonwealth, in which the several members are united by the reciprocal ties of government and subordination, and give rise to other persons, who propagate the same republic in the incessant changes of its parts.[8]

If Berkeley's spirit can be likened to the nucleus of an atom, the mind as conceived of by Hume is comparable to an atom deprived of its nucleus and in which the electrons are constantly exchanged (if such a thing were possible). Hume thus creates a new conception of the mind which takes its place in the history of thought beside such con-ceptions as the atomistic, the Platonic, the Aristotelian, and the Cartesian. A system of perceptions, in Hume's sense, is presumably not a perception. But if the Empiricist Theory of meaning rules out as nonsense any expression that does not refer to a perception, will it not thereby disqualify the expression "a system of perceptions" as well? This question did not occur to Hume.

Berkeley on physics. Of the three great empiricists, it was the theologian Berkeley who showed the most active critical interest in contemporary science. One motive behind his critique was his eagerness to discredit the accepted scientific world picture in order to make room for his own theological metaphysics. His critique is of interest, however, even to those who do not share that desire. In his critique of science, Berkeley in fact showed both common sense and perspicacity along with some queer prejudices. Not without reason he has been considered as a precursor of Mach and the other positivist critics of science towards the end of the nineteenth century.

In the *Principles* and in *On Motion* (*De Motu*, 1721)

---

[8] Ibid. (p. 261). Hume's theory of mind is anticipated by the Hylas of Berkeley's *Dialogues*. Cf. *The Works of George Berkeley*, vol. i, p. 450.

Berkeley criticized Newton's theory of absolute space and time. Newton thought that the centrifugal effect of rotational motion can only be explained by assuming the rotation to be a rotation relative to absolute space. Berkeley anticipated Mach when he suggested that the system of the fixed stars could play the role assigned by Newton to absolute space.

Berkeley makes an interesting classification of the constituents of physical theories. He distinguishes:

(i) observations of individual phenomena;
(ii) "laws of nature", which express regularities in the sequence of phenomena, and which we discover by observation, experiment, and analogical (inductive) inference;
(iii) "mathematical hypotheses", which are not laws of nature in sense (ii).

Those notions inaccessible to direct observation such as 'force', 'gravity', and 'attraction', belong to the realm of mathematical hypotheses. They are "useful for the reasoning about and calculation of motion and bodies moved, but not for understanding the simple nature of motion itself or for designating distinct qualities."[9] Just as Mach was later to deny the existence of atoms, so Berkeley rejected the corpuscular philosophy which attempted to explain phenomena on the hypothesis that bodies are composed of minute particles.

Berkeley on mathematics. Berkeley had a somewhat curious interest in, and dislike of, higher mathematics. He complains that the assumption of "the infinite divisibility of finite extension" renders the study of mathematics "so difficult and tedious".[10] In the *Principles*, as well as in two other works, *The Analyst* (1734) and *A Defence of Free-thinking in Mathematics* (1735), he attacked the use of "infinitesimal" magnitudes in the calculus. This critique gave rise to a lively debate in which many defended the infinitesimals, though some (e.g. MacLaurin) accepted Berkeley's critique. But Berkeley misunderstood the relevance of his criticism: he failed to see that Newton was

---

[9] Berkeley, *De Motu*, §17.
[10] Berkeley, *A Treatise Concerning the Principles of Human Knowledge*, §123.

correct even on those occasions when he expressed his reasoning badly. And even when discussing mathematics, Berkeley's aim was ultimately theological: thus he claimed that those who granted the mysteries of higher mathematics should have no difficulty in accepting those of revelation and faith.

Hume on evaluation. Hume shows a strong tendency to assume both that moral judgements—judgements about good and evil, virtue and vice, right and wrong, etc.—do not belong to the province of knowledge and science, and also that this is the case because such judgements can be neither true nor false. But here, as elsewhere, his explicit arguments are both intricate and ambiguous.

In all previous attempts to justify moral doctrines, the same logical fault can be observed:

> In every system of morality, which I have hitherto met with, I have always remark'd, that the author proceeds for some time in the ordinary way of reasoning, and establishes the being of a God, or makes observations concerning human affairs; when of a sudden I am surpriz'd to find, that instead of the usual copulations of propositions, *is*, and *is not*, I meet with no proposition that is not connected with an *ought*, or an *ought not*. This change is imperceptible; but is, however, of the last consequence. For as this *ought*, or *ought not*, expresses some new relation or affirmation, 'tis necessary that it shou'd be observ'd and explain'd; and at the same time that a reason should be given, for what seems altogether inconceivable, how this new relation can be a deduction from others, which are entirely different from it. But as authors do not commonly use this precaution, I shall presume to recommend it to the readers; and am persuaded, that this small attention wou'd subvert all the vulgar systems of morality, and let us see, that the distinction of vice and virtue is not founded merely on the relations of objects, nor is perceiv'd by reason.[11]

This principle of Hume's, that inferences from *is* to *ought* are illegitimate, is still the subject of debate within moral philosophy.

According to Hume, feeling is constitutive of all moral evaluation. As long as we merely observe facts, we are not conscious of values. It is when we come to approve or disapprove of things that they first appear to us as good or bad,

[11]Hume, *A Treatise of Human Nature*, III i 1 (pp. 469–70).

right or wrong, etc. When Hume tries to formulate this view in more precise terms, he outlines several distinct theories, the differences between which he seems to be unaware of.

(1) At times he compares moral qualities such as 'vice' and 'virtue' to "sounds, colours, heat and cold, which, according to modern philosophy, are not qualities in objects, but perceptions in the mind".[12] Moral qualities would thus have the same status as the so-called secondary qualities have according to the mechanistic world view. The "modern philosophy" which Hume refers to here taught that it is *false* to say that material things have colours and other secondary qualities. Is Hume, in this passage, leaning toward an analogous view about moral properties?

(2) Another theory is perhaps hinted at in statements such as this: "The very *feeling* constitutes our praise or admiration. . . . We do not infer a character to be virtuous, because it pleases; but in feeling that it pleases after such a particular manner, we in effect feel that it is virtuous,"[13] which can be interpreted as asserting that feeling, of a particular kind, constitutes a "moral sense" related to vice and virtue etc. as, say, the sense of sight is related to colours. If this view is combined with (1), feeling, of this particular kind, becomes a moral sense that always errs. But the quotation is, I think, also open to another interpretation. Hume asserts more than once that feelings or "passions" cannot be either true or false.[14] So, if praise and blame are feelings, it follows that they can be neither true nor false.

(3) When Hume develops his own utilitarian moral theory, he assumes a psychological definition of moral predicates: "The hypothesis which we embrace is plain. . . . It defines virtue to be *whatever mental action or quality gives to a spectator the pleasing sentiment of approbation*; and vice the contrary. We then proceed to examine a plain matter of fact, to wit, what actions have this influence."[15] Hume's complex position contains the seeds of several distinct theories of value. In his book *The Place of Value in a World of Facts* (1938), Wolfgang Köhler developed a theory of type (1). Theories of type (2) are often referred to today

[12]Ibid. (p. 469).   [13]Ibid. (p. 471).   [14]Ibid. (pp. 459–60).
[15]Hume, *Enquiries*, p. 289 (*Enquiry Concerning Morals*, Appendix I).

as "emotive theories of value". Such theories have been defended in this century by Hägerström, Russell, Carnap, Ayer, Stevenson, and others, and since the days of Hume psychological theories of type (3) have also had many spokesmen.

Hume on religion. Whereas Locke and Berkeley were religious believers, Hume was an atheist who, under cover of ironical reverence for revelation and faith, fought against what he took to be religious superstition. In the *Treatise* he refuted what he called the "metaphysical" arguments for the immortality of the soul. In the *Enquiry* he attempted to prove that we cannot have good reasons for believing in the occurrence of genuine miracles, or in the existence of a just providence which rewards and punishes after death. In the posthumous *Dialogues on Natural Religion* (1779) his critical view of religion was further developed.

Berkeley on stereoscopic vision. This survey of the empiricist critique would not be complete unless Berkeley's *An Essay towards a New Theory of Vision* (1709) were also mentioned. On Berkeley's theory, what we immediately perceive by sight is only an expanse of colours. That we ascribe to the elements of this expansion a varying distance from ourselves, that what we see appears to have a dimension of depth, depends upon our knowledge, gained by experience, that such and such visual impressions correspond to such and such tactile sensations. A man born blind who suddenly gained his sight would not be informed by his sight of the distance of things seen. What Berkeley says could be given a genetic interpretation to the effect that normal stereoscopic vision develops from an original non-stereoscopic vision under the influence of tactile experiences. But this is not what Berkeley intends to say. His view is, literally, that seeing itself is never stereoscopic, but is merely accompanied by ideas of tactile experiences which constitute our notion of distance from us. This descriptive phenomenological theory, which runs counter to obvious facts, has been surprisingly long-lived. (As late as 1928, in *The Logical Structure of the World*, Carnap maintained that the visual field is spatially two-dimensional.) The theory was dear to Berkeley since in his eyes it was a further reason in favour of his "immaterialism".

22. HUME'S ANALYSIS OF CAUSATION AND NECESSITY

Causal terminology plays an important part in our everyday speech; we also encounter it at almost every step within the history of philosophy. To this terminology belong expressions such as 'A is a cause of B', 'A depends on B', 'A produces B', 'A affects B', and so on. (To define exactly the scope of this terminology is quite obviously impossible.) Such terminology occurs very often in the writings of those thinkers who played a part in the development of the mechanistic world picture. The general determinist outlook was often expressed by phrases such as 'Everything has a cause', and a common view on the mind–body relationship was expressed by saying, 'Minds and bodies cannot act upon, or influence, each other'. Quite possibly, Hume, if pressed, would have acknowledged that 'cause–effect' and other forms of expression from this causal terminology have a variety of uses, and that, in his analysis, he concerned himself with only one particular usage. Anyhow, to begin with, let us try to discern the use of 'cause–effect' that Hume was thinking of.

A. *The use of the word 'cause' that interests Hume*

Hume gives some examples of situations in which, on his view, causation occurs, and also examples of reasonings that involve the notion of causation. Some of the situations he mentions are these: two smooth pieces of marble, when joined, "will adhere together in such a manner as to require great force to separate them in a direct line, while they make so small a resistance to a lateral pressure";[16] a flame radiates heat; a certain vibration gives rise to a certain sound; a billiard ball that hits another one will make it roll in a certain manner. Among the reasonings involving a belief in cause–effect relationships mentioned by Hume are the following: When I believe that the sun will rise tomorrow, or that immersion in water will suffocate me, I rely on assumed causal connections. "A man finding a watch or any other machine in a desert island, would conclude that there had once been men in that island";[17] in so doing he

[16]Ibid., p. 28a (*Enquiry Concerning Understanding*, §4, part I).
[17]Ibid., p. 26.

also invokes a presumed causal relationship. When we explain why we believe that Caesar was killed on the Ides of March, we argue in something like the following way:

> Here are certain characters and letters present either to our memory or senses; which characters we likewise remember to have been us'd as the signs of certain ideas; and these ideas were either in the minds of such as were immediately present at that action, and receiv'd the ideas directly from its existence; or they were deriv'd from the testimony of others, and that again from another testimony, by a visible gradation, 'till we arrive at those who were eye-witnesses and spectators of the event. 'Tis obvious that all this chain of argument or connexion of causes and effects, is at first founded on those characters or letter, which are seen or remember'd . . .[18]

It is not always quite clear how Hume thought his abstract reasonings about causation could be applied to the cases of causation, or of causal reasoning, that he adduces.

Hume also describes in abstract terms certain features of the cause–effect relationship he has in mind. The most important of these features are, I think, the following:

(a) If *A* is a cause of *B*, *A* and *B* are always distinct things.

(b) If *A* is a cause of *B*, then if *A* occurs, *B* also occurs.

(c) If *A* is the cause of *B*, *B* (or *B*'s existence) cannot be logically inferred from *A* (or *A*'s existence). There is no contradiction in assuming *A* (or *A*'s existence) and denying *B* (or *B*'s existence). Or, as Hume says, it is perfectly "conceivable" that *A* should occur without *B* occurring. Likewise it is impossible to discover *a priori*, by the mere use of reason, that *A* will be accompanied by *B*. If *A* is a ground of which *B* is the logical consequence, we can, whenever *A* is given, infer *B* simply by the use of logic. Hume's observation (d) thus implies a sharp distinction between the cause–effect relationship, on the one hand, and the logical relation between a ground and its consequence, on the other hand. (This distinction was not always observed by rationalists such as Spinoza and Leibniz.)

(d) If *A* is a cause of *B*, *A* precedes *B* in time.

(e) If *A* is a cause of *B* there obtains, Hume says in the *Treatise*, a "contiguity" in space and time between *A* and

[18]Hume, *A Treatise of Human Nature*, T. I iii 4 (p. 83).

B. Apparently, however, this is meant to hold only when A is, let us say, the "direct" cause of B. A can also cause B indirectly, by directly causing a C_1 that directly causes a C_2 . . . that directly causes a C_n that directly causes B ($n \geqslant 1$). Apparently Hume demands that, in such a causal chain, contiguity in space and time should obtain between each cause and its direct effect. In the *Enquiry*, however, Hume makes no mention of contiguity when analysing causation.

These features (a)–(e) are all present in those cases where we "legitimately" judge that A is the cause of B. However, our judgement that such is the case asserts something more:

(f) When we say that A is the cause of B, we say that there is a 'necessary connection' between A and B. The statement that there is a necessary connection between A and B can obviously be interpreted in several ways. It can be taken to mean either that

(i) 'it is necessary that if A occurs, then B occurs';

or that

(ii) 'it is necessary that if B occurs, then A occurs';

or that

(iii) 'it is necessary that A occurs if and only if B occurs'.

Hume's somewhat negligent choice of expressions sometimes invites the one, sometimes the other of these three interpretations. The dominant idea, however, seems to be (i); (f) is thus equivalent to:

(g) When we say that A is the cause of B, we say that it is necessary that if A occurs, then B occurs.

In the *Treatise* Hume summarizes his characterization of the notion of causation which he is going to investigate by saying that it is composed of the three ideas of temporal priority of the cause, contiguity in space and time, and necessary connection. In the *Enquiry*, contiguity is left out. The interpretation of causation presupposed in the *Enquiry* can, with a certain liberty of expression, be stated thus:

D_1. A causes B = Df A is followed by B in time, and A is necessarily connected with B.

The above explanation of what Hume meant by causation suffers from a very serious, but unavoidable, obscurity. The sentential schema, "A causes (or is a cause of, or is the cause of) B", is transformed into a determinate statement when we replace the letters "A" and "B" by expressions with a determinate meaning. Our everyday language allows us to replace these letters by expressions of very different kinds. We can, e.g., say:

(iv) That Hitler was a fanatical antisemite was the cause of millions of Jews being murdered in the Third Reich.

(v) Virus contagion is the cause of infantile paralysis.

(vi) Goethe caused the Werther fever.

(iv) is obtained from our sentence schema by putting sentences in the place of the letters "A" and "B". We obtain (v) by replacing the letters by general names (there are many cases of virus contagion and of infantile paralysis), and (vi) by putting the name of a person in the place of "A" and the name of a widespread historical phenomenon instead of "B". Hume is as permissive as everyday language in this respect. It is very doubtful, however, whether one can give a formally exact and philosophically clarifying explanation of causation which covers all the possibilities of substitution permitted by common usage.

B. *The subjective origin of the idea of necessary connection*

The definition D_1 involves the concepts of temporal precedence and of necessity. In this context Hume does not see any problem in temporal precedence, but the notion of necessity intrigues him. In order to clarify the import of this notion Hume sets himself the task of finding that impression, or those impressions, from which it has been derived.

The isolated observation of a process A–B does not give us any impression of necessity. In the isolated case we perceive only that A is in a certain manner followed by B. As a matter of fact, however, we do not, or we should not, judge that *A* is the cause of *B* on the basis of the mere observation of *A-B*. When labelling *A* as the 'cause' of *B*, we consider *A* as the representative of a species of events, say α, and *B* as a representative of another species of events, say β (I here formalize Hume.) It is only when every event of species α has, in our past experience, always been followed by an event of species β that we say that *A* is the cause of *B*. The repetition of similar instances of α–β does not, Hume asserts, add anything new to any one of them. But it does make a change to our mind. We form the habit of passing from the idea of an instance of α to the idea of a corresponding instance of β: we "feel" a "determination" or "propensity" of the mind to pass from one object to its usual attendant. This determination, or propensity, exists only in the mind. Our feeling of it is an impression of reflection, not one of sensation. In judging that the cause is necessarily connected with its effect, we somehow mistake the internal impression for a feature of the external objects:

'Tis a common observation, that the mind has a great propensity to spread itself on external objects, and to conjoin with them any internal impressions, which they occasion, and which always make their appearance at the same time that these objects discover themselves to the senses.[19]

The result of Hume's analysis thus becomes that the necessity in the causal relationship is an illusion which psychology can explain. Necessity exists only in the mind, not in objects.

C. *Causation and constant conjunction*

If Hume had adhered rigidly to the result of the above analysis, he would, it seems, have had to eliminate the notion of cause, and the entire causal terminology, from philosophy and science. He does not do so. The above analysis is an expression of Hume's scepticism, but Hume was never consistently a sceptic. Actually, Hume gives a "philosophical" definition of the cause–effect relationship which he thinks sufficiently agrees with common usage and is philosophically unobjectionable. When we judge that an event *A* is the cause of another event *B*, we have in mind our past experience of

[19]Ibid. (p. 167).

the fact that events of the same kind as *A* have always been conjoined with events of the same kind as *B*. By induction from this fact we may, and do, infer that every event of the first kind is always conjoined with an event of the second kind: "Similar objects are always conjoined with similar. Of this we have experience. Suitably to this experience, therefore, we may define a cause to be *an object, followed by another, and where all objects similar to the first are followed by objects similar to the second.*"[20] Trying to express Hume's view in more formal terms, one may suggest the following formulation:

> D_2.   *A* is the cause of *B* = df *A* is followed by *B*, and there are species α and β such that *A* belongs to α and *B* belongs to β and every event belonging to α is followed by an event belonging to β.

This is the definition that Hume himself makes use of when discussing, e.g., the problem of interaction between mind and body.

Terms such as "necessary", "possible", and "impossible" are today usually called modal terms. An interesting feature of Hume's "philosophical" definition of causation is that it can be seen as an attempt to replace a certain modal statement by a non-modal statement. From one point of view, Hume's ambition is to eliminate all modal terms with a "physical" or causal sense from our vocabulary. The modern debate on 'dispositional terms' (Carnap), 'counterfactual conditionals' (Goodman), and 'nomological statements' (Reichenbach) is concerned with very much the same problem and can be seen as a continuation of Hume's line of investigation.

Another interesting feature of Hume's "philosophical" definition is that it makes every assumption of a cause-effect relationship involve the assumption of a general law. This view has been restated in modern philosophy by a large number of writers, most well known among whom is the logical empiricist C. G. Hempel. The correctness of this view with respect to those sciences where 'laws' are rare but causal explanations common is a matter of dispute.

[20]Hume, *Enquiries*, p. 76 (*Enquiry Concerning Understanding*, §7, part II).

D. *Hume on the interaction between body and mind*

Many seventeenth-century philosophers denied the possibility of interaction between body and mind. From his analysis of causation Hume infers:

that to consider the matter *a priori*, any thing may produce any thing, and that we shall never discover a reason, why any object may or may not be the cause of any other, however great, or however little the resemblance may be betwixt them.[21]

The falling of a pebble may, for ought we know [*a priori*], extinguish the sun; or the wish of a man control the planets in their orbits.[22]

This consideration tears asunder all the speculative arguments against interaction. To decide whether interaction occurs, all we have to do is to enquire whether D_2 is applicable to the relation between bodily and mental events. Our everyday experience shows this to be the case: "every one may perceive, that the different dispositions of his body change his thoughts and sentiments." Since constant conjunction is causation, we can conclude "that motion may be, and actually is, the cause of thought and perception."[23]

If Hume's definition D_2 is granted, Hume's conclusion is difficult to avoid. Perhaps it is worth mentioning that Hume's definition and his conclusion have no consequences regarding the deterministic postulates (P1) and (P2) formulated in chapter I. In the seventeenth-century debate on mind–body interaction, the validity of these postulates was an important issue; but it does not seem to have interested Hume.

E. *Hume's experience*

Hume's analysis of causation is frequently cited as a classical example of a critical, rational, conceptual analysis. In what precedes, I have tried to give a picture of Hume's arguments. I think that Hume's conception of causation also has what might be called an emotional aspect.

Spinoza saw the world as a process in which one situation of necessity gives rise to the next. This outlook is linked with the deterministic postulate which was part of the

[21]Hume, *A Treatise of Human Nature*, iv 5 (p. 247).
[22]Hume, *Enquiries*, p. 164 (*Enquiry Concerning Understanding*, § 12, part III).
[23]Hume, *A Treatise of Human Nature*, I iv 5 (p. 248).

mechanistic world picture. But his outlook is not simply identical with the intellectual acceptance of that postulate. The outlook also implies that the world to Spinoza's eyes is coloured by what we feel when we feel ourselves to be under compulsion. From one point of view, Spinoza's entire philosophy was an attempt to show how the rational man can achieve a spiritual freedom even in a world of compulsion.

Although Hume was usually as convinced as Spinoza that whatever happens occurs in accordance with laws of nature, he sometimes gives expression to a way of experiencing the world that is diametrically opposed to Spinoza's. In the *Enquiry* he says:

We have sought in vain for an idea of power or necessary connexion in all the sources from which we could suppose it to be derived. It appears that, in single instances of the operations of bodies, we never can, by our utmost scrutiny, discover any thing but one event following another; without being able to comprehend any force or power by which the cause operates, or any connexion between it and its supposed effect. The same difficulty occurs in contemplating the operations of mind on body—where we observe the motion of the latter to follow upon the volition of the former, but are not able to observe or conceive the tie which binds together the motion and volition, or the energy by which the mind produces this effect. The authority of the will over its own faculties and ideas is not a whit more comprehensible: so that, upon the whole, there appears not, throughout all nature, any one instance of connexion which is conceivable by us. All events seem entirely loose and separate. One event follows another; but we never can observe any tie between them.[24]

Hume goes on to state his view that it is the habit of the mind, "upon the appearance of one event, to expect its usual attendant", which makes us feel a connection in the imagination.[25]

The question whether events are "loose and separate" or not hardly has any answer. The feeling, however, that events are loose and separate is a distinct feeling which I believe anyone can induce in himself with a little effort. This experience of Hume's is a secularized variant of a religious view which occurs in many medieval thinkers

[24]Hume, *Enquiries*, pp. 73–4 (*Enquiry Concerning Understanding*, § 7, part II).
[25]Ibid., pp. 75–6.

(Christian, Arabic, and Jewish), and which is found in the seventeenth century in Malebranche and in the eighteenth in Hume's precursor Berkeley. The religious view signifies, crudely speaking, that events in the world are not tied together among themselves but are held together merely by God's omnipotence. If God is erased, Hume's experience remains.

VI

Experience and the External World

23. INTRODUCTION

The discussion of which some glimpses will be given in this chapter centres upon a problem which can be roughly indicated by the question, "How are our sense perceptions related to the external world?". Those thinkers who belong to, or are influenced by, the empiricist tradition originating with Locke have been much preoccupied with this problem.

The problem has a long history. In antiquity it was considered by the Atomists, whose doctrine made reality so very different from what it appears to be to the senses, and by the sceptics who questioned man's capacity to obtain any knowledge of an external reality (if there were one). In the Middle Ages, the Ockhamist school showed a tendency toward a similar scepticism. In the seventeenth century the "Pyrrhonian" arguments of the ancient sceptics attracted general interest in the philosophical world. When Descartes, through his method of systematic doubt, hoped to reach an indubitable foundation for philosophy (finding it in the *Cogito*), he made himself doubt the reliability of his senses and the existence of bodies—a doubt he then overcame by his trust in God's veracity. According to Leibniz, only the monads, a kind of spiritual point, strictly speaking exist. In an interesting little essay *On the mode of distinguishing real phenomena from imaginary* (*De modo distinguendi phaenomena realia ab imaginariis*), he tried to show how, and in what sense, one can nevertheless discriminate between "real phenomena", i.e. veridical sense perceptions, and "imaginary", i.e. illusory ones. This essay is perhaps the first sketch of a phenomenalistic interpretation of our knowledge of the external world and anticipates thoughts that others were later to present in greater detail. The corpuscular theory of matter which was widely held in the seventeenth century recreated the situation in which the Atomists of antiquity found themselves: the material world as it really is is very different from what it appears to be according to our senses. In this chapter, I shall consider some of the arguments concerning the problem that were presented by Locke, Berkeley, and Hume, but with some side glances toward related arguments by others. Most space will naturally be given to Berkeley, who debated the problem with extraordinary energy, inventiveness, and bias.

It is common to distinguish between two philosophical views concerning the present problem, views which are by tradition denominated "naïve" and "critical realism". In Locke there are arguments that can be considered as a critique of naïve realism, and he settled for a form of critical realism that was a version of the mechanical world view. Berkeley took up the issue at the point where it was left by Locke. He thought that the arguments that show naïve realism to be an untenable theory apply with equal force to critical realism, which also has further difficulties of its own. He wished to replace the critical realism, implied by the mechanical world view, by a theory nowadays usually classified as "phenomenalist". In §§ 24 and 25 I shall try to give one possible formulation of what is usually vaguely meant by naïve realism (a formulation which I think fits in with the thinking of classical empiricism) and set forth some of the arguments against it. In §§ 26 and 27 I shall analogously try to give a statement of what is usually vaguely meant by critical realism (a formulation likewise tailor-made to fit classical empiricist thought) and some of the arguments against it. In § 28 I shall attempt to explain Berkeley's phenomenalism; in § 29 I shall consider, in terms of principle, the possibilities of phenomenalism; and in § 30 I shall take a brief look at the subsequent fate of phenomenalism.

The reasonings of the empiricists have an apparent clarity and simplicity; they talk about everyday perceptual phenomena with a minimum of esoteric terminology. Unfortunately, the clarity is largely only apparent. For anyone who looks for sharply stated problems and closely reasoned arguments for or against the one or the other solution, study of their writings turns out to be strenuous work with many disappointments. In the following sections, as always in this history, I have felt free to proceed with a certain liberty. With the reasonings of the empiricists in view, I have tried to state some problems and some theses, and I have then tried to extract relevant arguments from their writings.

24. NAÏVE REALISM

A formulation as good as any other of a "naïvely realistic" position is, I think, this:

(1)   External objects are, on the whole, as they appear to our senses.

The thought vaguely expressed by (1) could, I think, also be expressed as follows:

(2)   External objects have, on the whole, those qualities that they appear to have in normal sense perception.

With the reservation hinted at in (2), an object that visually appears to be round *is* round, one that visually appears to be red *is* red, and so on, according to (2). It is important to understand "is" here in the sense appropriate to naïve realism. When saying that a piece of cloth "is" red, we may very well mean that it will appear to be red when seen under certain specified conditions. The definition of such an "is" would run like this:

(i) x is$_2$ ϕ = Df When seen (felt, etc.) under conditions C x will appear to be$_1$ ϕ.

Such an "is$_2$", however, is *not* the "is" that naïve realism is here understood to involve. It is instead that "is$_1$" ("be$_1$") that occurs in the definiens of (i). External objects are supposed to "have" the sensibly given qualities in exactly that sense in which they appear to "have" them.

In Berkeley's *Dialogues*, Hylas, who enters the discussion as a naïve realist, makes a number of somewhat crudely formulated statements to the same general effect as (2):

Whatever degree of heat we perceive by sense, we may be sure the same exists in the object that occasions it.[1]

Each visible object hath that colour which we see in it.[2]

[1] *The Works of George Berkeley*, vol. i, p. 384.   [2] Ibid., p. 392.

Since "naïve realism" is not a view defended by any historically identifiable persons but merely a position constructed by epistemologists for discussion and, usually, for critique, a debate as to its true import easily turns into a debate about the pope's beard. It is clear, however, that (2) becomes a position that can be taken seriously only if it is somehow made precise what objects (the so-called "external objects") it is concerned with and what the reservations ("on the whole", "normal") amount to. Since no such rigorous statement was made, or clearly implied, by the British empiricists, we shall not worry now about how it should be framed.

Naïve realism, as stated in (2), implies a view as to the nature of the external world, the physical universe. Objects such as chairs and tables literally have the kind of spatial extension that we experience in visual perception. The external world as the sum total of all external objects (including, of course, my own body) also literally has that kind of spatial extension: it is the one, enormously large, spatially extended object of which all spatially extended external objects are parts. Processes in the external world also literally have the kind of temporal duration that I sensibly experience, for instance, when seeing a sheet of paper being turned by my hand on the desk in front of me. Many material objects in the world also literally have, for instance, colours such as those I now see.

In discussing the empiricist theory of ideas we met the notion of a sense-datum, a modern notion which, I think, essentially coincides with what the empiricists meant by the "idea" (Locke, Berkeley), or the "perception", "impression" (Hume), that is present to my mind when I perceive something with my senses. As sense-data are usually understood, they literally have the sense qualities they are perceived as having. When, e.g., I see a red rose, I perceive a sense-datum which literally *is* red: it literally is_1 what the rose appears to be_1. The empiricists assumed that their "ideas" fulfilled this condition, too. When a theory of sense-data is assumed, the naïve realism of (2) obtains a new implication.

Let us assume a naïvely realistic position of the kind (2), and let us also assume a sense-datum theory. Let us presuppose that the conditions, alluded to in (2), are fulfilled, and that the object which I see, say a red rose, has all the qualities that it visibly appears to have. According to the sense-datum theory, all these qualities are also possessed by the sense-datum involved in my seeing the rose. This sense-datum cannot be identical with the whole rose: it presents the rose only as seen from one particular point of view. But this sense-datum will be indistinguishable, in terms of visible qualities, from the part of the surface of the rose that is visible from this particular point of view. When the naïve realism (2) is combined with a sense-datum theory, we are thus naturally led to adopt the view:

> (3) Under favourable conditions, the sense-datum involved in our seeing (feeling, etc.) an object coincides with a fragment of that object and, hence, is itself a fragment of the external world.

Conversely the assumption (3) may itself, of course, be a reason for believing in (2). One of the assertions with which Hylas, initially a naïve realist, opens the debate in Berkeley's *Dialogues* is that "sensible things"—which here, I think, means much the same as "sense-data"—have a "real existence" or a "subsistence exterior to the mind, and distinct from their being perceived", an assertion which Berkeley's alter ego, Philonous, then refutes.[3] I think Hylas can be understood to assert something like (3).

Adopting the terminology of the classical empiricists, we could restate (3) in roughly the following way:

> (4) Under favourable conditions, the "ideas" or "impressions" we have in sense perception themselves exist in the external world.

The form of naïve realism which presupposes a theory of sense-data can be roughly illustrated in diagram (F).

I here represents the contents of consciousness, the "ideas" or "perceptions", *S* represents sense-data or "sensations" (obtained under favourable conditions), and *EW* represents the external world.

---

[3] *The Works of George Berkely*, vol. i, p. 384.

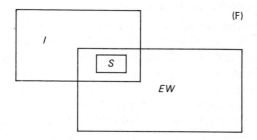

25. SOME ARGUMENTS AGAINST NAÏVE REALISM

Locke distinguished between what he called "primary" and "secondary" qualities of bodies. As primary he acknowledged "solidity, extension, figure, motion or rest, and number", sometimes adding "texture" also.[4] The secondary qualities of bodies are the "powers" they have to create in us such "sensations" as colours, sounds, tastes, etc. After Locke it has become customary to let the term "secondary quality" stand for those very sensible qualities that the "powers" Locke speaks of make us perceive. I shall here employ the term in this established non-Lockean sense even when discussing the views of Locke. Speaking thus, we may say that, according to Locke, bodies literally have primary qualities but never literally have any secondary qualities (although they have the powers to make us sense them). The view:

(1)   Colours, tastes, smells, sounds, degrees of warmth and coldness, etc., are not literally properties of bodies, and are not found in the external world,

was quite common in seventeenth-century philosophy. It is found in Galileo, Hobbes, Descartes, Gassendi, Boyle, and many others, and it was, in fact, an accepted ingredient of the mechanistic world view. Apparently, (1) seemed more or less self-evident to Locke. The space he devotes to arguing for it in the *Essay* is minimal. Some arguments, however, are hinted at in passing, and some of them were taken up and elaborated by Berkeley and Hume. Three arguments found in Locke will now be discussed.

[4] Locke, *An Essay Concerning Human Understanding* II viii 9.

A. *The argument from variation*

This argument, which was already well known in antiquity, points to the fact that the qualities one and the same object appears to have to different observers, or under different circumstances of observation, are very often incompatible with each other although we cannot assume that the object itself has undergone any change. Locke uses the example of a piece of porphyry which looks red and white when illuminated but colourless in the dark. Arguments of this type are also given by Berkeley and Hume—although, on their view, they apply also to Locke's primary qualities.[5]

All reasonings of this type start from observations such as these:

(i) In case c, the object o appears to have the quality q:.

(ii) In case c', the same object o appears to have the quality q'. One assumes that the object o has not undergone any qualitative change from case c to case c'.

(iii) o has the same qualities in c that it has in c'.

Hence:

(iv) If o has q in c and q' in c', it has q and q' simultaneously.

On the strength of the (presumed) fact:

(v) Nothing simultaneously has, or can have, q and q',

one can infer:

(vi) Either o does not have q in c, or it does not have q' in c'.

This, of course, is not the same as:

(vii) Neither does o have q in c, nor does it have q' in c'.

The similarity between the perceptual situations (i) and (ii) is often thought to be a reason why, if we grant (vi), we must also assent to (vii). For, say, any visible object o and any colour q, we can encounter, or plausibly imagine,

[5] Cf. Berkeley, op. cit., vol. i, pp. 265, 388–9, 393–8, 398–9, 400, 417–18; Hume, *A Treatise of Human Nature*, I iv 2 (pp. 210–11); I iv·4 (pp. 226–7); Enquiries, p. 152 (*Enquiry Concerning Understanding*, §12, part I).

a situation such as (i) and (ii) describe. The conclusion, then, is that no objects have colours, and similarly for the other secondary sense qualities.

The argument from variation is, of course, not a genuine "proof" of the thesis that no external objects, no "bodies" ever have any one of the qualities classified as secondary. As always in philosophy, we must reckon with the very real possibility that the argument suffers from semantic short-comings. Even disregarding this possibility, we have already noticed that the step from (vi) to (vii) is guided only by analogy. Hume expresses this very clearly:

Now from like effects we presume like causes. Many of the impressions of colour, sound, &c., are confest to be nothing but internal existences, and to arise from causes which no ways resemble them. These impressions are in appearance nothing different from the other impressions of colour, sound, &c. We conclude, therefore, that they are, all of them, deriv'd from a like origin.[6]

How much confidence can we put in this analogical inference? Discarding it, can we believe that "bodies" under specific circumstances reveal their real secondary qualities to us in sense perception?

B. *The argument from pain and pleasure*

This argument, barely sketched by Locke, is put forth at length by Berkeley in the *Dialogues* and again mentioned by Hume. The argument is primarily applied, by all three, to our sensations of heat, but Berkeley applies it also to tastes and odours.[7] The course of the argument as stated by Berkeley is this:

(i) Pain and pleasure are, by common consent, not qualities in bodies.

(ii) Certain degrees, or kinds of Q (temperature, taste, smell) *are* pains or pleasures.

Therefore:

(iii) These degrees, or kinds, of Q are not qualities in bodies.

[6] Hume, *A Treatise of Human Nature*, I iv 4 (p. 227).
[7] Cf. ibid., I iv 2 (pp. 192–3); Locke, op. cit. II viii 16 (vol. i, p. 173); Berkeley, op. cit., vol. i, pp. 384–91.

One may again, arguing by analogy, pass from (iii) to:

(iv) No degrees, or kinds, of Q are ever qualities in bodies.

A critical point in this argument is, of course, assertion (ii). Is it correct to say, e.g., that an intense degree of experienced heat is *identical* with a degree of pain, or would it not be more accurate to say that the two are intimately associated? Berkeley is aware of this possible objection but rejects it, maintaining that upon putting your hand near the fire you perceive "but one simple sensation".[8]

C. *A causal argument*

According to Locke's mechanical world view, our sensations are caused by particles acting upon our senses. These particles act only through their "different motions and figures, bulk and number", i.e. those properties which are treated of in Newtonian mechanics.[9] Although Locke does not present his thought here in the form of a formal argument, he apparently thinks that, since the secondary qualities have no "resemblance" to the "motions" which are the causes of our perceiving them, they must be assumed not to exist in the bodies from which these "motions" originate.[10] The argument is presented so sketchily by Locke that it is very hard to make out its point. Possibly, the argument should be understood as inferring the non-objectivity of secondary qualities from the Newtonian description of material objects. Possibly, also, its point is that since the particles acting on, say, our eyes and causing our seeing cannot be supposed literally to transport the colour of the rose from the rose to the eyes and thereby to the mind, it is difficult to believe that the colour seen actually inheres in the rose. If this is taken to be the gist of the argument, it is akin to some of the causal arguments of the ancient sceptics. In a more explicit and more sophisticated manner, the same line of thought has been expounded by Bertrand Russell and by C. D. Broad in our century.

[8] Berkely, op. cit., vol. i, p. 385   [9] Locke, op. cit. II viii 13.
[10] Ibid. II viii 15–22.

26. MECHANIST CRITICAL REALISM

Anyone convinced by arguments such as those we have met in the previous section can make a first retreat to some position of critical realism. The mechanist philosophy which had so many adherents in the seventeenth century, one of whom was Locke, involves one such position. It combined the two assertions:

(1) No external objects (bodies) ever have any secondary qualities,

and:

(2) External objects have spatio-temporal properties (and relations) of the kind that they appear to have.

(The first and the second "have" in (2) should be taken in the same sense.) The world as conceived of by this critical realism is thus essentially that of naïve realism stripped of its secondary qualities. Assumption (1) could be combined with the belief that:

(3) External objects, on the whole, have those spatio-temporal properties (and relations) they appear to have in normal sense perception.

Surveying the "qualities that are in bodies", Locke first mentions: "The bulk, figure, number, situation, and motion or rest of their solid parts. Those are in them [the bodies], whether we perceive them or not; and when they are of that size that we can discover them, we have by these an idea of the thing as it is in itself; as is plain in artificial things."[11] When, in the *Dialogues*, Hylas has been forced to abandon his original naïve realism, he still maintains that: "the very texture and extension which you perceive by sense, exist in the outward object or material substance."[12] If a sense-datum theory is combined with this form of critical realism, (3) will imply something like this:

(4) Under favourable conditions, those spatio-temporal properties (relations) which are found in the sense-datum we have when seeing an object belong also to the object itself.

[11]Ibid. II viii 23.   [12]Berkeley, op. cit., vol. i, p. 398.

The critical realism of Locke, and of the mechanist philosophy, can be very roughly illustrated in a diagram (G),
which may be compared with diagram (F) on p. 125 above,
illustrating naïve realism:

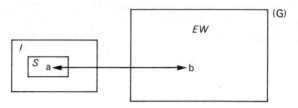

I is here the contents of my consciousness, my "ideas" or
"perceptions", *S* are the sense-data or "sensations", and
EW is the external world. The arrow from *a* in *S* to *b* in
EW signifies that *b* is the external object, or "body", that
corresponds to the sense-datum *a* and with which *a* more
or less agrees in point of the so-called primary qualities.

27. BERKELEY'S CRITIQUE OF MECHANIST
CRITICAL REALISM

A. *On Berkeley's terminology and method*

Locke's version of mechanist critical realism—hereafter
referred to as *MCR*, for short—is the starting-point for
Berkeley's discussion of our knowledge of the external
world. Berkeley employs a slightly esoteric terminology.
He distinguishes between the notion of "material substance"
and that of "sensible thing". He also distinguishes between
the philosophical claim that material substances exist (matter
exists) on the one hand, and the commonsense belief in the
existence of chairs, tables, trees, and stars, on the other
hand. In Berkeley's language, when naïve realism has been
abandoned, the philosophical claim, "Material substances
exist", amounts to about the same as *MCR*. By "sensible
things" Berkeley understands roughly the same as "sense-
data". When he speaks of the commonsense belief, he has
in mind primarily those assertions that we make in everyday
life about physical phenomena, but to some extent he is
prepared to give equal treatment to the propositions of

physical science. In order to simplify my exposition, I introduce the term "*m*-proposition" as a common designation of this entire class of propositions, the truth of which Berkeley considers to be beyond dispute.

Berkeley wishes to refute the philosophical theory that material substances exist, i.e. the theory *MCR*. He stresses that his refutation leaves the belief in the existence of "sensible things" unaffected. He also emphasizes that the refutation is not intended to question the truth of those *m*-propositions that in everyday life we find reason to accept or which science arrives at. *MCR* provides, on Berkeley's view, a certain philosophical interpretation of the *m*-propositions. From the conviction that *MCR* is an illusion, Berkeley infers that the interpretation of the *m*-propositions that MCR provides is incorrect. Berkeley then tries to clarify what is the correct interpretation of these propositions. We shall now study his arguments against *MCR* and then, in §28, his own "phenomenalistic" interpretation of the *m*-propositions. Some of Berkeley's arguments were repeated by Hume, who also proposed a form of phenomenalism.

B. *Some of Berkeley's arguments*

Berkeley does not separate, as sharply as I shall, the critique of naïve realism from that of *MCR*. I find the separation instructive, and I shall here consider some of his arguments merely as arguments against *MCR*. In the *Dialogues*, especially, Berkeley shows an untiring imagination in varying his attack on *MCR*. I shall select here the arguments I think most interesting. A critique of *MCR* can aim at showing:

I.   *MCR*'s unequal treatment of primary and secondary qualities is unfounded.

The main reason for this thesis is what I shall call:

The measure-for-measure argument

Consider any so-called primary quality, say geometrical shape, or size. The argument from variation applies to it with exactly the same force as it applies to secondary qualities. In the *Dialogues*, Berkeley's spokesman, Philonous, asks:

Was it not admitted as a good argument, that neither heat nor cold
was in the water, because it seemed warm to one hand, and cold to
the other? . . . Is it not the very same reasoning to conclude, there
is no extension or figure in an object, because to one eye it shall
seem little, smooth, and round, when at the same time to the other,
great, uneven, and angular?[13]

This argument is also found in Hume's *Enquiry*.[14]

Both Berkeley and Hume also assert against *MCR*:

II. Primary qualities cannot occur without secondary
qualities.

To establish this thesis Berkeley and Hume both appeal to
what I shall call:

The argument from inconceivability

When presented in more pedantic detail than Berkeley and
Hume cared for, the argument runs like this:

  (i) What is possible is what is conceivable.
  (ii) What is conceivable is what we can form an idea of.
  (iii) We cannot form the idea of an extended object
        without providing it, in our imagination, with some
        secondary qualities.

Imagining a triangle, we must visualize its sides as marked by,
say a colour contrast. Together, (i)–(iii) entail thesis II.[15]

This argument is based on a notion of "possibility" which
appears much too narrow for the context. I may perhaps
be unable to visualize in my imagination a triangle without
colours entering into my picture, but I am still able to
understand the statement, "There exists a colourless triangle
in a colourless milieu", and the assertion hardly suffers
from any logical contradiction.

Both Berkeley and Hume argued in favour of the even
stronger thesis:

III. No immediately perceived quality, primary or secondary,
can exist in a body.

[13]Ibid., p. 399.
[14]Hume, *Enquiries*, pp. 154-5 (*Enquiry Concerning Understanding*, §12,
part I).
[15]Berkeley, op. cit., vol. i, p. 404; Hume, *A Treatise of Human Nature*, I iv 4
(pp. 228–9).

Their reason for this thesis was what I shall call:

The quality–idea argument

Suppose that a quality q, a colour, say, or a shape, is "immediately perceived":

(i) The quality q is immediately perceived.

Now, by the theory of ideas outlined in the previous chapter:

(ii) Everything that is immediately perceived is an idea.

Therefore:

(iii) q is an idea.

Again by the theory of ideas:

(iv) An idea can exist only in a mind.

From this and the supposedly trivial presupposition:

(v) No material substances are minds,

the desired conclusion is drawn:

(vi) q cannot exist in a material substance.

Since the validity of this argument is independent of the choice of q, to accept the argument is to accept thesis III.[16]

According to one classical-empiricist explanation, the principle (ii) is tautological, "idea" being defined as "what is perceived immediately". If we stick to this explanation, we find that (iii) is a mere restatement of (i) in a different phraseology. In one passage Berkeley explains the phrase, "The idea i is in the mind m", to mean the same as "i is (immediately) perceived by m".[17] If this explanation were correct, the dictum (iv) would say no more than that only minds can (immediately) perceive. If (vi) follows from (iv) and (v), it ought to say that no material substance can (immediately) perceive q. But what Berkeley, and after him Hume, wanted to prove was that no material substance can have the quality q.

As we saw in the previous chapter, the empiricists' talk of ideas being "in the mind" has some rather mysterious surplus

---

[16]Hume, *A Treatise of Human Nature*, I iv 2 (pp. 189–90); Berkeley, op. cit., vol. i, pp. 261, 411, 420, 442–3.

[17]Berkeley, op. cit., vol. i, p. 470.

meaning beyond that given to it by their own terminological explanations. The quality–idea argument derived,
I think, its seeming force from the surplus meaning.

Berkeley, and after him Hume, also maintained:

IV. If material substances did exist, we could never acquire
any knowledge about them.

One reason for this thesis is what I choose to call:

The argument from possible non-existence

Suppose that matter, or material substances, did not exist.
Berkeley asks: "whether it be not evident you might for
all that be affected with the same ideas you now are, and
consequently have the very same reasons to believe its
existence [the existence of matter] that you now can
have?"[18] He thinks that this consideration deprives all the
arguments for the existence of bodies of their strength.

If "might" is understood in a sufficiently weak, purely
"logical" sense, and if, thus, in judging what is possible
we disregard all known psycho-physical connections and
other scientific laws, Berkeley is probably right in saying
that a world of experience such as mine might exist even
if there were no matter. In the same very weak sense of
"might", it is probably true, e.g., that every thing that
happens within a sphere with the tip of my nose at its centre
and a radius of 3 yards might exist even if there were nothing
beyond this sphere. All the reasons that events within the
sphere (light rays, soundwaves, the arrival of things "from
the outside", etc.) afford for the belief that there are things
outside the sphere might be present even if the belief were
false.

What Berkeley's argument shows is that the question of
the existence of material substances cannot be logically
decided on the basis of a description of my experiences.
But is this more relevant than the fact that the existence
of a world beyond the sphere just mentioned cannot be
logically decided on the basis of a description of the events
within the sphere? Although these events no doubt play
an essential part in the process through which I obtain

[18]Ibid., p. 435, Cf. ibid., p. 268.

knowledge of what happens outside the sphere, I do not obtain this knowledge solely by *inference* from the events within. Isn't the relation between my experiences and my knowledge of the external world of a similar kind?

However, from the point of view of the empiricist theory of knowledge in its subjectivist version (cf. p. 91), the basis for all my knowledge of matters of fact consists in my knowledge of certain sense-data and of other experiential contents. From this point of view, the argument from the possible non-existence of material substances is relevant. Its relevance is increased if, as Berkeley as well as Hume sometimes seems to do, one acknowledges only strictly demonstrative reasons as reasons that are at all trustworthy.

Another argument for thesis IV which is hinted at by Berkeley and more explicitly stated by Hume is what I shall call:

The argument from induction

This argument, too, relies heavily on the basic ideas of the empiricist theory of knowledge in its subjectivist variant. Since material substances, or external objects, are not immediately perceived by us, whatever knowledge we may have of them must be reached by inductive reasoning from past experience. The premisses of such reasoning will all be concerned with "ideas" (Berkeley) or "perceptions" (Hume) only. Hence, the same must hold of its conclusion. Inductions from premisses about the realm of "ideas" or "perceptions" can never lead to conclusions beyond that realm.[19]

Let us consider an inductive pattern that might possibly seem to provide a means for inferring the existence of an external object. It could look like this:

a_1 of kind A is accompanied by b_1 of kind B
a_n of kind A is accompanied by b_n of kind B
$\cdots\cdots$
a_{n+1} is of kind A

[19]I find this argument hinted at in passages such as: Berkeley, op. cit., vol. i, pp. 262–3, 415–16, 435; Hume, *Enquiries*, p. 153 (*Enquiry Concerning Understanding*, §12, part I); *A Treatise of Human Nature*, I iv 2 (pp. 193, 198, 212).

Therefore, there is a b_{n+1} of kind B that accompanies a_{n+1}.

The Argument from Induction asserts, I think, not only that the entities $a_1 \ldots, a_{n+1}, b_1 \ldots, b_{n+1}$, will all be "ideas" or "perceptions", in an empirically founded inference of this type, but also that its premises and its conclusion must be understood to assert that such is the case. If to be an "idea" or a "perception" is the same as to be "immediately perceived", this amounts to the claim that "A" should be read as "A and immediately perceived" and "B" as "B and immediately perceived" in the above pattern of inference. If this line of thought is carried out consistently, does one not arrive at the view that any assertion about an a that is immediately perceived must involve the assertion that a is so perceived? Is this a plausible view?

Their theory of ideas did provide Berkeley and Hume with a final argument against naïve realism, mechanist critical realism, and any theory that recognizes objects beyond ideas or perceptions—although Berkeley, inconsistently, made an exception for spirits. According to the theory, we can never in any way whatever be conscious of anything but ideas or perceptions, nor can we speak in a meaningful way about anything but them.[20]

28. BERKELEY'S PHENOMENALISM

A. *Berkeley's intentions*

Since we know that tables, chairs, and stars exist, and since both naïve and mechanist critical realism are false, how should our assertions about tables etc., what I have called the m-propositions, be understood? Berkeley saw this problem and sketched some solutions of it. Of an adequate interpretation of the m-propositions Berkeley required:

  (i) m-propositions must, on an adequate interpretation, be capable of being known with certainty.
  (ii) m-propositions must not, on an adequate interpretation, presuppose the existence of anything but "ideas"—and "spirits".

[20]Cf. Berkeley, op. cit., vol. I, pp. 257–8; Hume, *A Treatise of Human Nature*, part IV, §§ 2–6.

If the arguments against the knowability of material substances are granted, and if we leave out the spirits from (ii),
(ii) appears as a corollary to (i) within the framework of
Berkeley's thought. The spirits are a sore point, here as in
so many other contexts of Berkeley's philosophy. Point (ii)
was concisely expressed by Berkeley in the dictum, *esse est
percipi* (to be is to be perceived), which he sometimes ex-
panded into the thesis that to be is either to be perceived or
to perceive, this in order to make room for spirits.

Berkeley sketches two interpretations which he apparently
considers adequate in the sense of meeting requirements (i)
and (ii).

B. *The categorical interpretation*

This interpretation consists of an identification of the things
that are spoken of in the *m*-propositions with the "sensible
things" that are the immediate objects of our sense perceptions. What Berkeley understands by "sensible things"
are, as previously noted, very much the same as the sense-
data of modern philosophy or, perhaps, certain combinations
of such sense-data or of sensibly given qualities. Houses,
mountains, rivers, are nothing but "the things we *perceive*
by sense, and what do we perceive besides our own ideas
or sensations . . .?"[21] An apple is a "collection" of "ideas"
received through the several senses, such as "a certain colour,
taste, smell, figure, and consistence".[22] There is much obscurity in these and similar explanations offered by Berkeley.
Some aspects of his thought become clearer through a study
of the manner in which he replies to certain objections.

One possible objection to the categorical interpretation
is that, say, a tree is believed by common sense to exist
continuously for a long time whereas it is observed only
now and then. If the tree is nothing but an idea, or a collection of ideas, the interrupted existence of our ideas seems
to make the existence of the tree equally interrupted. In
certain passages, Berkeley accepts this consequence.[23] In
other passages, however, he tries to show that it does not
follow from his theory. Even if there is no idea of the tree

[21]Berkeley, op. cit., vol. i, p. 259. [22]Ibid., p. 258.
[23]Ibid., pp. 281-2.

in any human mind, there may exist one in the mind of God. Berkeley apparently makes the bizarre and often ridiculed assumption that God perceives the tree exactly as long as it is believed by common sense to exist and that God thus ensures the truth of common sense.[24] Both re-actions of Berkeley to the present objection presuppose that the tree exists at a time if and only if somebody, poss-ibly only God, perceives the tree at that time. (Does an interpretation of the *m*-propositions that involves appeal to theological hypotheses make these propositions more capable of being known with certainty, than an interpreta-tion which assumes the existence of "material substances"? Berkeley was not troubled by this question.)

The second objection is that, on the view of common sense, several people can see the same tree but that each of them will have his own visual sensations. If a tree is identical with a certain idea, does it not follow that the several persons see as many distinct trees? Berkeley replies that when several people are said to see the "same" thing, the word "same" is not used in its strict philosophical sense. Its "vulgar" sense here is such that different persons can perceive the same thing.[25] Here Berkeley seems to approach the view proposed by Bertrand Russell, his pupil in our century, that the tree is a certain class of related sense-data. (If, as the empiricist theory of ideas maintains, *I* can perceive only *my* ideas, and refer through *my* words only to them, how can the present problem arise at all?)

C. *The conditional interpretation*

The first of the two objections just mentioned is also met by Berkeley in an entirely different way. Astronomy has established that the earth is a planet circling around the sun, but "the motion of the earth is not perceived by sense." How, then, can astronomy be right? Berkeley replies:

. . . the question, whether the earth moves or not, amounts in reality to no more than this, to wit, whether we have reason to conclude from what hath been observed by astronomers, that if we were placed in such and such circumstances, and such and such a position or dis-tance, both from the earth and the sun, we should perceive the former

[24]ibid., pp. 284, 424–5.   [25]Ibid., pp. 463–8.

to move among the choir of the planets, and appearing in all respects like one of them: and this, by the established rules of nature, which we have no reason to mistrust, is reasonably collected from the phenomena.[26]

The *m*-proposition, "The earth circles around the sun", is here interpreted as a conditional proposition, "if we were in such and such a position, we would perceive such and such." This interpretation is distinct from what I have called the categorical interpretation, and it is open to objections of its own. As G. E. Moore, among others, has pointed out, an obvious deficiency in this interpretation is that it construes certain propositions about physical facts as conditionals, "If P then Q", where at any rate P is again a statement of physical fact.

29. ON PHENOMENALISM

Berkeley's theory is of a phenomenalist character. Like most of the words classifying philosophical theories, the word "phenomenalism" is rather vague. It is applied to theories maintaining that (i) our knowledge does not reach beyond "phenomena", conceived of as contents of consciousness, or (ii) the "world" itself is nothing but such phenomena, or (iii) the statements about the world that are acceptable to common sense or science are, to a greater or lesser extent, interpretable in terms of such phenomena. On all three scores, Berkeley's theory exhibits an obviously although not consistently phenomenalist tendency. The problem of giving a phenomenalist interpretation of our beliefs about the world is analogous to another, historically even more venerable, problem, viz. that of carrying out a nominalist interpretation of language. The two problems have a common structure. Two sets of statements are given, S_1 and S_2, such that S_1 is included as a part in S_2. The statements in S_1 refer exclusively to a kind of entities E_1, whereas the statements in S_2 at least apparently refer to a larger domain of entities E_2, of which E_1 is only a part. The problem is to find a method of translation (say, a system of definitions) whereby each statement A in S_2 can be transformed into a statement A_1 in S_1 in such a manner that some

[26]Ibid., pp. 289–90. Cf. ibid., pp. 258–9, 456.

sort of equivalence obtains between A and A_1. In the case of medieval nominalism, E_1 consists of (the) "singular things", whereas, in addition to them, E_2 contains the entire hierarchy of "species" and "genera", and other "universals". In the case of a consistent phenomenalism, E includes nothing but subjective phenomena (in the language of the British empiricists: "ideas", "perceptions", "sensations"), whereas E_2 embraces also all the entities pertaining to the external world.

The phenomenalist as well as the nominalist programme of interpretation can be seen as an expression of that instinct for theoretical parsimony that Ockham voiced in his famous "razor". The successful completion of the phenomenalist programme, or the nominalist one, would in a sense simplify our picture of the world and our language.

Obviously, both phenomenalism and nominalism are very big and rather indefinite orders. Exactly what sort of equivalence should the methods of translation ensure? Exactly how should the domains of entities E_1, E_2 in each case be delimited? As long as human language, knowledge, and science continue to develop, the systems S_1, S_2 will remain open and variable. The orders can at most be effected in rather small successive portions. It is clear *a priori* that those philosophers who have tried to present, in a book or two, a phenomenalistic interpretation of our knowledge of the external world have overestimated their resources. What they have achieved can at most be a more or less stimulating incitement to further thought. This prediction concerning the writings of phenomenalists is completely confirmed by a closer study. It is fully valid with respect to those post-Berkeleyan philosophers who are mentioned in the next section.

30. THE LATER FATE OF PHENOMENALISM

In the chapter of the *Treatise* entitled "of scepticism with regard to the senses", Hume presents certain views of a phenomenalistic nature. The *Treatise* contains many passages in which Hume restates Berkeley's opinion that we cannot cognitively reach beyond our own ideas or perceptions. The present chapter, however, opens with a declaration that " 'tis vain to ask, *Whether there be body or not?*" " since "that is a point which we must take for granted in all our reasonings." Hume proposes instead to investigate the question, *"What causes induce us to believe in the existence of body?"*[27] His aim, more precisely stated, is to trace those features of our experience, of our "sensations", that make us postulate a connected spatio-temporal world, containing more or less permanent things, in addition to the sensations that are fragmentary and transient. Hume thinks that these features are the "coherence" and the "constancy" that our sensations so frequently exhibit. The phenomenon of "coherence" is described by Hume as follows.

We remark a connexion betwixt two kinds of objects in their past appearance to the senses, but are not able to observe this connexion to be perfectly constant, since the turning about of our head, or the shutting of our eyes is able to break it. What then do we suppose in this case, but that these objects still continue their usual connexion, notwithstanding their apparent interruption, and that the irregular appearances are join'd by something of which we are insensible?[28]

An example of the phenomenon Hume has in mind would be this. I fix my eyes upon a ball that is rolling across the floor, and I then receive a sequence of perceptions which we may symbolize by the sequence of letters, $A_1 B_1 C_1 D_1 E_1 F_1$. This sequence of perceptions is of a type of which I have met many other instances: I have, e.g., many times looked at objects rolling over a plane. Let us represent these sequences schematically thus:

(i) $\begin{array}{l} A_1 B_1 C_1 D_1 E_1 F_1 \\ A_2 B_2 C_2 D_2 E_2 F_2 \end{array}$

Now, at some other time, I again watch a ball rolling across the floor, but this time I now and then close my eyes or turn away my head. I then get an interrupted sequence of perceptions, say:

(ii) $A_n \ldots C_n \ldots F_n$

It is such a combination as (i) and (ii) that Hume thinks of when speaking of the coherence of our sensations. Its immediate effect, according to Hume, is that our imagination

[27]D. Hume, *A Treatise of Human Nature* (p. 187).   [28]Ibid. (pp. 197–8).

completes the sequence (ii) so as to make it conform with the sequences (i). In our imagination we transform (ii) into: A_n (B_n) C_n $(D_n$ $E_n)$ F_n, where (B_n), $(D_n$ $E_n)$ are the terms interpolated by our imagination. (What Hume calls the constancy of our sensations is in fact only a special case of this coherence, and we may bypass that notion here.)

Considered as a contribution to the interpretation of the m-propositions—a point of view actually foreign to Hume— what Hume says is even more indefinite than what Berkeley said. The modern Oxford philosopher H. H. Price has, how- ever, worked out some interesting phenomenalist theories on the basis of Hume's exposition.[29]

Kant's attitude to what I have called the m-propositions is so obscure that any schematic account must lead astray. He does, I think, operate with a phenomenalistic theory: the spatio-temporal world is a world of "phenomena"; and "phenomena", in one of the Kantian senses of the word, are contents of perceptions. "Experience", according to one thought in Kant, is the part of the sum total of our contents of consciousness that consists of what we regard as "experiences of real objects". When Kant enquires into "the conditions for the possibility of experience" one poss- ible interpretation of his undertaking is that he tries to discern those properties of this part that make us consider it as consisting of "experiences of real objects". His theory about these conditions touches the same problem area that Hume touched with his theory of the coherence and con- stancy of our sensations. Kant's theory, however, is far more complex than Hume's.

In the nineteenth century, phenomenalist ideas played an important role in philosophical thought, and they were often developed under the influence of Berkeley, Hume, or Kant. In British philosophy phenomenalism had a de- fender in John Stuart Mill who declared material objects to be "permanent possibilities of sensation". On the con- tinent, one of the most influential statements of a phe- nomenalist position was made by the Austrian physicist and philosopher Ernst Mach in *The Analysis of Sensations* (*Die Analyse der Empfindungen*, 1885). In our century,

[29] H. H. Price, *Hume's Theory of the External World* (Oxford, 1940).

Bertrand Russell has sketched a phenomenalist interpretation of the *m*-propositions in several works, especially in *Our Knowledge of the External World* (1914) and in *The Analysis of Mind* (1921). In far greater detail than anyone had attempted before him, Russell presents a (fragmentary) method of translation in the form of a number of definitions. Even more ambitious is Rudolf Carnap's *The Logical Structure of the World* (*Der logische Aufbau der Welt*, 1928), which aims at showing that all scientific statements can, by suitable definitions, be translated into a *Principia Mathematica* language, whose domain of individuals consists exclusively of the author's own "elementary experiences", and whose extra-logical vocabulary consists of a single predicate, denoting a relation between the experiences. Under the influence of authorities such as Mach, Russell, and Carnap, phenomenalism was in vogue in the twenties and thirties among those philosophers who were in sympathy with the logical-empiricist movement.

VII

Kant on Synthetic *a priori* Judgements

31. INTRODUCTION

A. *The critique of reason and the metaphysics of Leibniz and Wolff*

As a young man Immanuel Kant (1724–1804) was strongly influenced by the metaphysical speculation in the spirit of Leibniz which flourished in Germany during the former part of the eighteenth century, the foremost spokesman of which was Christian Wolff (1679–1754). The physical world with which we establish contact through our senses is, on Leibniz's view, a subjective world of appearances, in a sense an illusion. In order to gain knowledge of the true reality we must use our reason and rely on abstract arguments. These arguments show that reality is really an infinite multiplicity of simple perceiving substances, the monads, which are literally in time but are not in space of the (intuitive) kind we experience in perception. (On this point, however, Leibniz's statements are difficult to interpret. There are passages in which he appears to consider the monads as points of physical space.) Kant's critique of reason must be considered against the background of this metaphysics against which it was a reaction but with which it was also secretly allied. The parallel distinctions:

the senses—reason,
phenomena—things in themselves,

are taken over in the critique from Leibniz, although Kant modified both the concepts and the terminology. Like Leibniz's monads the critique's things in themselves are not in space, but Kant takes a further step and also denies their being in time. The monads of Leibniz are of a spiritual nature, a kind of mind, even if sometimes of a very rudimentary sort. In his moral philosophy Kant says that the thing in itself that corresponds to our temporal mind has free will and hence, we may assume, is some sort of personality. Whereas Leibniz thought that he could rigorously prove his doctrine of monads, the Kant of the critique maintained the impossibility of a "scientific" metaphysics.

In some of his earlier writings, Kant propounded modifications of Leibniz–Wolffian themes. In the *New Light on the First Principles of Metaphysical Knowledge* (*Cognitionis Metaphysicae Nova Dilucidatio*, 1755) he attempted, e.g., to give an alternative to the doctrine of the pre-established harmony. In the *Physical Monadology* (*Monadologia Physica*, 1756) he sketched a new version of the monadology, which brought it closer to atomic theory and which was related to the theory of Boscovich. A few years after the Lisbon earthquake of 1756, a catastrophe which shook the faith in Providence of many, in *Considerations on Optimism* (*Betrachtungen über den Optimismus*, 1759), Kant thanked the best of all beings for having, for the greatest well-being of the whole, chosen him, who in himself was unworthy, to be a humble member of the most perfect of all projects. In *The Only Possible Foundation for a Demonstration of the Existence of God* (*Der einzig mögliche Beweisgrund zu einer Demonstration des Daseins Gottes*, 1763) he gave his own *a priori* proof of God's existence.

In the sixties there appears in Kant's writings a gradually increasing distrust of this type of speculation. In *Dreams of a Ghost-Seer, Seen in the Light of Dreams of Metaphysics* (*Die Träume eines Geistersehers, erläutet durch Träume der Metaphysik*, 1766) Kant adopts a sceptically ironic attitude toward the visions of Swedenborg as well as to the systems of metaphysics, while still being fascinated by both and not definitely rejecting either. One of the many ironical epithets he gives to metaphysicians is "constructors in the air of all kinds of thought worlds". Kant considered 1769 a decisive year in his development: "The year 69 gave me great light." In a work of 1770, *The Form and Principles of the Sensible and the Intelligible World* (*De Mundi Sensibilis atque Intelligibilis Forma et Principiis*), he speaks for the first time of space and time as forms of sensible intuition, but he also discusses God, the interaction of substances, and the relation of the mind to the external world in very much the same vein as before. Then followed ten years of philosophical silence, broken in 1781 by the publication of the work that has given Kant a place in the history of philosophy, the *Critique of Pure Reason* (*Kritik der reinen Vernunft*). It is the theories that he presents here and in his later writings that are usually referred to as Kant's "critical" philosophy, and it is these theories that I shall dwell upon in this and the following chapter. Besides the 1781 work (second revised edition 1787), the following five books are the most important documents of the critical philosophy: *Prolegomena to Any Future Metaphysics that May Claim to be a Science* (*Prolegomena zu einer jeden künftigen Metaphysik, die als Wissenschaft wird auftreten können*, 1783), *Foundations of the Metaphysics of Ethics* (*Grundlegung zur Metaphysik der Sitten*, 1785), *Critique of Practical Reason* (*Kritik der praktischen Vernunft*, 1787), *Critique of the Faculty of Judgement* (*Kritik der Urteilskraft*, 1790), and *Religion within the Bounds of Mere Reason* (*Die Religion innerhalb der Grenzen der blossen Vernunft*, 1793).

One of the problems that Kant wants to settle in the critique of reason, is simply "Is metaphysics as a science possible?"; and he thinks he can muster sufficient grounds for a negative reply. Only concerning the phenomena that constitute the spatio-temporal reality of the empirical sciences and concerning their forms, space and time, is scientific knowledge possible. Metaphysics, which is an attempt to gain knowledge of something beyond these phenomena, is therefore an impossibility. However, Kant's attitude to metaphysics is hardly unambiguous. For the critical Kant there is also a world of things in themselves beyond phenomena; and, as we have seen, Kant makes various assertions about them. Sometimes Kant appears to suggest that the impossibility of metaphysics is the impossibility of positive knowledge about the things in themselves but not of negative knowledge, and that he himself stops at negative assertions. Although knowledge about the beyond is unreachable, Kant maintains that our practical reason, i.e. the reason through which we recognize our duties, demands that we entertain certain metaphysical beliefs. Morals require of us a moral perfection which we are unable to attain to on this side of the grave but which we may approach as a limit during an infinite existence: hence we must believe in the immortality of the soul. As we approach moral perfection, we deserve—practical reason says—our corresponding share of happiness; hence we must believe in a God who justly portions out happiness in the life hereafter. Kant's critical attitude toward metaphysics seems, in fact, to be dictated by two very different motives. On the one hand, he was genuinely suspicious of metaphysical speculation and dogmatic theology. On the other hand, by referring the metaphysical problems from the domain of knowledge to that of practical reason and faith, he wished to make religion immune to the attacks from the side of "reason" which it so often had to suffer during the Enlightenment.

In the sequel I shall not devote any separate section of my presentation to Kant's critique of metaphysics. In part the critique coincides with a line of thought that we have encountered in Berkeley and in Hume: we have no knowledge of anything but (quoting Kant) "the play of ideas (*Vorstellungen*) in our consciousness"[1]—there belong all the phenomena of nature—and metaphysics, which desires to see what is going on behind this play of ideas, is therefore impossible.

B. *The critique of reason, Newtonian science, and Hume's scepticism*

Besides the Leibniz–Wolffian metaphysics, natural science was the major interest of the young Kant. He had thoroughly, although in a non-mathematical manner, absorbed the principles of Newtonian mechanics, and in several early writings he made independent applications of them. In 1754 he suggested that the tides have changed the rotational velocity of the earth, an idea which was accepted in science only a hundred years later when rediscovered by others. In 1755 he sketched his theory of the origin of the planetary system from a whirling nebula, a theory later independently developed by Laplace at the end of the century. In 1756 he gave an explanation, which in its essentials still stands, of

[1] Kant, *Kritik der reinen Vernunft*, A 101.

the course of the periodic winds. And so on. Kant, who in his critique of reason stuck so rigidly to Euclidean geometry, was far more imaginative in this respect in his youth. In his very first treatise, which he published at the age of twenty-two, he considered three-dimensional Euclidean space as a special case of n-dimensional space and said: "A science of all these possible kinds of space would unfailingly be the highest geometry that a finite understanding could undertake."[2]

Newtonian mechanics is, besides Leibniz–Wolffian metaphysics, the main ground from which the critique of reason grew. The second great problem of the critique, "How are synthetic *a priori* judgements possible?", arose for Kant when he tried to become philosophically clear about Newtonian mechanics and the mathematics it presupposed. Let us try to understand how the problem arose.

Kant declared that it was Hume's discussion of causality that roused him from his "dogmatic slumber"[3] and led him to the lines of thought which resulted in the critique. According to what I have called the Empiricist theory of knowledge, as formulated by Hume, the consideration of "relations of ideas" and experience are the two sources of human knowledge. In terms of his own conceptual apparatus, Kant understood this as the doctrine that all human knowledge is either "analytic" (roughly, pure or applied logic) or "*a posteriori*", i.e. based on observation and induction. The "laws of nature", e.g. the Newtonian laws of mechanics, are, according to Hume, of the latter kind. On the strength of the thesis that induction at most makes its conclusions probable, Hume inferred that laws of nature can never be rigorously established, that we can never have a guarantee that what is considered to be such a law will not be refuted by future experiences. Kant considered this conclusion of Hume's as something of a philosophical catastrophe.

Neither arithmetic nor Euclidean geometry nor "the pure science of nature" (to which Kant reckoned a number of general physical principles that he regarded as self-evident) is applied logic, according to Kant. If Hume were right,

---

[2] Kant, *Gedanken von der wahren Schätzung der lebendigen Kräfte*, § 10.
[3] Kant, *Prolegomena* (Leipzig: 1920), p. 7.

our knowledge in these disciplines would rest on the fragile foundation of observation and induction. Kant himself, however, was convinced that the theorems of these disciplines were truths that no future findings would ever be able to shake. Their validity seemed to him to be in some way a presupposition for the very possibility of empirical science. The great task he set himself was to create secure philosophical foundations for the exact sciences of his time. In order that the foundations should be firm, arithmetic, Euclidean geometry, and the pure science of nature must be placed on a safe footing, and to this end Hume's scepticism had to be refuted.

In conscious opposition to Hume and to the entire empiricist school, Kant tried to show that, besides the analytical (logical) and synthetic *a posteriori* (empirical) knowledge, there exists a third kind of human knowledge which he called "synthetic *a priori*". This third kind is in Kant's eyes more of a mystery than the other two, and so he was led to raise the question, "How are synthetic *a priori* judgements possible?"

Hume's sceptical conclusion struck at all general statements about "facts". Translated into Kant's terminology, which will soon be explained, it concerns all general "synthetic" statements. If one is intent upon refuting Hume's scepticism, one might conceivably try to show that certain knowledge is possible with regard to all the statements that are affected by this scepticism. This, in itself rather absurd, approach is not the one chosen by Kant. He seems to accept Hume's view of induction. What he endeavours to show is only that some among the statements hit by Hume's scepticism can become the object of certain knowledge. This he tries to do by showing that for these statements we invoke a source of knowledge other than logic and empirical induction, viz. the synthetic insight *a priori*. If I have not misunderstood Kant's epistemology, it is hardly an attempt to solve what has previously been labelled "Hume's problem".

The question, "How are synthetic *a priori* judgements possible?", is stated in a technical terminology peculiar to Kant. After having delved into the significance of this terminology in §§ 32 and 33, I shall, in § 34, try to give a somewhat more profound analysis of the question.

32. *A PRIORI* AND *A POSTERIORI*

A. A priori *and* a posteriori

Kant's problem turns on the concept of "synthetic judgement *a priori*", formed by combining the concepts "synthetic judgement" and "*a priori* judgement". To understand these concepts we must first take cognizance of Kant's theory of different kinds of knowledge or certainty.

Our knowledge of the truth of a proposition is knowledge *a priori* if it is based exclusively on reflection and intuition ("Anschauung *a priori*", Kant says). That the statement, 'All bodies have extension', is true, we know, according to Kant, just by apprehending the meaning of the notions involved. This knowledge is thereby an example of what he calls "direct discursive knowledge *a priori*". It is direct since it is not the result of a proof. It is discursive since it is entirely founded on the apprehension of the contents of certain concepts. That two points in space can always be joined by a straight line, we realize, according to Kant, by considering in the space we see with the mind's eye (of which we have an "intuition *a priori*") two points, and then mentally joining them by a straight line. This geometrical knowledge is an instance of what Kant calls "direct intuitive knowledge *a priori*". It is direct for the same reason as the previously mentioned knowledge: it does not result from a proof. It is intuitive since it rests on a non-empirical intuition of space. All such knowledge which is not gained by demonstration, is, on Kant's view, either discursive or intuitive. We come to know more complex theorems in, e.g., mathematics by deriving them from simpler theorems, of which we have a direct knowledge *a priori*, be it discursive or intuitive. Such knowledge is therefore what Kant terms "indirect knowledge *a priori*." All knowledge *a priori* is, on Kant's scheme, either direct, and then either discursive or intuitive, or indirect.

The opposite of knowledge *a priori* is knowledge *a posteriori*, i.e. what would today be called empirical knowledge. Our knowledge of the truth of a proposition is *a posteriori* if it is founded on experience, on sense perception, "the external sense", or on introspection, "the internal sense". (Kant's theory of the external and the internal sense is an obvious parallel to the British empiricists' doctrine of "sensation" and "reflection".) That there is a writing desk in front of me, I know directly by what I see. That King Charles XII of Sweden was shot in 1718, I know indirectly, by inferences from what I see and hear, historical documents and remnants, other people's written and oral testimony.

Kant's presentation does not clearly determine to what category knowledge of mixed origin should be referred, i.e. one that is based on premisses *a priori* as well as on empirical data. Most of the knowledge found in the empirical sciences is of this kind. Mathematical physics, for example, constantly relies both on mathematics and on experience. Kant's failure to make a precise statement on this point no doubt produces a lacuna in his system. With the reservation implied by this I take Kant to mean that any knowledge among whose grounds are any empirical data is *a posteriori*. Only knowledge which rests exclusively on reflection and intuition is *a priori*. The only sources of knowledge available to us, Kant thinks, are conceptual reflection, intuition and experience. By the definitions of '*a priori*' and '*a posteriori*', all human knowledge is thus either one or the other.

As far as I know, this investigation of Kant's into the varieties of knowledge hardly has any equal in earlier philosophy. Leibniz, for instance, operates with the terms '*a priori*' and '*a posteriori*' much more crudely than Kant in his best moments. But at the same time it is difficult not to be puzzled by Kant's analysis. Is it only a piece of empirical psychology? Or is it, at least in part, something else? Then what? How should one go about testing whether Kant is right or wrong? Such questions obtrude upon Kant's reader, but they get no answer from Kant.

B. *Degrees of knowledge*

The misgivings just expressed also make themselves felt with regard to the views that I shall now present. Kant states in many different ways a view, which, without subtlety, could be formulated thus: knowledge *a priori* possesses the highest possible degree of certainty. In contrast to *a posteriori* knowledge, knowledge *a priori*, Kant says, has

an "apodeictic certainty", or is accompanied by an "awareness of necessity", or is "universally and objectively necessary
(valid for everybody)". He also says that one ought to prefer
knowledge *a priori* to knowledge *a posteriori* in those cases
where the same proposition can be an example of either,
apparently because the former knowledge has greater certainty.

When this view is applied to some of the examples Kant
gives of intuitive knowledge *a priori*, it appears rather strange.
By joining, in my spatial imagination, two points by a straight
line, how can I obtain absolutely certain knowledge that
any two points in the world can be thus joined?

This view is however essential to Kant's argument in the
critique. Only since knowledge *a priori* has supreme certainty
can the classification of some synthetic statements effectively
save them from Hume's scepticism.

C. A priori *and* a posteriori *truth*

Relying on this theory of the varieties of certainty, Kant
makes a division of the truths we can know. The same
proposition may sometimes be the object of certainty *a
priori* as well as certainty *a posteriori*. Whereas the mathematician has knowledge *a priori* of the general impossibility
of solving equations of a higher degree than 4 by radicals,
the non-mathematician may know the same theorem empirically, e.g., by trusting the authority of Abel. Any true
proposition of which human beings can obtain knowledge
a priori, Kant terms a proposition *a priori*. Abel's theorem
is thus *a priori*, notwithstanding the fact that there are
many who know it only *a posteriori*. A true proposition,
of which human beings can only have knowledge *a posteriori*,
is called by Kant a proposition *a posteriori*. Since all human
knowledge is either *a priori* or *a posteriori*, all true propositions that we humans can come to know are also either
a priori or *a posteriori*.

33. ANALYTIC AND SYNTHETIC TRUTH

The distinction between proposition *a priori* and propositions
a posteriori is of a psychological or epistemological nature:
it concerns only those true propositions that are accessible
to human knowledge, and it is based on a distinction between

different kinds of certainty or knowledge. In addition to this division, true propositions are divided by Kant into analytic and synthetic.[4] This division is, I think, in contrast to the previous one, intended to apply to all true propositions whatsoever, whether we can know them or not, and it is of a logical, not of a psychological or an epistemological, nature.

Before we consider Kant's attempts to define these concepts, it may be illuminating to take a look at some of the propositions with which he exemplifies them.

Some examples of analytic truth

(A1) All truths of the form, 'Everything that is X and A and Y is A' where X and/or Y may be missing, or which by a substitution of synonyms can be brought to this form, or which are logically equivalent to such a statement, for instance:

   (i)   The human being is a human being,
   (ii) All bodies are extended (here 'body' is synonymous with extended substance'),
   (iii) Substance is what can exist only as subject,
   (iv) No bodies are unextended.

(A2) Various propositions which are not of the above kind, for instance:

   (v) $a = a$, or 'The whole is equal to itself',
   (vi) $(a + b) > a$, or 'The whole is greater than its parts' (Euclid's fifth axiom),

---

[4] By crossing the two concept pairs, true–false, and analytic–synthetic, one obtains four categories:

   (i)   true analytic proposition,
   (ii) false analytic proposition,
   (iii) true synthetic proposition,
   (iv) false synthetic proposition.

Did Kant wish to define the concepts 'analytic' and 'synthetic' so that there exist propositions of all four categories, or did he intend his definitions to render some of the categories empty? Kant's writings are not quite unambiguous on this question. With regard to category (ii) as well as (iv) there are passages where he seems to admit them, but there are also passages—and they are in the majority —in which he seems to rule them out. The definitions I shall state are perhaps less general than they ought to be in order to give a faithful rendering of Kant's thinking.

(vii)   If equals are added to equals, the results are equal (Euclid's second axiom).

Some examples of synthetic truths

(S1) All "perceptual judgements", i.e. "empirical judgements with merely subjective validity", for instance:

(viii)   I, who see a tower, perceive in it a red colour,
(ix)   When touching the stone I feel heat.

(S2) All "experiential judgements", i.e. "empirical judgements with objective validity", for instance:

(x)   The tower is red,
(xi)   The stone is hot.

(S3) "The laws of nature", e.g., the laws of Newton's mechanics.

(Possibly, (S3) is conceived by Kant as a subset of (S2).)

(S4) The theorems of "the pure science of nature", including "the analogies of experience" among which figure a principle of causality and a principle of conservation of matter.

(S5) Those theorems of geometry that do not follow from the definitions—for instance:

(xii)   The straight line is the shortest between two points,
(xiii)   The sum of the angles of a triangle is equal to two right angles,

(S6) Those theorems of arithmetic that do not follow from the definitions—for instance:

(xiv) $7 + 5 = 12$.

(S7) Those metaphysical truths that do not follow from definitions—for instance:

(xv)   God exists.

(S8) All assertions to the effect that something exists. (Naturally, (xv) belongs also under this heading.)

Kant usually describes the difference between the analytic

and the synthetic in something like the following terms: in an analytic judgement the predicate does not contain anything that is not already thought in the subject concept, whereas the predicate in the synthetic judgement goes beyond what is contained in the subject concept; in an analytic judgement the predicate can be produced by analysis of the subject concept, something not possible in the case of a synthetic judgement; the predicate in an analytic judgement is connected with the subject through identity—i.e. by being identical with a part or the whole of the subject concept, something not true of synthetic judgements. When saying things like this Kant seems to have in mind particularly those analytic truths that fall within our previously listed category (A1): the predicate A is there, in an obvious sense, a part of the subject concept 'X and A and Y'. Indeed, what Kant says invites the interpretation that to be analytic is just to belong to (A1):

Def. A. S is analytic = Df S belongs to category (A1).

What Kant, as we have seen, says in explanation of the synthetic would correspondingly seem to imply a definition like this:

Def. S. S is synthetic = Df S is a true proposition, which contains exactly one subject and one predicate and which does not belong to category (A1).

Of course, Kant is free to define analytic and synthetic in any way he chooses. But not any definition will correspond to the actual use he makes of these concepts. Definitions A and S do not so correspond. It has often been pointed out that the stated definitions apply only to propositions in which one can discern exactly one "subject" and one "predicate" whereas not all true propositions are of this kind. The above definitions could, of course, be made to effect a division of all true propositions by dropping from S the requirement that the synthetic proposition contain exactly one subject and one predicate. But the definition A of the analytic in itself appears hopelessly inadequate for Kant's purposes. When Kant explains analyticity, in the manner set forth above, with reference to propositions of the form, "All *A* are *B*", he actually states that the notion is intended to have a wider application.

Kant often repeats the idea that analytic propositions are true by virtue of a common logical principle, the law of contradiction, or that they can be derived from this principle. By subordinating the analytic propositions under this law, he obviously wished to characterize them as true on purely logical grounds. Simultaneously he declares that the synthetic truths are not guaranteed by logic: "explanation of the possibility of synthetic judgements is a task with which general logic has nothing to do at all."[5] Although Kant himself did not consider these ideas as representing alternative definitions of the concepts, one may well suspect that Kant intended at least two different distinctions when separating the analytic from the synthetic, that the previously stated definitions express one of his intentions, while another finds expression in his talk of the different relations that the two kinds of judgement bear to logic. We thus suggest also these definitions:

Def. A*. S is analytic = Df S follows from the laws of logic.

Def. S*. S is synthetic = Df S is a truth which does not follow from the laws of logic.

The notion of "the laws of logic" is indefinite. How logic is to be delimited from other related formal disciplines appears today, when there exists such an abundance of "logics", to be very much a matter of taste. The narrower the limits of logic are drawn, the smaller becomes the class of truths that are analytic by A*, and the larger will be the class of truths that are synthetic by S*. Thus, our new definitions are indefinite, but it is still clear that they are more reasonable than the previous ones. They are also of interest since this interpretation of Kant's doctrine came to play an important role in later discussions. When, e.g., Frege and Russell maintained in opposition to Kant that arithmetic is analytic, they presupposed the notion given by *A**.

[5] Kant, *Kritik der reinen Vernunft*, A 154/B 193.

34. HOW ARE SYNTHETIC *A PRIORI* TRUTHS POSSIBLE?

When we cross the concept pairs, analytic–synthetic, *a priori–a posteriori*, we get a division of all truths that may become objects of human knowledge into four categories. A truth of that sort may be:

    (a) analytic *a priori*
    (b) analytic *a posteriori*
    (c) synthetic *a priori*
    (d) synthetic *a posteriori*

According to Kant, analytic truths are always *a priori*: truths that follow from logic can always be grasped by pure thought. Thus, category (b) is empty.

As we have already seen, Kant understood Hume's position to mean that all truths are either of category (a) or of category (d). In view of Hume's analysis of induction, it follows that general synthetic laws never have any certainty. It is to avoid this conclusion that Kant classifies some such laws as belonging to category (c). There are in fact, Kant maintained, truths that do not hold by virtue of logic, which nevertheless we can come to know without the help of experience. Although Kant was convinced of the existence of knowledge of this kind, he had a feeling that it was something of a riddle: "A secret is thus concealed here, and only by clearing it up can we render certain and reliable the progress into the limitless field of the knowledge of pure understanding: we must with sufficient generality show the basis of the possibility of synthetic *a priori* judgements."[6]

Kant's question, "How are synthetic judgements *a priori* possible?", expresses a feeling of mystification before these judgements. The theoretical significance of the question, however, is far from clear, and in the great Kant-exegetical literature, it has been interpreted in innumerable ways. Like so many classics of philosophy, the *Critique of Reason* is complex and many-faceted, and probably no interpretation that ascribes to Kant an unambiguous aim can claim to be *the* correct interpretation. Different lines of thought in the critique may require essentially diverging interpretations, and even what Kant presents as one connected argument may

---

[6] Ibid. A 10.

have distinct aspects to which no one clear-cut interpretation can do justice. When, in the sequel, I shall expound just one kind of interpretation, I am well aware that there is a certain arbitrariness in this procedure.

The question, "How are synthetic *a priori* propositions possible?", can, I take it, be restated in the form, "How is it possible to have an *a priori* knowledge of synthetic propositions?". The question could be understood as requesting an explanation of how such knowledge comes into being in the human mind. Kant's description of the complex machinery that he believes that the human cognitive faculty involves often invites such an interpretation. Kant appears to explain how our various kinds of knowledge arise when our consciousness, through a series of operations, "synthesizes" the originally unorganized sense impressions. In so far as Kant is doing this, his explanation is not really a genetic one, I think. It is rather an instance of that quasi-genetic mode of thought that we first encountered in the late Pythagorean philosophy of Plato. The process Kant describes in that line of thought, which I shall call his "Copernican revolution" and shall deal with in §38, both is and is not a genuine process: it goes on outside time. Neither a genuinely genetic nor a quasi-genetic explanation however, seems to be what is primarily demanded by Kant's question.

Kant, who liked to think of himself in the role of a philosophical judge, says in one place that it is not the question, *quid facti*, but the question, *quid iuris*, that interests him. It is not so much the "facts" in the case as the validity of the legal claim that he wishes to establish.[7] His question would then seem to mean: With what right do we think that we know such and such synthetic propositions in an *a priori* manner? An obvious way of answering such a question is to give an *a priori* proof of the propositions in question. I think that a major aim of Kant's critique is precisely to sketch such a proof. Kant already had at hand an abundance of *a priori* proofs of what he took to be synthetic propositions, e.g., in mathematics. I think Kant did not regard such proofs as meeting his demand since

[7] Ibid. A 84/B 116.

they rest on premisses that are of exactly the same kind as their conclusions. Kant had a tendency to think that the synthetic propositions *a priori* that intrigued him were descriptive of "nature" and its forms, space and time, and his problem was very much: "How can we know anything in advance about nature?". To derive some *a priori* propositions about nature from other such *a priori* propositions, did not solve this general problem. It occurred to Kant that it might be possible to prove the *a priori* propositions about nature from premisses dealing, not with "nature", but with our "cognitive faculty". The proofs that Kant is out to find are thus proofs based on premisses that are both *a priori* and, in some sense or other, epistemological. As a third characteristic of the proofs that Kant is looking for one may, albeit with some hesitation, add a kind of generality: he wishes to prove the basic propositions of a given synthetic discipline *a priori* in a rather uniform manner more or less at the same time.

In the following I shall, in this spirit, interpret one aspect of Kant's solution to the problem, "How are synthetic *a priori* propositions possible?". Let me call this aspect so interpreted "the criticist deduction". (This is a term that does not occur in Kant, which I feel free to use in this context.) Although this aspect is intimately interwoven, in Kant's presentation, with another aspect which I shall call "the Copernican revolution" and which will be treated in §38, I shall here try to keep them apart.

35. SYNTHETIC *A PRIORI* PROPOSITIONS AS CONDITIONS FOR THE POSSIBILITY OF EXPERIENCE

The possibility of experience is thus what lends objective reality to all our knowledge *a priori*.[8]

The highest principle of all synthetic *a priori* judgements is therefore: each object [phenomenon] stands under the necessary conditions of synthetic unity of the multiplicity of perceptions in a possible experience . . . the conditions of the possibility of experience in general are simultaneously conditions of the possibility of the objects of experience and thus possess objective validity in a synthetic *a priori* judgement.[9]

[8] Ibid. A 156/B 195.   [9] Ibid. A 158/B 197.

The words here quoted are a summary Kant gives of his investigation into the judgements that puzzle him. Let us try to analyse the significance, or one aspect of the significance, of the indicated line of thought.

A. *Phenomena and experience*

"Experience" as conceived of by Kant is the "synthetic unity", the sum total, of all "phenomena". Kant uses the words "phenomenon" and "experience" in what I think are two distinct senses, which, however, for him appear to be one. I shall call them the phenomenalist and the realist sense.

1. *The phenomenalist sense*

. . . phenomena are not things in themselves but the mere play of our ideas [*Vorstellungen*], which in the end are nothing but determinations of the inner sense [roughly, introspection].[10]

There is only *one* experience, in which all perceptions are conceived to have an all pervading and law-bound connection: just as there exists only *one* space and *one* time, in which the forms of phenomena and all situations of being and not-being take place. If one speaks of different experiences, they are only just as many perceptions belonging to one and the same general experience. The pervasive and synthetic unity of the perceptions is just the form of experience, and it is nothing but the synthetic unity of phenomena in accordance with concepts.[11]

If this unity did not have "a transcendental foundation" (what Kant meant by this must here be left an open question) "it would be possible that a chaos of appearances filled our soul without experience ever arising from it."[12]

In these quotations Kant seems to identify "phenomena" with certain perceptions (or contents of perceptions), and "experience" is the conceptually interpreted and ordered sum total of these perceptions. Like all notions in Kant, these are rather elusive. Perhaps Kant's meaning could be made slightly more tangible thus: that we, to use the terminology of Leibniz, can distinguish between real and imaginary phenomena, between adequate normal perceptions on the one hand and dreams, hallucinations, etc., on the other hand,

[10]Ibid. A 101.   [11]Ibid. A 110.   [12]Ibid. A 111.

depends upon the fact that our mental life has a character that the mental life of any sentient being does not necessarily have. We can imagine a being whose experiences were so fragmentary and chaotic that it would find it impossible to make that distinction. Those perceptions in which we see the manifestations of real phenomena constitute a subset of our total set of experiences, a subset characterized, *inter alia*, by a certain internal structure or, as Kant says, "synthetic unity". I suggest that what Kant means by "experience", from one point of view, is just the indicated subset. That a set of experiences constitutes an "experience", in Kant's sense, I interpret to mean that *inter alia*, it has the indicated structure. When Kant says that each one of us has only one experience, I understand this to mean that each of us has only one set of experiences of this kind.

2. *The realist sense* At the same time "experience" is, in Kant, more or less synonymous with "nature", the empirical reality in space and time. "Phenomenon" is, analogously, almost synonymous with "natural phenomenon" or "something that forms part of nature". This aspect of the concept is especially obvious in the *Prolegomena*:

The possibility of experience in general is therefore at the same time the general law of nature, and the principles for the former are themselves laws of the latter. This is so because we do not know nature save as the sum total of phenomena, i.e. the ideas within us, and hence cannot derive the law of their connection otherwise than from the principles of the connection of these (the ideas) within us, thus from the conditions for their necessary association in one consciousness, which constitute the possibility of experience.[13]

B. *A fundamental idea in Kant's deduction*

Kant speaks of "the fact of experience" as a basic datum of epistemology. It is an indisputable fact, he asserts, that I have (he has) experience, "the experience" that is mine (his). Let us call it E. By his critique of metaphysics, Kant thinks that he has established the thesis:

(a) All my knowledge is exclusively concerned with the phenomena in E (including their forms, space and time).

[13]Kant. *Prolegomena*, § 36.

From (a) follows:

> (b)   The synthetic *a priori* propositions are exclusively concerned with the phenomena in E.

Given a synthetic *a priori* proposition P, we may—to make the argument more perspicuous—consider it rewritten in the form, 'E has the characteristic C_p'. We know:

> (c) E is an (my) experience.

Now the crucial step in Kant's criticist deduction is the endeavour to show that from (c) we can derive:

> (d) E has the characteristic C_p,

and hence the very synthetic *a priori* proposition P.

If all the premisses made use of in the course of the argument are *a priori*, P has been shown, by the very existence of the argument, to be itself *a priori*. Within that set E of perceptions (natural phenomena) that constitutes my experience (nature), there can never arise any counter-instances to P, and so, by virtue of the argument, we can know for sure, and in advance, that experience (nature) without exception conforms with P.

C. *Some brief critical remarks*

In order to perform the task expected of them, the premisses of the Criticist Deduction must all be *a priori* and, furthermore, at least some of them must be synthetic. As we have seen, an analytic proposition according to one of Kant's ideas, is one that holds by virtue of the law of contradiction (the laws of logic), and what can be derived from analytic premisses will itself hold by virtue of this law (these laws) and hence be analytic. Since the argument is to prove synthetic *a priori* propositions there have to be some synthetic propositions among its premisses. But then, how are these synthetic *a priori* propositions possible? As far as I am aware, Kant has not considered the question. And yet, in view of their strength, the synthetic premisses of the Criticist Deduction ought to pose a riddle even more than the more ordinary synthetic *a priori* propositions.

As a matter of fact, Kant worried very little about the

character of the premises he employed. He hardly ever saw that there was a problem here. When Kant speaks of "the fact of experience", he even seems to intimate that this is an empirical fact. As we have already mentioned, proving in advance propositions about nature from epistemological premises appeared to Kant an important theoretical gain. Perhaps he thought that we are in an especially good position to know such premises since they deal with what is closest to us, our own minds.

In so far as "the fact of experience" is to be understood as a fact known by us about the course of our perceptions, how meagre it must be! Any unpredictable drowsy nod will cut off the influx of sensations, and some misfortune can any day reduce my mental life to the "chaos" that Kant contrasts with an orderly experience. Don't we actually know far more about, say, the course of the planets than about that of our perceptions? Agreeing to this Kant might nevertheless maintain that as long as our well-ordered experience lasts, it will exhibit certain characteristics, and that these are such that experience will never give us reason to abandon the synthetic *a priori* propositions. But if the known fact of experience is a meagre one, its implications must be correspondingly weak. Are not the synthetic propositions that Kant tries to derive from this fact far too strong?

In so far as "experience" for Kant coincides with "nature", the Criticist Deduction is turned into a monstrosity. If our knowledge of "the fact of experience" is really just our knowledge of "the fact of nature", and if this fact entails those synthetic *a priori* propositions about nature which are a problem for Kant, then this knowledge must be an advance knowledge about nature which is even stronger than any of those propositions and even more in need of explanation.

If Kant had been asked how he could know *a priori*, say, the principle of causality, he could have answered by presenting the Criticist Deduction of it, now supposing that the deduction is water-tight. But Kant thinks that this and other pieces of knowledge *a priori* are more or less common human property, associated with the nature of human reason and belonging, e.g., to unphilosophical mathematicians and physicists. How can the fact that Kant has found an *a priori* proof of a synthetic proposition help us to understand how people who are ignorant of this proof know that proposition *a priori*? Is not their knowledge just as mysterious as ever?

36. HOW ARE ARITHMETIC, GEOMETRY, AND THE PURE SCIENCE OF NATURE POSSIBLE?

In this section I shall briefly consider Kant's attempt to deduce arithmetic, Euclidean geometry, and what he calls the pure science of nature. From the fact:

(i)   *E* is an (my) experience,

it follows, on Kant's view:

(ii)   *E* is a spatially and temporally ordered multiplicity of phenomena.

Kant relies on the spatial ordering when showing how geometry is possible and on the temporal ordering when showing how arithmetic is possible. Both orderings are relevant to the possibility of the pure science of nature.

A. *How is geometry possible?*

The space that Euclidean geometry describes is, Kant thinks, given to us in two different ways, both in an "*a priori* intuition" and in those sense perceptions wherein we experience phenomena with spatial extension and location. When Kant talks of our *a priori* intuition of space, I guess he has in mind such spatial configurations as a geometer may imaginatively visualize as an aid in his reasoning.

Now it appears quite evident to Kant that the theorems of Euclidean geometry hold for the space that we intuit *a priori*. It is so evident to him that he does not even bother to state it as a premiss for his argument, although it is one.

Next Kant assumes that the *a priori* intuited space is also a "form" of our sense perceptions. By this, Kant seems simply to say that the same geometrical theorems that we find by studying the intuited space hold also for those spatial configurations we experience in sense perception.

When the mathematician has obtained a theorem by the combination of intuition and deduction which constitutes the method of geometry, he can thus take it for granted that the theorem is true also of the space of perception. Now, what empirical science studies is nothing but phenomena. In this context, Kant must, to clinch the argument, mean by this that science deals only with contents of perceptions. Thus, Euclidean geometry is true also of physical space.

In condensed form, the argument would look roughly like this:

(a) Euclidean geometry is true of the *a priori* intuited space *S*.

(b) This space *S* is a form of our sense perceptions.

(c) The phenomena of physics are nothing but the contents of our sense perceptions.

(d) Hence, the space *S* is also the space of the phenomena of physics, the physical space.

(e) Therefore, Euclidean geometry is true of the space of physics.

The argument is of course worthless.

B. *How is arithmetic possible?*

In an analogous manner, Kant tries to show that the theorems of arithmetic are generally valid for all phenomena. Arithmetic, according to Kant, has an even wider application than geometry: whereas geometry holds for everything that is in space, arithmetic is true of everything that is in time, whether or not it is also in space. Arithmetic is thus applicable not only to external phenomena but also to our mental states. Kant thinks that arithmetic is somehow essentially associated with time, that the arithmetician comes to know the basic propositions of his science by considering how unit is added to unit in his *a priori* intuition of time.

C. *How is pure science of nature possible?*

One of the most important principles of what Kant regards as "pure science of nature" is a principle of causality, of which he gives various, more or less informative, formulations. Here are three:

Every alteration has a cause.[14]

All changes occur in conformity with the law of the connection between cause and effect.[15]

All that happens is always determined in advance by a cause in accordance with immutable laws.[16]

Kant's principle of causality is obviously closely related to similar principles which we have encountered in the work of Hume, and also the deterministic postulate (P) of the mechanist world view.

Kant undertakes to show that the principle of causality is a condition for the possibility of experience, i.e. that from the fact of experience:

(1) E is an (my) experience,

we may deduce, say:

(n)   In E all that happens is always determined in advance by a cause in accordance with immutable laws.

Let us follow Kant a few steps on the road from (1) to (n). From (1) Kant infers:

(2)   If A and B are two events in E, then either A precedes B, or A and B are simultaneous, or B precedes A.

He then asks how we can decide in a given case which of the three alternatives in (2) obtains. To elucidate the question Kant considers two distinct situations. In the one I stand looking at a house, I let my eyes wander over it and see first one part, then another. In the other situation I watch a boat gliding down a river. First I see the boat higher up, then I see it further down. Suppose that in the first situation I have the perceptions $p(a_1)$, $p(a_2)$ and in the second the perceptions $p(b_1)$, $p(b_2)$ where a_1, a_2, b_1, b_2 stand for what is being perceived. The reason why, in the first situation, we say that a_1 and a_2 are objectively simultaneous is, Kant says, that we can reverse the order of the perceptions: instead of the sequence $p(a_1)$–$p(a_2)$ we could also have the sequence

[14]Kant, *Kritik der reinen Vernunft*, B3, B5.
[15]Kant, *Kritik der reinen Vernunft*, B 232.
[16]Kant, *Prolegomena*, §15.

$p(a_2)-p(a_1)$. The reason why, in the second situation, we say that b_1 objectively precedes b_2, is that the sequence of perceptions is here irreversible: the order $p(b_2)-p(b_1)$ cannot occur. The irreversibility amounts to a rule concerning the temporal order of perceptions, and since the principle of causality also deals with laws or rules, Kant thinks that he has herewith advanced a derivation of (n) from (1). Here my understanding of Kant's argument ceases, and I can only refer the reader to the original passage of the *Critique of Pure Reason*.

37. FINAL REMARKS

The *Critique of Pure Reason* is, from one point of view, one of the classic documents of scientific and philosophical conservatism. For an adherent of Kant's critique, the outlines of the scientific explanation of the word are established once for all. Research can only fill in more and more details in the sketch of the world whose correctness is guaranteed by pure reason. The critique is thereby in sharp contrast with Hume's empiricism which admits the possibility that any statements that contain an element of prophecy may be refuted by future observations.

It is of course necessary to distinguish the two questions:

(i)   Are those propositions that Kant held to be synthetic *a priori* really so? (Are they true? Are they synthetic? Can they be known *a priori*?)

(ii) Do there exist at all any synthetic truths *a priori*, and if so, what are they?

Even if the answer to (i) had to be negative, the reply to (ii) might still be affirmative.

Ever since the days of Kant these questions have been the subject of a lively debate which has not yet reached its conclusion. Concerning arithmetic, some extreme empiricists, among them John Stuart Mill, have maintained that a proposition such as $7 + 5 = 12$ is an empirical generalization, based on observations of what happens when a group of seven things is brought together with a group of five things. According to the so-called logicist theory, which was first stated by Frege in the *Foundations of Arithmetic* (*Grundlagen der Arithmetik*, 1884) and then rediscovered by Russell in the *Principles of Mathematics* (1903), the arithmetical truths are analytical in the sense that they can be derived by means of suitable definitions within a formal logic. The logicist construction of arithmetic was later refined in various ways. Even though this theory is not generally accepted and, in particular, its philosophical value has been doubted, it puts a strong question mark against Kant's theory. On the other hand, the founder of the so-called intuitionist school in modern mathematics, the Dutchman L. E. J. Brouwer (1881–1966), has sketched a theory which in some respects is similar to Kant's. Like Kant, he thinks that arithmetic is based on an intuition of time, that the arithmetician makes, and describes, a kind of mental construction in the medium of time. Finally, according to certain so-called formalist views arithmetic is just a game with the arithmetical symbols, and, as such, it falls outside the domain of application of the Kantian distinctions.

Geometry is a theory—today a large family of theories—with many aspects. It can be considered as a set of "sentential functions", where the basic geometric concepts ("point", "line", etc.) play the role of variables (parameters). If so, then it is neither true nor false. It can be interpreted as a special branch of arithmetic, as Descartes in effect interpreted Euclidean geometry by the introduction of coordinates. Or it can be looked upon as a material theory about a space given somehow or other, in a literal sense. When geometry is understood as a theory about the space of physics, according to the prevailing opinion today, its propositions do not have a status fundamentally different from that of other propositions in physics: the choice of a geometry must, in principle, be justified in the same empirical manner as the choice of, say, a mechanics. As is well known, according to certain modern physical theories, physical space is non-Euclidean, or, better, can with advantage be described by a non-Euclidean geometry.

Most of the propositions that Kant listed as synthetic *a priori* principles of "the pure science of nature", have met with the fate of disappearing from science. Two of the most interesting of these propositions were the principle of the conservation of matter and the principle of causality. Hardly any physicists today would be prepared to subscribe to either of these principles in a form that Kant would be able to recognize.

Concerning question (ii), it is of interest to note that the positivist Vienna Circle of the twenties and the movement of logical empiricism to which it gave rise viewed the thesis that all *a priori* knowledge is analytic as an expression of a fundamental philosophical insight.

Really well-founded answers to questions (i) and (ii) cannot be given unless one first makes the significance of the terminology employed far more clear and precise than it is in Kant. When it is asked concerning a given statement, say Kant's "7 + 5 = 12", to what category it belongs, we must also make quite clear what use or interpretation of the statement we have in mind. The answer to the question how to classify the statement will thus depend both on how the Kantian distinctions are specified and on how the statement is interpreted. Since several specifications and several interpretations may be equally reasonable, it is only too possible that the same statement can be classified in several distinct ways. It is also possible that certain statements, under certain reasonable specifications and interpretations, will be found to have no place in a Kantian classification.

Concerning the 'analytic–synthetic' distinction, modern logic has made many interesting contributions to its clarification, especially with regard to particular formalized languages. In many ways, however, it is still not very clear. If it is made to depend on an idea of logic, or of logical truth, we must acknowledge that we have no general criterion by which to judge whether a theory is 'logic', or a proposition a 'logical truth'. The situation with respect to the epistemological distinction '*a priori–a posteriori*' is even less satisfactory. The clarification of these concepts may well be a task in the accomplishment of which the philosopher should look, not only to logic, but also to psychology and the history of science.

In his attempt to solve the problem of the possibility of the synthetic *a priori* Kant was led to consider the problem of the "conditions of the possibility of experience" or, as we may say, the "necessary conditions of experience". We have seen that "experience" is an ambiguous word in Kant's writings, signifying both a certain sum total of perceptions and the empirical reality, "nature". Let us here fasten upon the former meaning of the term. Here, also, we must distinguish two questions.

(a)   Are those propositions which Kant regarded as synthetic *a priori* also necessary conditions for experience?

(b)   Are there perhaps other such conditions, and, if so, what are they?

Kant's affirmative answer to (a) is so loosely argued that it hardly merits serious attention. Since the overwhelming majority of his synthetic *a priori* propositions say nothing about what somebody (he, you, I) experiences, it is difficult offhand to imagine that they can be reasonably construed as necessary conditions of experience. Question (b), however, seems to be an interesting problem, one which, before Kant, was considered by Leibniz and by Hume. This question, too, is in need of precise formulation before it can be fruitfully discussed, preferably by philosophers and psychologists in co-operation. The question is not guaranteed a unique answer—there may be several, essentially different kinds of experience.

VIII

Kant's Copernican Revolution
and its Aftermath

38. KANT'S COPERNICAN REVOLUTION

In the preceding chapter I tried to present one aspect of Kant's argument in the critique of reason in isolation from its other aspects. In this section I shall make the picture somewhat more complete by presenting another aspect, which might be called Kant's "Copernican revolution".

Hitherto it has been assumed that all our knowledge must conform to objects. But all attempts to extend our knowledge of objects by establishing something in regard to them a priori, by means of concepts, have, on this assumption, ended in failure. We must therefore make trial whether we may not have more success in the tasks of metaphysics, if we suppose that the objects must conform to our knowledge. This would agree better with what is derived, namely, that it should be possible to have knowledge of objects a priori, determining something in regard to them prior to their being given. We should then be proceeding precisely on the lines of Copernicus' primary hypothesis. Failing of satisfactory progress in explaining the movements of the heavenly bodies on the supposition that they all revolved round the spectator, he tried whether he might not have better success if he made the spectator to revolve and the stars to remain at rest.[1]

This attempt to alter the procedure which has so far prevailed in metaphysics, by completely revolutionising it in accordance with the example set by geometers and physicists, forms indeed the main purpose of this critique of pure speculative reason.[2]

Those "objects" of which Kant is speaking here are not things in themselves but phenomena. The Copernican revolution which Kant attempts is thus a theory according to which phenomena are conditioned by our knowledge, or some of the properties of phenomena are dependent upon the nature of our cognitive faculty.

[1] Kant, *Kritik der reinen Vernunft* B xvi, trans. N. Kemp Smith (Oxford, 1968), p. 22.   [2] Ibid. B xxii (Kemp Smith, p. 25).

The best way to present this theory is, I think, to illustrate it by diagrams. We begin with diagram (H).

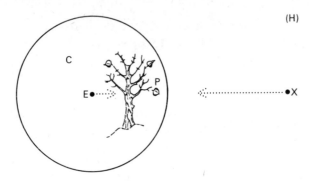

(H)

The tree we see, which science studies (P) is merely a phenomenon in our consciousness (C). To this phenomenon corresponds an otherwise unknown thing in itself (X) outside consciousness. The pure Ego (E), or the unity of the transcendental apperception, is a sort of active centre in consiousness. The perception of the tree, and therewith the tree as a phenomenon, comes into existence when the thing in itself acts upon consciousness, creating sense impressions which are then processed.

The sense impressions derived from the thing in itself are raw material for the mind's activity which, according to Kant, takes place on two different levels or in two distinct stages. Another diagram (I) may illustrate this.

The sense impressions that the thing in itself impresses

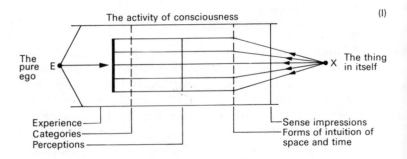

(I)

upon consciousness are conceived of by Kant as certain minimal perceptible and mutually isolated units. In perception, however, we experience not such isolated units but spatially and temporally ordered wholes. The spatial and temporal order in which the impressions are arranged in perception is the first result of the activity of consciousness. Consciousness has here ordered the impressions by means of its two forms of intuition, space and time. Since geometry and arithmetic are descriptions of these forms, they necessarily hold for all perceptions, all phenomena. At a later stage, the perceptions are ordered by means of certain concepts inherent in consciousness, the so-called "categories" (e.g. substance, causality). Thereby arises that "synthetic unity" of a multiplicity of perceptions which is experience. The synthesis of the perceptions by means of the categories occurs in such a manner that our synthetic *a priori* statements (e.g. the principle of causality) will necessarily hold for all experience. Considering the synthetic *a priori* statements as laws, Kant can thus say that our cognitive faculty lays down the laws for experience, for empirical phenomena.

Although, in Kant's critique, what I have here called the Copernican revolution is presented in the same breath as what I have called the Criticist Deduction, they are really, I think, two distinct trains of thought. The Criticist Deduction, as I understand it, by itself says nothing about how it happens that there is experience. It merely states the fact that there is, and then submits the notion of experience to an analysis. The Copernican revolution, on the other hand, describes the mental machinery that produces experience. I think it is important to separate the two lines of thought, since the Copernican revolution appears the incomparably more problematic of the two.

The Copernican revolution may be taken to point to the undeniable fact that human knowledge is not obtained by revelation but is the result of a complex interplay between human beings and the surrounding world, where the nature of man is just as important as the nature of the world. The Copernican revolution, however, gives a most baffling picture of this situation. It faces a series of problems which have often been subsequently pointed out.

(1) According to a fundamental idea of Kant's, we can have no synthetic knowledge about things in themselves. How, then, can Kant claim to know that there is a correspondence between phenomena and things in themselves, and that the latter act upon consciousness?

(2) On Kant's view, space and time exist only as forms of our intuition and thereby as forms of the phenomena. Both things in themselves and the pure ego must therefore be outside time and space. How then can Kant maintain that things in themselves act upon consciousness? How can he say that the ego processes the sense impressions? Is he considering here some sort of timeless activity?

(3) What is the consciousness and the ego that Kant is referring to? Often he seems to say that it is a consciousness such as his and yours and mine. My consciousness, however, undoubtedly evolves in time. How can this fact be reconciled with the theory that time and space are only forms for the phenomena that appear in consciousness? Sometimes Kant seems to mean that the consciousness with which he is concerned is some kind of supra-individual consciousness, a "general consciousness" (*Bewusstein überhaupt*) or a "transcendental consciousness". But what kind of thing is that? How is it related to individual minds? How can we, on Kant's own assumptions, know anything about it?

(4) In what sense does Kant maintain that the tree perceived by me is "in" my consciousness (or "in" some other consciousness)?

If one holds on to Kant's idea that time and space are only forms of the phenomena, the Copernican revolution will be seen to make the mind into a factory working outside of space and time.[3]

---

[3]In the nineteenth century a number of psychological and even physiological interpretations of Kant's theory were suggested. On one kind of psychological interpretation, Kant aimed at describing how a human being's picture of the world is shaped through an interplay between the sensations he receives from without and a certain (innate) psychological constitution. A physiological interpretation sees in Kant's theory an indication of the interplay between external stimuli and the central nervous system. According to interpretations of these kinds, Kant's critique of reason is essentially a contribution to the genetic explanation of the individual's world conception. It seems rather obvious that such interpretations must do violence to, or radically disregard, large parts of the *Critique of Pure Reason*.

Within some neo-Kantian schools of philosophy toward the end of the

39. GERMAN TRANSCENDENTAL PHILOSOPHY

Kant's theory of the factory of consciousness can easily be transformed from epistemology into mysticism. This happened in the work of the three German so-called transcendental philosophers, Fichte (1762–1814), Schelling (1775–1854), and Hegel (1770–1831). Kant himself was no mystic: he was an Enlightenment philosopher, influenced by Pietism, who wished to keep science and religion in what he took to be their proper spheres. His philosophical standpoint is so complex that it can be interpreted and developed in the most divergent directions. The way in which the transcendental philosophers refashioned it was connected with the mental climate of the time. While the philosophers of the Enlightenment generally saw themselves as interpreters and apostles of Newtonian science, the Romanticists revolted against the world picture that mechanism offered and favoured mythical-poetical-religious pictures. In their youth, transcendental philosophers also welcomed the French Revolution as the harbinger of a new era, and "freedom" remained for them an honoured word. In the course of the years, however, their doctrines became, both politically and religiously, more and more conservative, and they thereby participated in the reaction against the revolution and against Napoleon's attempt to reorganize Europe. In Schelling and Hegel the mysticism was nourished by interest, strong in Germany around the turn of the century, in the pantheist and mystic Spinoza. Both were also intensely interested in the German sixteenth-century mystic Jacob Böhme. The dialectical method that Hegel practised can be traced back to the Neo-Platonist Proclus of late antiquity. The transcendental philosophers can be reckoned as standing at the periphery of the great mystic tradition

nineteenth century, Kant's theory was interpreted in a more methodological fashion. What he says about sense impressions and categories was understood to point to the fact that scientific theory, especially within the exact sciences, goes far beyond the data of experience, and that the rational choice between theories is not uniquely determined by the data. Sometimes thoughts of this kind were combined with positivistic ideas about the data of experience as the only reality accessible to science and about the scientific theory as a mere tool for handling the data. Such interpretations are also, I think, far from Kant's own intentions.

in European thought which was carried on by the Pythagoreans, by Plato and the Neo-Platonists, and by neo-Platonizing mystics of the Middle Ages and the Renaissance.

The thing in itself, which we have seen to be an anomaly in Kant's system, was abolished by Fichte who thereby made consciousness a self-supplying factory outside time and space. Indeed, in Fichte consciousness even becomes a factory that builds itself. "The ego posits the ego", and "The ego posits the non-ego [i.e. experience, nature]", are the two basic theses of his philosophy. In so far as what Fichte calls "the ego" or "the I", really is *I*, I myself, we all carry within ourselves the freely creating, original source from which we ourselves and all that we are ever confronted with spring.

Schelling criticized Fichte for considering nature as a "non-ego", as something whose essence is opposed to the essence of the mind. Nature, the young Schelling taught, is akin to spirit, and the opposition between subject and object, which is characteristic of spirit, recurs in nature as an all-pervasive polarity between opposite forces. At a later stage of his thinking, Schelling replaced Fichte's "I" as the ultimate source of everything by something which is an identity of spirit and nature or is "indifferent" with respect to these categories. In the end he identified this source with a personal God. World history is the history of how God, through the manifestation of opposites, becomes separated from himself and finally returns to himself. (A sober German history of philosophy, Ueberweg-Heinze, says that Schelling's writings are full of beautiful-sounding words which are often devoid of any reasonable meaning.)

Hegel, too, sees in history the evolution of "the Idea", or "Spirit", or "God". According to Hegel, however, Spirit or the Idea is "Reason", its evolution is a "rational" process, and by his own reason the philosopher can reconstruct this process more or less *a priori*. A basic scheme of thought in Hegel's philosophy can be illustrated as in diagram (J). The Idea "in itself", which is the object of study of Hegel's "logic", is an abstract system of concepts. When the Idea leaves itself to embody itself in its opposite, "nature" arises. In and through nature "Spirit" develops through a complex

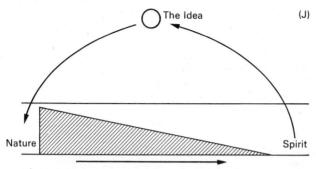

sequence of stages (subjective spirit: soul, consciousness, reason; objective spirit: laws, morals, "Sittlichkeit") into absolute spirit (art, religion, philosophy). In philosophy, i.e. Hegel's own philosophy, the Idea finally returns to itself as "the thought that thinks itself". In the history of man-kind, which is the carrier of this evolution of Spirit, Hegel saw "the march of God".

The method that Hegel used in his sketches of various phases of this process is the so-called dialectical method, the immediate inspiration for which he got from similar ideas in Kant, Fichte, and Schelling. In his dialectics Hegel employs two operations, the "negation" of a thing and the "synthesis" of two things. When a thing is negated, we get its opposite or "anti-thesis". What is negated or syn-thesized can be almost anything, propositions, concepts, phenomena, events, etc. Let us for the sake of brevity use $n(a)$ to signify the Hegelian negation of a and $s(a, b)$ to signify the Hegelian synthesis of a and b. If I have read Hegel correctly, he uses these operations in accordance with two distinct formal schemata which can suitably be called the linear schema and the tree schema.

(a) *The linear schema.* When Hegel's thinking follows this schema, he applies the two operations alternately so as to obtain sequences, or processes, of this form:

t_1 ("the thesis", "the first")

$t_2 = n(t_1)$ ("the antithesis", the second", "the first negation")

$t_3 = s(t_1, t_2)$ ("the synthesis of the first and the second",
"the third")

$$t_4 = n(t_3),$$
etc.

Hegel identifies the "synthesis" with the "negation of the negation", a view which, in the present symbolism, amounts to the equation:

$$s(a, n(a)) = n(n(a)).$$

Using this idea, the above linear dialectical process can (also) be represented simply as the progression:

$$t_1, n(t_1), n(n(t_1)), n(n(n(t_1))), \text{etc.}$$

(b) *The tree schema.* When Hegel applies this schema, he let each term in an original triad, thesis–antithesis–synthesis, generate a new such triad, and this process is continued *ad libitum*.

	t_1	t_2	t_3	
	t_{11}	t_{12}	t_{13}	
t_{111}	t_{112}	t_{113}		etc.

$t \ldots _2$ is here the negation of $t \ldots _1$, and $t \ldots _3$ is the synthesis of $t \ldots _1$ and $t \ldots _2$. In *A Study of Hegel's Logic* (Oxford, (1950), G. R. G. Mure gives a tableau, depicting a dialectical tree of Hegels with no less than six generations.

Hegel's dialectical method raises many questions which receive no answers in his writings. The two dialectical operations are quite mysterious, and Hegel's way of applying them appears completely arbitrary. Why did Hegel dialectically arrange certain concepts, events, or phenomena in one way rather than another? I can only point here to some ideas that Hegel associated with the dialectical method.

(1) Hegel often employs what I have called the quasi-genetic mode of thought. An earlier term in a dialectic evolution transforms itself into, or is supplanted by, the succeeding term without this necessarily being a happening in time.

(2) In other cases, particularly in his philosophy of history,

Hegel assumes that the dialectic process somehow mirrors a course of events in time: what comes later in dialectics is also later in time.

(3) The dialectic order is often conceived of as a progress towards a richer content. Sometimes the terms of the dialectic process are thought of as distinct aspects of a common phenomenon, and the aspects become more and more concrete. In particular, he thinks of the synthesis as more concrete than the synthesized terms.

(4) The dialectic process goes from the "lower" to the "higher", from what, in some sense, is less valuable to what is more.

(5) The triad thesis-antithesis-synthesis is sometimes coloured by dramatic-religious associations. The thesis and antithesis may appear as powers in conflict, and the conflict is then settled through the synthesis. Or the antithesis is a kind of desertion of the thesis, and the synthesis brings about a reunion or reconciliation.

Hegel's assumption that dialectics is the proper method of philosophy comprises some characteristically Hegelian views on reality:

(i) Reality is contradictory, since the thesis (A) as well as the antithesis (non-A) are aspects thereof.

(ii) Reality is a rational process which we can reconstruct by the aid of reason, or is an assemblage of such processes.

(iii) Reality is an evolution from the lower to the higher.

Propositions (ii) and (iii) Hegel expressed in the famous words that "the real is the rational." As he grew older, Hegel became more and more conservative, and gradually the rationality of reality came to mean for him that the contemporary Prussian political system was the height of rationality. Of course, propositions (ii) and (iii) lend themselves to other interpretations. The future political changes—which must come—are "rational", too. According to (iii), they are for the better, and on the strength of (ii), the philosopher can predict and welcome them. On this point, the conservative Hegelian "right wing" and the radical Hegelian "left wing", to which Marx and Engels belonged, parted ways.

The transcendental philosophers exerted a far-reaching influence throughout Europe on general culture, on literature, religion, and politics, on the feeling of life and the conception of man. It is impossible to give a just appreciation of this influence in a few words, and no attempt to do so will be made here. From a purely intellectual point of view, the transcendental philosophy meant a dangerous lowering of standards in philosophy, a lowering which in many quarters has not yet been repaired. The lowering concerns the ability to state problems, the demands made in respect of proof, verification, logical rigour, and linguistic clarity; it concerns the ability to distinguish between a theoretical presentation and the expression of emotions; in short, the difference between irresponsible phrase-making and a critical-scientific attitude.

Hegelian ways of thinking and talking today still play a prominent role in the philosophy of Germany and of the Latin and socialist countries.

APPENDIX

IX

Socialism and Dialectical Materialism: Karl Marx and Friedrich Engels

40. INTRODUCTION

The terms "socialism" and "communism" are used to designate a family of political views, parties acting on them, and such forms of society as agree, or pretend to agree, with them. The word "socialism" is ultimately derived from the Latin "socius" meaning 'ally' or 'comrade'. The word "communism" has for its root the Latin "communis" meaning 'common'. In what may be regarded as a common core significance of the two words, a communist or socialist advocates a social order in which some form of common or social (state) ownership to some extent replaces private ownership. But the words are actually used in a bewildering multiplicity of fashions. Today in the West "socialism" is frequently employed as a wider term, covering a whole series of diverging political opinions, whereas "communism" brings to mind more-or-less orthodox forms of Marxism and especially the views held by political parties who label themselves communist. When, as here, the words are used in a purely historical context, they can be suitably construed as synonymous carriers of their common core of meaning.

Socialist or communist views were already held by some of the Greek sophists. The oldest book in existence that sets forth a communist ideal is the *Republic* by Plato, written in the first half of the fourth century BC. In the hierarchic society it describes, the so-called guardians, the ruling élite, are without property and family; they live at the expense of the state, they mate at periodical festivals, organized by the state, and their children are brought up in the care of society. Plato is an early example of the fact that a socialist need not be a democrat: the contemporary Athenian democracy is vigorously attacked in the *Republic*, and the ideal society is intended as an alternative to democracy.[1] Early Christianity exhibits certain socialist traits, and in the history of Christianity many sects have tried to bring about religious communities on a communistic basis. The late Renaissance gave birth to two great socialist utopias, both inspired by Plato: the *Utopia* (Nowhere) by the Englishman Thomas More (1478–1535) and the *Sun State* by the Italian Tommaso Campanella (1568–1639).

Socialism thus has a more than 2,000-year-long history as a political dream. Around 1800 interest in socialist ideas intensified. The French Revolution had shown that revolutionary changes in society were possible, and it had done so in the name of freedom, equality, and fraternity. The growth of industrialization often brought about stark misery among the workers who were forced to move from the countryside into the cities. Industrialism and the accompanying rapid scientific and technological advances also gave rise to the dream of a future in which man (to use the words of Marx) would finally throw off the yoke of necessity and become the master of nature. In this situation socialist doctrines were put forth in France by Saint-Simon (1760–1825), Fourier (1772–1837), and Proudhon (1809–65), by Robert Owen (1771–1858) in Scotland, and by many others.

The version of socialism that came astronomically to surpass all other versions in historical efficacy, was formulated by Karl Marx (1818–83) and Friedrich Engels (1820–95), who were both born in Germany but settled in England. It has become known under the name of "Marxism" although "Marxism–Engelsism" would be a more adequate designation. Marxism can today look back upon a long history, during

[1] In the *Statesman*, a dialogue written later than the *Republic*, Plato creates one of his gradiose myths, one in which astronomico-theological and communist ideas are fused. The world alternates between what may be called forward and backward phases. We are living in a phase of the latter kind. In the forward phase, God himself steers the stars, all their courses are then reversed, and therewith also the processes on earth. Human beings rise aged from the soil, they get younger and younger, and smaller and smaller, to disappear in the end. In this phase the earth provides all living beings with nourishment in abundance, men and animals are friends, and there is no private ownership of women or children or anything else. Men could, if they so wished, devote themselves entirely to "knowledge and discussion". When God lets go of the stars, they turn about in their orbits, and an evil order such as ours is ushered in.

which it has been split into many factions: the "revisionist" social democracy which has chosen the road of gradual reform through parliamentary action, Lenin's and Stalin's version realized in Russia, the versions of Trotsky, Tito, Mao Tse-tung, and Fidel Castro, etc. The theoretical interpreters have also been legion. Here I shall discuss only certain ideas in Marxism as originally stated by the founding fathers, Marx and Engels.

Their theory consists of several strata derived from very heterogeneous sources:

1. A socialist programme, or vision of the future, for which Marx and Engels borrowed much from earlier and contemporary socialists.

2. A theory of, or a programme for, the realization of the vision, by revolution and the dictatorship of the proletariat. Here Marx and Engels drew inspiration from earlier revolutionaries. (It was the indefatigable French revolutionary Blanqui (1805–81) who coined the catchphrase "the dictatorship of the proletariat".)

3. A theory about the origin, the necessary course, and the final collapse of capitalism, which Marx developed in his major work *Das Kapital* (1867; volumes 2 and 3 posthumously, 1885 and 1894), and which is one of the most original elements of Marxism.

4. A theory of economic value, which was formulated in *Das Kapital* and which borrowed essential ideas from classical British economists, above all from Adam Smith (1723–90) and David Ricardo (1772–1823).

5. A theory about the moving forces in history and the phases of development of society. This theory is an original creation of Marx's although it has important points of contact with theories of Saint-Simon and also of his pupil Comte (1789–1857), and with early nineteenth-century French historical research (Guizot, Thierry, and others).

6. Some very general philosophical views which Marx and Engels themselves characterized as materialist and dialectical, and which they evolved in reaction against, and simultaneously under the influence of, Hegel's idealism. In their youth both Marx and Engels were greatly influenced by Hegel, and Hegel remained a philosophical enemy and

ally of whom they never lost sight. In the eyes of Engels, Hegel and Saint-Simon were the two greatest thinkers of their age. The belief in evolution, which in those days was in the air, was transmitted to Marx and Engels by Hegel; and from him they also gained a dialectical jargon, the emptiness of which they never quite understood—and Engels far less than Marx. In Hegel's writings they also encountered radical formulations of an idealism they thought it important to combat. It is not without interest to make the thought experiment in which Marx and Engels, *ceteris paribus*, are brought up in the spirit, not of Hegel, but of British empiricism or French positivism. The accidental circumstance that in their youth they encountered Hegel put the mark of heavy-footed scholasticism on a century's communist preaching and debate. But then, without the inspiration from Hegel's historical dynamism, would the materialist philosophy of history ever have occurred to them?

All these ideas Marx and Engels managed to unite in their system of "scientific socialism". But actually, neither of them was a genuinely systematic writer. Their enormous literary output—around forty heavy volumes in the (still incomplete) edition of the Russian Marx–Engels institute— contains no connected presentation of the system. Not even the various parts of the system are given a systematic presentation. When trying to establish Marx's views on important questions one often has to rely on scattered passages in his writings.

For their followers the works of Marx and Engels have become something of a Holy Writ in which it is believed that the answers to the questions of the day may be found. Just as every Christian can find his own opinions in the Bible, each Marxist can find support for his own views in the fathers of Marxism. In the course of the years, Marx and Engels changed their views on many questions, their statements are frequently forceful rather than nuanced and clarifying, and the problems they knew were, of course, those falling within the horizon of their time. Many of those problems are still with us, but we have also got new problems. Just as we little know what Jesus would have thought about today's female ministers of the Swedish state church, so do we little know how Marx and Engels would have reacted to modern political democracy and the welfare state, to the present socialist states, to our problems concerning population increase and environment deterioration, etc. They knew a capitalist reality and had a socialist dream; we know also a socialist reality which has its effect on our dreams for the future.

From the point of view of free rational deliberation, it is unfortunate that Marxism presents its socialist programme as a universally valid inference from an esoteric and mystifying philosophical system. It is the consequences of the attempt to realize that programme in a given case that ought to govern our judgement on the attempt in that case.

No attempt to evaluate the effects of Marxism on world history will be made here. Nor shall I, in this non-political book, take a stand either for or against any of the various forms of socialism or capitalism.

41. MATERIALISM AND DIALECTICS

Marx never gave a systematic form to his ideas about the nature of knowledge and of the universe. His interest in such questions was much stronger in his youth than during the years he devoted to the shaping of his theory on capitalism and to the organization of the international labour movement.[2] When trying to reconstruct his opinions on these very general questions, one is forced to bring together statements from various contexts. Engels, however, saw in Marxism a general philosophy. In books such as *Anti-Dühring* (1877-8), *Ludwig Feuerbach* (1888), and *The Dialectics of Nature* (1873-83, published 1925), he attempted to state its basic tenets. It is difficult to know to what extent and how whole-heartedly Marx shared the philosophy sketched here by Engels.

[2] Those simultaneously Hegelian and anti-Hegelian philosophical views that Marx and Engels held in the middle forties are stated in a series of writings, especially Marx's *Economic–philosophical Manuscripts* (written in 1844 and published in 1932) and the two works co-authored by Marx and Engels, *The Holy Family* (1845) and *The German Ideology* (written in 1845-6 and published in 1888). Among modern western Marxists it is a common view, which I do not share, that these youthful writings express Marx's most interesting philosophical views. It is in them that the Hegelian notion of "alienation" (*Entäusserung, Entfremdung*) plays such a large role. In the present discussion I have mainly utilized the later and "more mature" writings of Marx and Engels.

Since Plekhanov, it is customary in Russian Marxism to distinguish between "dialectical materialism" ("diamat"), which is a general theory about the nature of reality and our knowledge, and "historical materialism" ("histmat"), which is a theory about the development of society. This terminology is foreign to Marx, but he considered himself a "materialist", and he operated with certain "dialectical" ideas derived from Hegel. Here, I shall try briefly to explain what Marx's "materialism" and "dialectics" implied. I shall also take into consideration some of the views of Engels who is so much more explicit on these questions of general philosophy.

A. *Materialism*

What Marx and Engels called their materialism was a many-faceted reaction against idealism, especially in the form it received in the hands of Hegel. The opposition between idealism and materialism as conceived of by the fathers of Marxism has, *inter alia*, the following four aspects:

(1) Idealism includes an epistemological subjectivism, according to which the world we know is a system of our experiences. Materialism, on the other hand, is an episte-mological realism, teaching that "matter", "the material world", exists independently of mind.

(2) According to idealism there exists something beyond empirical reality, be it Kant's things in themselves, Fichte's pure ego, the Absolute of Schelling, Hegel's Idea, or the Christian God. Materialism maintains that empirical reality is the one and all-embracing reality which follows its own immanent laws, without interference from without.

(3) From the point of view of Hegel's idealism, the history of mankind is the history of the march of the Idea through the ages. The deeds of the Idea, of the World Spirit, are done through the great empire-building heroes—an Alexander, a Caesar, a Napoleon—and by peoples, nations, thought of as independent beings, each with its own spirit manifesting itself in the traditional culture. According to materialism, there are no ideas but those occurring in the minds of men. If Hegel's talk of "the Idea" is given a realistic interpretation, his philosophy of history will, Marx and

Engels thought, amount to the view that men's consciousness steers the course of history. Turning Hegel upside down they obtained their own philosophy of history which they labelled materialist: consciousness is something secondary in history; what is primary is the material conditions of life.

(4) Now and then Marx also appears to give an ethico-political connotation to materialism: it coincides, he said in 1845, with humanism. What he meant seems to be that materialism, by doing away with the superworld and its demands, puts man himself in the centre of ethics and politics: it is the inborn possibilities of man that are to be realized in this world.

Neither Marx nor Engels had any elaborate theory about the relationship between matter and consciousness, body and mind. Engels said that thinking and perceiving are activities of the human body, and that the idea of a soul as an independent entity is an inheritance from savages.

B. *Dialectics*

Marx said that in the first edition of *Das Kapital* he had dressed up his thoughts in the terminology of Hegelian dialectics. Many dialectical features in Marx's writings are no doubt stylistic embellishments which could be pruned away without materially changing the theories. The validity of Marx's theory of capitalism, for example, does not seem to be essentially tied to the validity of dialectics. Engels treated the Hegelian dialectics with far greater and far more naïve respect. Some views in Marx and Engels which they themselves called "dialectical" and which were inspired by Hegel are the following:

(1) *Change, evolution, and final stage.* According to Hegel, reality undergoes a constant change: thesis is turned into antithesis and the two are united in a synthesis. Marx especially applied this thought to social reality, the economic-political conditions and their ideological reflections. Just as different forms of society have succeeded each other in the past, so our present social system will one day be replaced by another.

Hegel believed that the history of mankind represents a genuine evolution, a succession of stages in which the later is in some sense more perfect than the earlier or at least a necessary preparation for the realization of something more perfect. Marx shares this belief in evolution: each social system is during its apportioned time a necessary stage in the evolution of man from the primitive savage to the free citizen of the socialist society.

Here, too, Engels produced the more general formulations. Engels said that Heraclitus was right: everything in the universe is steadily changing, nothing is fixed and determinate. With a slight reservation in view of the possibility that there may be an end to human life on earth, he also maintains that the evolution of mankind proceeds without ever reaching a final stage: each stage is only a transition to the next. The fundamental contradiction in Hegel's philosophy is, in Engels's opinion, the combination of the doctrine of evolution with the thought that the Idea is reunited with itself in the last act. The former doctrine, on Engels's view, excludes the possibility of any last act. This is true also of the evolution of science and philosophy: there never appears any final truth, there are only theories which are steps on the road to still better theories.

Did not Engels see here the beam in the eye of Hegel but fail to notice the mote in his own and Marx's eyes? Neither Engels nor Marx has ever, I think, quite explicitly said that the socialist form of society is the last and most perfect; yet it is a thought that seems to be found between the lines in their writings. Nor have they, I think, said that their own economic-political theory is the final truth on the questions with which it deals. But the scepticism which the doctrine of evolution, as conceived by Engels, should have brought about is hard to find in their statements.

As a matter of fact, there exists a pattern of thought which is quite explicit in the young Marx, which can be glimpsed now and then in the mature Marx, and which runs more or less parallel to a pattern of thought in Hegel's philosophy of history. It may be illustrated as in diagram (K). Alienated man is man for whom work is an imposed necessity rather than a joy, man who through the division of labour is prevented from developing all his possibilities ("hunt in the morning, fish in the afternoon, herd cattle

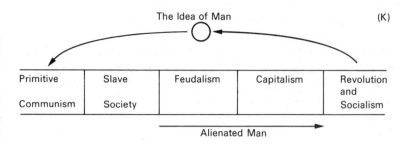

in the evening, write critique after the evening meal, just as I like, without ever becoming a hunter, a fisherman, a herdsman, or a critic",[3] man who lives in misery and dreariness. After reaching its high-point under capitalism alienation disappears with the advent of socialism. In socialist society man finally "returns to himself". In later days both Marx and Engels were to express thoughts that run counter to this light, and even somewhat Bohemian, optimism. Marx took into account the possibility that the division of labour might also be necessary in socialist factories, and Engels stressed the necessity for authority and obedience there. As early as the *Communist Manifesto* they argued in favour of a general obligation to work and of "industrial armies" in the socialist state.

(2) *The concept of Contradiction.* One of the best-known features of Hegelian and Marxist dialectics is the repudiation of the law of contradiction. The law was stated by Aristotle in the words that "it is impossible that the same both is and is not", or that "one side of a contradiction is false". In *Das Kapital* Marx mentions a number of contradictions which, he thinks, characterize the capitalist system; and Engels maintains that all change is contradictory. It seems, however, that there is here a fairly clear difference between the attitude of Marx and that of Engels.

Let us say that two assertions of which one denies what the other asserts constitute a logical contradiction. The two assertions, '2 + 3 = 5' and 'It is not the case that 2 + 3 = 5', are an instance of logical contradiction. It is of such contradictions that Aristotle asserts that one side is always

[3] K. Marx/F. Engels, *Werke* (Berlin 1962), vol. 3, p. 33.

false. Let us say that we assume the existence of a real contradiction if we suppose both sides of a logical contradiction to be true. If, e.g., we assume both that $2 + 3 = 5$ and that such is not the case, we assume the realm of numbers to contain a real contradiction. If the world did contain real contradictions, a correct description of the world would have to contain logical contradictions. And conversely, if a theory beset with logical contradictions were correct, the reality it describes would exhibit real contradictions.

If one believes that reality contains real contradictions, then one cannot unconditionally consider it as an objection to a theory that it involves logical contradicitions. It is interesting to notice that Marx, in *Das Kapital*, severely censures bourgeois economists for their logical contradictions, and this kind of criticism is also very common in the writings of Engels. In view of this fact, can Marx and Engels really have meant that there exist real contradictions? Did they perhaps assume that such contradictions exist, but not those contradictions that bourgeois economic theory implies? To suppose that *one* real contradiction but *not* another exists is a highly problematic position. The following inference is correct according to classical logic:

$$A$$
$$\text{Hence:} \quad A \text{ or } B$$
$$\text{not-}A$$
$$\text{Hence:} \quad B$$

From A and not-A we thus infer B. In exactly the same manner we can also infer not-B from A and not-A. Thus, from the logical contradiction, A, not-A, any other logical contradiction, B, not-B, can be inferred. Hence, to abandon the law of contradiction only on certain isolated points cannot be done without a thoroughgoing revision of logic as a whole. There is not even a trace of such a revision in Marx and Engels.

When Marx speaks of the contradictions inherent in capitalism, very often what he has in mind are not any real contradictions at all, in the present sense. What he thought of was what we may call dynamic contradictions (if we wish to stay close to the terminology of dialectics) but what would more appropriately be called dynamic oppositions. Two forces counteracting each other, two tendencies running in opposite directions, two strivings whose aims are irreconcilable—such phenomena can be said to constitute dynamic contradictions. This type of phenomenon is entirely distinct from real contradictions, and its occurrence does not upset the Aristotelian law. A theory correctly describing a system harbouring dynamic contradictions does not contain logical contradictions. The capitalist system, according to Marx, suffers from such dynamic contradictions: its tendency toward steadily increasing private accumulation and concentration of capital—to take one example among several—gives birth to opposite forces which in the end bring about the expropriation of private capital.

Engels, too, in many cases considers dynamic contradictions when he speaks of the contradictory nature of reality. But he also very emphatically declared his belief in real contradictions:

True, so long as we consider things as at rest and lifeless, each one by itself, alongside and after each other, we do not run up against any contradictions in them. . . . But the position is quite different as soon as we consider things in their motion, their change, their life, their reciprocal influence on one another. Then we immediately become involved in contradictions. Motion itself is a contradiction; even simple mechanical change of position can only come about through a body being at one and the same moment of time both in one place and in another place, being in one and the same place and also not in it. And the continuous origination and simultaneous solution of this contradiction is precisely what motion is.[4]

Engels here echoes the Eleatic philosopher Zeno, in one of his arguments against motion, that of the Arrow. Whereas Zeno took the supposed contradiction to refute the reality of motion, Engels, following Hegel, sees in it a proof of the contradictoriness of reality.

According to Engels even mathematical truth is contradictory. He thinks, e.g., that the following arithmetical propositions which contradict each other are equally correct in mathematics: '$a^{1/2} = \sqrt{a}$', 'A power of a number is never

[4]Ibid., vol. 20, p. 112.

a root of that number'. Marx, I think was more restrained by common sense in questions of this kind.[5]

(3) *The laws of dialectics.* Hegel distinguished between a lower, "reasonable" mode of thought (*Verstand*) and a higher, "dialectical", "rational" one (*Vernunft*). Engel's distinction between "metaphysical" and "dialectical" thinking is close to the Hegelian distinction. Some aspects of the distinction made by Engels can be roughly summarized in the following schema:

Metaphysical thinking	*Dialectical thinking*
considers things as at rest and lifeless	considers things in their motion (change) and life
conceives of reality as static	conceives of reality as process, evolution
considers things as isolated from each other (classifies, analyses)	considers things in their dynamic interplay
recognizes only new configurations of given elements	recognizes the occurrence of qualitative changes (inter alia "qualitative jumps")
strives for a non-contradictory description of reality	acknowledges the contradictoriness of reality.

Metaphysical thinking is accorded by Engels a certain limited validity, but it is in need of complementation through dialectical thought.

On Engels's view, Hegel discovered three fundamental laws of dialectical thinking, laws which are also laws of reality itself:

  (i) the law of the transformation of quantity into quality, and vice versa,

---

[5]In all justice it must be said that Engels himself had some qualms about *Anti-Dühring*, from which these views have been gathered, and which has become part of the Bible of orthodox Marxism. He confessed that it was not written on an inner urge, and that he was forced there to pronounce opinions on questions he had not mastered.

(ii) The law of the mutual penetration of opposites, and

(iii) the law of the negation of the negation.

Let us try to discern what these "laws" meant to Engels.

(i) The first law says that qualitative change cannot take place without a simultaneous quantitative change (addition or subtraction of matter or motion) and that a quantitative change at certain critical points may give rise to qualitative jumps. A phenomenon exemplifying the latter part of the law is the transformation of ice into water at 0 °C and also that of water into steam at 100 °C. In *Das Kapital* Marx gives the following example:

The owner of money and goods is actually changed into a capitalist only when the minimal sum invested in the production is far above the maximum of the Middle Ages. Here, as in natural science, the law which Hegel discovered in his *Logic* demonstrates its validity, viz. that purely quantitative changes at a certain point result in qualitative differences.[6]

(ii) The second law, to which Engels never gave a general formulation, is to the effect, it seems, that all change involves real contradictions. This law has often been construed, at least by later Marxists, as saying that each thing, each situation, even each concept, somehow involves what I have called a dynamic contradiction.

(iii) Neither does the third law receive any general formulation in Engels's writings. It deals with a kind of process that may suitably be called triadic, with which we are familiar from Hegel. By calling a process triadic I mean here that it consists of, or involves, three stages, A, the negation of A, and the negation of the negation of A. In *Das Kapital* Marx gives this example of a triadic process:

The capitalist mode of acquiring property, which results from the capitalist mode of production, brings about capitalist private property. This is the first negation of individual private property based on the labour of the owner. But, with the necessity of a law of nature, capitalist production begets its own negation. This is the negation of the negation.[7]

[6] K. Marx/F. Engels, *Werke*, vol. 23, p. 327.
[7] Ibid., vol. 23, p. 791.

Engels gives, *inter alia*, a botanical example. When a grain of barley grows, there appears in its place a plant which is the negation of the grain. The plant flowers, is pollinated, and produces new grains of barley, and when these have ripened, the plant dies. Therewith the plant is negated, and "as a result of this negation of the negation we again have the original grain, not as a single unit, but multiplied ten-, twenty-, and thirtyfold."[8]

The metaphysicians could object, Engels says, that the grain may also be negated by being ground to flour, and where then is the double negation? Engels's reply is to the effect that there may be many ways in which a thing or a concept can be negated but that for each thing or concept there is a particular negation which gives rise to a dialectic evolution. Engels also seems to maintain that the third law by itself does not tell us what this particular negation is. To find it we must study the thing or concept in question.

Engels also attributes a role to the third law in mathematics. For example, $-a$ is the negation of a, and $-a \times -a = a^2$ is the negation of $-a$.[9] Here, too, there are other ways of negating a: it may, for instance, be cancelled (in a formula, I suppose); and in order to obtain a triadic process it is necessary to find the right mode of negating.

Engels sometimes appears to consider dialectics as an independent scientific discipline on a par with formal logic. His own inept reflections concerning the three laws— repeated in a sterile manner by innumerable Marxists—hardly lend convincing support to this idea.

C. *The motive forces in the development of society*

We have already taken notice of the fact that, in opposition to Hegel, Marx and Engels maintained that the material conditions of life determine men's consciousness. To explain with any precision what this so-called historical materialism amounts to is a very difficult, if not impossible, task. It is based on the assumption of a fixed sequence of factors, let us abstractly say:

(i) $A, B, C \ldots$

[8]Ibid., vol. 20, p. 126.   [9]Ibid., vol. 20, pp. 127–8.

These factors can be discerned in any sufficiently developed society. In various passages in their writings, Marx and Engels have described the factors in several different, although related, ways. According to a frequent explanation, A is "the forces of production", i.e. the tools, the machines, the technical processes, the natural resources, etc., which are available. B is "the conditions (relations) of production" which together constitute the "economic structure" of society. Exactly what it is that belongs to the economic structure is not clear. Primitive tribal communism, the ancient slave society, feudalism, capitalism, and socialism—those forms of society that Marx and Engels particularly distinguished—all have their characteristic economic structures. According to certain statements, C is "the juridical and political superstructure", and D is "the social consciousness". According to other presentations, the sequence has just three terms, and the last, C, is described as "the superstructure", "the consciousness", "the ideology": it includes "the juridical, political, religious, aesthetical, and philosophical, ideological forms".[10]

Concerning this sequence (i) Marx and Engels advocate a thesis which, vaguely speaking, asserts that the character of B during a given historical epoch in the development of a society is determined by the character of A, and that the same relation holds between C and B. They also say such things as that the character of B can be explained only on the basis of that of A, that changes in B are conditioned by changes in A, etc.

As far as I can see, we are here confronted with two distinct theses, one of a synchronic and another of a diachronic nature. Let us first look at the synchronic thesis. It asserts something about the *simultaneous* natures of A, B, C in a society in a given epoch. Marx's and Engels's own formulations are so elastic that they lend themselves to the most divergent interpretations. To avoid getting entangled in subtle exegetical problems I shall here be content with delineating the two extreme poles of a scale on which most interpretations can be placed. One pole I shall call the strongest interpretation, the other the weakest.

[10]Ibid., vol. 13, p. 9.

The strongest interpretation of the synchronic thesis can be symbolized as in diagram (L).

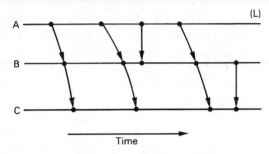

The *A*-line is intended here to symbolize the entire complex course of events that may be referred to the factor *A*, "the forces of production" during a certain epoch of a society. The *B*- and *C*-lines are to be interpreted analogously. The dots represent particular events, and the arrows stand for relations of cause and effect. Under the strongest interpretation all the relations of cause and effect have the same direction: they go from *A* to *B* and from *B* to *C*. This version of the thesis is inconsistent with our everyday experience: it simply cannot be true.

The weakest interpretation, which stands at the other end of the scale, can be illustrated by diagram (M).

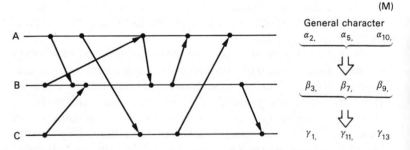

The lines, the dots, and the arrows between them, have the same significance as before. On the weakest interpretation the causal arrows go back and forth between the three layers. It is here assumed that "the general character" of *A* during an epoch can be described by some selection from the attributes α_1, α_2, α_3 . . . , likewise that of B by some selection from β_1, β_2, β_3 . . . , and that of C by some selection from γ_1, γ_2, γ_3. In the diagram it is further supposed that in the given epoch the general character of A can be described just by α_2, α_5, α_{10}, that of B by β_3, β_7, β_9, and that of C by γ_1, γ_{11}, γ_{13}.

What the synchronic thesis in the weakest interpretation asserts is that the general character of B is determined by that of A but not conversely and that likewise the general character of C is determined by that of B but not conversely. The determination of B by A might be construed here to mean:

(ii)   If A in the society S during the epoch E has the same general character as A in the society S' during the epoch E', then B in S during E has the same character as B in S', during E'.

The determination of C by B may then be understood analogously. The double arrow in the diagram stands for this determination. There is, as far as I can see, nothing absurd or evidently unrealistic in the way the weakest synchronic thesis combines a statement about particular A-, B- and C-events and a statement about the general characters of A, B, C during an epoch. As presented here, the weakest thesis is actually quite indeterminate. It acquires a definite meaning only when the relevant sets of attributes, α_1, α_2, α_3 . . . , β_1, β_2, β_3 . . . , γ_1, γ_2, γ_3 . . . , have been clearly specified. I am not familiar with any such specification in Marxist literature. Perhaps the synchronic thesis in the weakest interpretation is best understood as a conjecture that interesting relationships of type (ii) exist and as an exhortation to historical research to look for them.[11]

A historical-materialistic synchronic thesis which is not as patently false as the strongest and not as nearly empty

---

[11]Reasons of space have induced me to oversimplify here. It might be argued that the determination involved here can be construed as a causal determination not implying any such general rule as (ii). Whereas (ii) can be verified, or made plausible only by a comprehensive comparative study of different societies under different epochs, such a causal determination can, it may be argued, be established by a particular case study. A more careful discussion would obviously have to take into account this idea as well.

as the weakest must be looked for somewhere between these extreme poles. Here the interpreters, apologists, and critics of Marxism provide a wide field of possibilities.

A critical point in all variants of the thesis is, of course, the segmentation of history into so-called historical epochs. What is the general recipe for this segmentation?

The diachronic thesis, which is also part of historical materialism, says something about how changes in the factors *A, B, C* take place during the passage from one historical epoch to another. Marx and Engels think that the passage occurs in a definite manner. In the beginning of an epoch the conditions of production (*B*) are in harmony with the forces of production (*A*) and favourable to their development. By the very development of the forces of production, a conflict, a "contradiction", between the two factors gradually arises: the conditions of production become a hindrance to the further development of the forces. When the conflict has become sufficiently acute, the forces make the old conditions burst asunder, new conditions are established, and a new epoch commences. This diachronic view seems to presuppose some fairly weak interpretation of the synchronic thesis.

In *Anti-Dühring* Engels makes the following statement which he thinks is of central importance in dialectics:

. . . cause and effect are conceptions which only hold good in their application to individual cases; but as soon as we consider the individual cases in their general connection with the universe as a whole, they run into each other, and they become confounded when we contemplate that universal action and reaction in which causes and effects are eternally changing places, so that what is effect here and now will be the cause there and then, and vice versa.[12]

For anyone who takes this point of view it should be difficult to indicate any one factor as the ultimate moving force in history. To a dialectical materialist of this confession, history ought to appear as an infinitely complex interplay of different factors in which "causes and effects are for ever changing places." But does not historical materialism aim at putting a limit to just this substitutivity? It is hardly possible to free Engels entirely from the charge of inconsistency here.

[12]K. Marx/F. Engels, *Werke*, vol. 20, pp. 21–2.

The inconsistency, however, is very much mitigated by the indefinite character of the theses of historical materialism.

Marx and Engels regarded as an essential part of their view of history their famous statement that the entire history of mankind, ever since the primitive tribal society with its common ownership of the land was dissolved, has been a history of the struggle between classes. It is a statement that no doubt points to innumerable historical facts. In its general form, however, it unavoidably gives rise to such critical questions as: What is a "class"? What is a "struggle" between classes? If the statement is intended to exclude the possibility that "history" can be said, with equal right, to be many other things besides class struggle, it is obviously either absurd or involves an arbitrarily narrow definition of the term "history".

42. VALUE-CREATING LABOUR AND CAPITALIST EXPLOITATION

Marx's major work, *Das Kapital*, is very rich in content. It contains a historical sketch of the growth of modern capitalism, based on a great fund of facts. It gives a heart-rending picture of the sufferings and the exploitation of the landless agricultural workers and factory workers, especially in England during the first part of the nineteenth century. (This picture was largely drawn from the reports of the official English factory inspectors.) It also contains an economic theory, based on the labour concept of economic value, by which Marx thinks he can impart a deeper understanding of the fact of exploitation and of the growth of capitalism. It also predicts and welcomes the ultimate downfall of capitalism and the advent of socialism. Here I shall present only certain ideas which belong to the general foundations of Marx's economic history.

A. *The scope of the theory*

Marx may have thought that some propositions in his economic theory held good for practically all forms of human economic life. Of the theory as a whole, however, he assumed only that it was valid for a social system of the capitalist kind. According to Marx, capitalism is characterized by the following fundamental properties:

(1)   Commodities are to a large extent produced solely for the purpose of being traded for other commodities or sold for money.

(2)   There is a free market: no central social authority governs production and trade.

(3)   Labour power can be bought and sold freely like any other commodity on the market.

(4)   There is a large social class, the proletarians, who do not own any means of production, and who have no commodities to sell but their labour power.

(5)   There is another social class, the capitalists, who do not themselves work (produce) but who own the means of production, who buy the labour power of the proletarians, and who are constantly striving to increase their property, the capital.

To these properties I think we are entitled to add also a sixth which Marx patently took for granted:

(6)   Not only is the market, including the labour market, free, but the society, or the state, is on the whole economically passive, a *laissez-faire* society. It does not itself own means of production to any sizeable degree, nor does it influence the course of production by controlling the flow of the money capital, nor does it divert an important part of profits for purposes of its own by taxation and other similar means. And so on.

All these properties are rather indefinite, and they all admit of degrees. The market, including the labour market, is not just free or not free; it may be more or less extensively regulated by legislation. The nature of ownership is relative to legislation; it may include a larger or a smaller number of legal rights. The separation of the class of those who sell their labour power and that of those who buy it can be more or less clear cut. The owner of the means of production may contribute to a greater or lesser degree to the successful execution of production. He may also in varying degree answer to the notion of "the economic man" of classical economy. Political democracy, also, may be more or less well developed, and the democratically created authorities can constitute a more or less efficient counter-weight to the power of capital. Property (6) is quite obviously very much one of degree. By a series of almost insensibly small steps one may conceivably move from a complete *laissez-faire* situation to a highly state-controlled economy. In the capitalist society that Marx had before his eyes, England during the first part of the nineteenth century, those factors that can moderate the superior power of private capital were still very feeble, and Marx wrote in the conviction that the overwhelming power of private capital and the gross misuse of its power were inevitable characteristics of all capitalism.

B. *The inheritance from Adam Smith and David Ricardo*

In his economic thinking, Marx was much indebted to his predecessors, and especially to Adam Smith and David Ricardo. In *The Wealth of Nations* (1776), Adam Smith presented certain ideas concerning economy under free competition, ideas which were more sharply stated and further elaborated by David Ricardo in *The Principles of Political Economy and Taxation* (1817). These ideas underlie Marx's whole reasoning in *Das Kapital*, although they are not always stated by Marx with sufficient clarity at the points where they come into play. It is therefore virtually impossible to understand *Das Kapital* without a knowledge of certain fundamental notions in the economic theories of Adam Smith and David Ricardo. I shall here primarily follow Ricardo's *Principles*.

Smith and Richardo, like Marx after them, distinguished between the value in use, or utility, of a commodity and its value in exchange, or exchangeable value, which is somehow measured by its price. Without value in use nothing can possess value in exchange: that for which no one has a use will not be accepted in exchange for anything. But the value in exchange is no way proportionate to the value in use. The latter may even exist without the former: "Water and air are abundantly useful; they are indeed indispensable to existence, yet, under ordinary circumstances, nothing can be obtained in exchange for them. Gold, on the contrary, though of little use compared with air or water, will exchange for a great quantity of other goods."[13] According to Smith and Ricardo, as well as Marx, it is the value in exchange that is the central notion of economic theory.

Some commodities owe their value in exchange to their scarcity. However:

By far the greatest part of those goods which are the objects of desire are procured by labour; and they may be multiplied, not in one country alone, but in many, almost without any assignable limit, if we are disposed to bestow the labour necessary to obtain them. In speaking, then, of commodities, of their exchangeable value, and of the laws which regulate their relative prices, we mean always such commodities as can be increased in quantity by the exertion of human industry, and on the production of which competition operates without restraint.[14]

In the focus of Ricardo's interest stand, thus, those goods that are produced on a very free and very competitive market. Labour is considered as being, more or less, one such commodity.

In a free competitive market the agents restlessly compete in pursuit of the highest possible profit on their invested money. The profit is "the remaining value or overplus" which is left "after paying the wages for the labour necessary for their production [the production of the goods], and all other expenses required to put the capital in its original state of efficiency."[15]

The rate of profit is the ratio between the profit and the capital employed. Capital will always flow from the spheres of production with a low profit rate to spheres in which this rate is high. By this movement of capital, a unique common rate of profit is established, in the neighbourhood of which the individual rates of profit will stay, on the whole. This profit rate is something the agents on the market will expect to obtain, and Smith and Ricardo include it in the cost of production. The common rate of profit may change with time. There are, in Ricardo's opinion, factors that, unless counteracted, tend to make it fall.

When a given commodity is produced in insufficient quantity to satisfy the demand for it, its price will naturally

[13] *The Works and Correspondence of David Ricardo* (Cambridge, 1951), vol. i, p. 11.   [14]Ibid., p. 12.   [15]Ibid., p. 91.

rise above the cost of production. The production of this commodity will then yield a higher profit rate than the production of other commodities. Hence, capital will flow into the production of it, the marketed supply of it will be enlarged, and its price will sink. When the price sinks so far as to make the rate of profit less than the common rate, capital will again withdraw from this particular sphere of production and the price will again rise. The actual prices, or market prices, will therefore oscillate around the cost of production. The value around which the market price of a commodity thus oscillates is called, by Smith and Ricardo, the "natural" price of the commodity. When speaking of the "value in exchange", or "price", of a commodity, Ricardo wishes to be understood as referring to this natural price, not to the actual market price.

On Ricardo's view, it is the costs of production, not the relation between supply and demand, that determine the prices of goods. The effect of the relation between supply and demand is merely either to raise the market prices above, or to depress them below, the costs of production. Such deviations are always accidental and temporary. The natural prices are, of course, themselves subject to change. This also holds of the natural price of labour. Smith and Ricardo also assume that the natural prices of goods, produced under free competition, are in some sense average prices.

So far I have not mentioned Smith's and Ricardo's perhaps most famous idea concerning value. The exchange value, or natural price, of a commodity is, they maintain, determined by the total quantity of labour that has gone into the production of it. Further, the value rises or falls as this quantity of labour is augmented or diminished; indeed the ratio between the natural prices of two commodities is equal to the ratio between the corresponding quantities of labour. (When prices are counted in money, this rule must of course be applied only to prices counted in the same money.. The rule cannot, e.g., be applied indiscriminately to prices in one currency at different times, since the currency will most probably have changed what today we would call its buying power.)

The reasons that made Smith and Ricardo accept this view—which had been advanced by other economic thinkers before them—are not at all clear. Smith made the following psychological reflection:

The real price of everything, what everything really costs to the man who wants to acquire it, is the toil and trouble of acquiring it. What everything is really worth to the man who has acquired it and who wants to dispose of it, is the toil and trouble which it can save to himself, and which it can impose upon other people.[16]

In this reflection there is also a hint of a moral or legalistic notion: If I exchange *a* for *b* with you, where *a* and *b* have cost the same labour, the things exchanged are really worth the same and the transaction is just or fair.

One reason for adopting the labour theory of value was undoubtedly, at least for Smith, the desire to find an unalterable standard of value outside the price system. As long as we confine our horizon to the price system, or to the system of exchange relations, we can merely observe that the ratio in which commodities are exchanged varies; but we cannot say whether any one commodity has "absolutely" risen or fallen in value. The amount of labour that the production of a commodity requires at various times was thought to provide the absolute standard that allows us to settle such questions. If we now further suppose that things exchanged for each other are, on the average, of equal absolute worth, we arrive at a form of the labour theory of value.

Both Smith and Ricardo emphasize that in estimating the quantity of labour that the production of a commodity has required, we must take into account not only the labour immediately or last employed, but also the labour that the production of the raw materials, the tools, the factory buildings, etc. have cost. It is of interest to consider whether the assumption of a proportionality between natural prices and quantities of labour is consistent with the assumption of identity between natural prices and costs of production.

In consonance with the ideas of Smith and Ricardo, we may suppose that there is a unique positive profit rate, say *p*. Let us assume that a commodity has required a quantity

[16] Adam Smith, *The Wealth of Nations* (London, 1904), vol. i, p. 32.

of labour a_1 and that its natural price is c_1. Another commodity is produced by means of the first commodity (which is totally consumed in the process) and another quantity of labour a_2. The natural price of the latter commodity will then be $(1 + p)$ times the sum of c_1 and the price of a_2. Let us assume that, in the present situation, the price of labour is proportionate to its quantity, i.e. if x is the price of the labour quantity y, then $x = k.y$. By suitable choice of units for measuring price and/or quantity of labour, we may make $k = 1$ and $x = y$. The natural price of the second commodity will thus be $(1 + p)(c_1 + a_2)$. If we now introduce the assumption that there is a constant ratio r between natural prices and quantities of labour, we obtain the following:

$$(i) \qquad \frac{c_1}{a_1} = \frac{(1 + p)(c_1 + a_2)}{a_1 + a_2} = \mathrm{T}$$

It is easily seen that this can hold for arbitrary choices of $a_1 > 0$ and $a_2 > 0$, only if:

(ii) $r = 1$,

and:

(iii) $p = 0$.

The closer (i) agrees with economic reality, the nearer to zero the profit rate will hence be.

The above argument shows that the thesis of the general proportionality between natural price and quantity of labour is, in a clear-cut sense, inconsistent with the assumption that natural price coincides with cost of production.

Summing up, we may say that the natural price, as conceived by Smith and Ricardo, has the following characteristics:

(i) it coincides with the cost of production, defined so as to include the common profit;
(ii) it is the price at which the commodity would be sold if demand and supply were to match each other exactly;
(iii) it is the value around which the actual market prices oscillate, their deviations being only temporary;

(iv) it is, in some sense, the average price;
(v) it is, in some sense, a fair price, corresponding to what the commodity is really worth;
(vi) the ratio between the natural prices of two commodities coincides with the ratio between the corresponding quantities of productive labour.

(The thinking of Smith and Ricardo is highly complex, and this bare outline does not, of course, pretend to do justice to that complexity.)

C. *Exchange value and quantity of labour in Marx*

Marx accepted the theory on exchange values and market prices found in the work of Adam Smith and David Ricardo, and, like them, he thought that the notion of the exchange value is of central importance in economic theory. Even more emphatically than Ricardo, Marx asserted that the exchange values, or real values, of commodities are proportional to the quantities of labour required for their production. The quantity of labour that has been necessary for the production of the goods, which is "embodied", "materialized", or "crystallized" within them, is, he says in metaphysical terms, the "substance" whose form of expression is the exchange value. In the first volume of *Das Kapital* this tenet is put forward almost as if it were an *a priori* truth. That two quantities of goods have the same exchange value must, he says, depend upon the fact that they have some more deep-seated property in common, and the only such property there is is their being the result of equal amounts of labour.

The inconsistency we have seen involved in the Ricardian labour theory of exchange value made itself felt also within Marx's economic system. In the third volume of *Das Kapital*, Marx was actually forced to give up the assumption that the 'natural prices' of commodities are, in general, proportional to their values as measured in labour time. This assumption is there replaced by the weaker assumption that, for each sphere of production where the 'organic composition' (a concept explained in §E) is the same, 'natural prices' can be obtained from values by multiplying them by a common factor of proportionality. In the first volume of *Das Kapital*, however, Marx argues on the whole as if the more general assumption were actually correct.

What does Marx mean by "labour"? How should the "quantity" of given labour be measured? And how can one, in a complex process of labour, distinguish just that labour that has been used to produce one particular commodity? Clear answers to these and related questions are not found in Marx's writings, but we may note the following ideas:

(i) By labour or work Marx means only work done by human beings, by their muscles, nerves, etc. He also shows a tendency to identify work with manual work and with "production". A machine or a horse cannot do any work, in the sense that interests Marx in his theory of value.

(ii) Marx sometimes says that the quantity of a given labour is measured simply by the units of time in which it has been done. But he also distinguishes between "simple" and "complex" labour. One hour of complex work can, according to this idea, represent a quantity of labour as big as many hours of simple work. Marx assumes that the quantity of labour that an individual worker accomplishes during an hour can be identified with a certain number of simple labour hours. Sometimes Marx intimates that this calculation is carried out by the market, apparently assuming that wages are in principle proportional to quantities of labour. Marx also thinks that capitalist industry, by subordinating men to machines, tends to degrade all labour into simple labour.

(iii) It is a fact that two instances of what would be regarded as the same commodity can have been produced under very different conditions: the one may have required many more hours of work than the other. How then can the exchange value of this commodity be determined by the labour? Marx says that the exchange value of, say, this pound of potatoes is determined by that quantity of labour that under the prevailing conditions is on the average required to produce 1 lb. of potatoes. That quantity is also called by Marx the quantity of labour that is "socially necessary" for producing 1 lb. of potatoes.

(iv) Marx's talk of "the socially necessary quantity of labour" sometimes has another significance. When calculating the quantity of labour which is "socially necessary" for producing 1 lb. of potatoes, one should, Marx sometimes intimates, first find out how many pounds of potatoes society needs just now (how many can be sold), then calculate the labour time that under prevailing conditions is necessary for the production of this quantity, and finally divide this time by the amount of potatoes actually being produced. If there is an overproduction of potatoes, then the real value of potatoes will sink, according to this line of thought. If too few potatoes are grown, the real value will conversely rise. This idea of Marx's is of a certain interest. According to Marx's "official" point of view, what essentially determines the prices is the quantity of labour or (as he sometimes also says) the cost of production. We have now seen that in his very definition of the quantity of labour Marx imports a reference to supply and demand.

(v) The production on the loom of a yard of linen—to take an example of the kind that Marx used to discuss—is only the final stage in a very long and complex process which branches out almost indefinitely in various directions in the past. The linen has been cultivated, and, with the help of various tools, it has been transformed into yarn. The loom has been manufactured by means of diverse tools, and the factory has been built with tools. All the tools that have been employed here have themselves been made with other tools. Marx stresses that in calculating the value one should add to "the quantity of labour finally employed" (here, say, the work at the loom) the labour that has been employed in producing the raw material, the tools, the buildings, etc. How far back in the history of mankind one ought to go Marx does not specify, and it would obviously be a difficult thing to do.

(vi) Marx sometimes expresses the idea that, in calculating the value of a commodity *at a given time*, we should take into account only the quantities of labour that *at that time* are necessary for the production of those commodities that are being used in the production of the first commodity. According to this line of thought, the value has no historical dimension.

(vii) The work that the manufacture of the loom has cost

belongs to the pre-history, not only of the yard of linen that is just now being woven, but also of all linen that is ever woven on the loom. Marx decides that in calculating the value of this yard one must estimate how many yards will in all be made on the loom during its lifetime, say n yards, and then include in the value of this yard an nth part of the work that the manufacture of the loom has cost. In weaving this yard an nth part of the value of the loom is being "consumed", or "transferred" from the loom to the yard.

(viii) In a modern complex industrial enterprise in which many different workers and many different machines may simultaneously be engaged in the production of many types of goods, the task of calculating the amount of labour that goes into the production of one particular type of commodity may appear truly baffling. Sometimes Marx seems inclined to think that in many such cases only the amount of labour that goes into the production as a whole can be meaningfully discussed.

(ix) The real value of labour power also consists, in principle, in the labour necessary for its production. Here, however, Marx does not stick too closely to the principle. The value is to be measured by the labour necessary for the "production and reproduction" of the labour power, and in this labour Marx includes what is necessary for maintaining the worker's family and bringing up his children. In measuring this labour one must take into account the mode of life that, according to the standards of the time, a worker is considered entitled to. In one passage in *Das Kapital* (vol. I, ch. 17), Marx presents the view that one should consider the normal number of normal working days in a worker's life, calculate the value of a life with this number of normal days, and then divide that value by the number of working days that the capitalist actually gets out of the worker—a number which because of overwork and premature decrepitude or death is usually much smaller: the result of this calculation is the real value of the real working day. (In this connection Marx maintains that the capitalist normally pays the worker less than the real value of his working day and thus cheats him, an idea which is otherwise foreign to Marx.)

It may be worth noting that Marx did not arrive at his

theory of real value and its role in economic life through any empirical (statistical) investigations concerning prices and quantities of labour. His reasons are purely *a priori*. The theory is derived from ideas that Marx found in the classical English economists, ideas which in turn were inspired by earlier speculations concerned with natural law. Although Marx officially objected to the mixing of economic analysis with moral considerations, his entire work is an indictment of capitalism. Thus the theory of real value has, for Marx, a moral implication. The real economic value is created by the productive labour of the workers, the proletarians, and in this labour it finds its measure.

D. *Exchange value and just prices*

According to Marx, exchange value plays a role in the formation of prices. Less explicitly, Marx also seems to attribute a quite different role to exchange value, one connected with the old idea of a "just price", a *iustum pretium*. When man at a more primitive stage of civilization agreed to trade a thing he had produced for something produced by another man, he self-evidently, Marx thinks, required that the respective labour times should be equal. When, under our economic system, goods demanding the same labour time are traded for each other, the transaction is, in a sense, fair: neither of the parties is cheating the other. When the capitalist buys the labour power of the proletarian at its real value, the capitalist, although he is the gaining party, is still, in a sense, within his rights. Engels praises Marx especially for having shown how the capitalist can exploit the proletarian without actually cheating him, i.e. without buying his labour power below its real value. I think we can attribute to Marx belief in the principle that the trading of one commodity for another is, in a sense, a just economic transaction if and only if the exchange values of the commodities are equal.

The inserted words, "in a sense", are important here. In the first stage of the socialist society, this principle will be strictly observed, although labour power will no more be a thing that can be sold and bought, as under capitalism. In the consummated socialist system, however, the principle will no longer have any application.

E. *Surplus value and related concepts*

Since the entire system of exchange values is always changing, an individual capitalist can make a profit through speculation: he may, e.g., buy iron when it is cheap and sell it when it fetches a high price. Such transactions, however, only imply, Marx observes, that the real value is redistributed among the speculating capitalists. How is it possible that, not merely an individual capitalist makes a profit, but that the capitalist class as a whole increases its capital? This is made possible, Marx maintains, by the fact that something which, properly speaking, is not a "commodity", is treated as such in the capitalist society, viz. human labour power.[17]

The very essence of the capitalist system consists, on Marx's view, in the following process: for an amount of money c the capitalist buys certain means of production (factory, machines, raw materials) p:

(i) p is bought for c.

For another sum of money v he buys the labour power l of the worker:

(ii) l is bought for v.

The use of the labour power l in combination with the means of production p results in the production of the goods g:

(iii) The use of l and p produces g.

Finally the capitalist sells g for a price that we may suppose to be $c + v + \Delta v$:

[12]The commodity that the capitalist buys from the worker is not his "labour" but his "labour power", i.e. his ability to work. One of Marx's reasons for this curious and terminologically cumbersome distinction is expressed in the following argument. For the production of, say, eight hours of work are required exactly eight hours of work. If labour were a commodity, therefore, the real value of eight hours of work would be eight hours of work. This conclusion is nonsense, Marx asserts, and it also contradicts the fact that the value of what the worker sells changes from time to time. The commodity that he sells, hence, cannot be his labour, but must be his labour power. Labour is no commodity and has no value. Only the labour power has a value. The argument is puzzling, and nothing essential in Marx's theory would have to be changed if the assumption that the worker sells his labour were incorporated in it. The value of the labour A, i.e. the amount of labour necessary to produce A, could by definition be identified with the amount of labour which, on Marx's theory as it stands, is required for the production of the labour power whose consumption yields A.

(iv) g is sold for $c + v + \Delta v$.

(That the process here is assumed to begin and end with sums of money is not essential.) "Δv" is the symbol used here by Marx himself. The use is not in accordance with common practice in the calculus (Marx's "Δv" does *not* signify a small increase in the wages v); but the choice of the symbol reflects Marx's conviction that the designated quantity arises solely from the labour, bought with v, not from the means of production.

The quantity Δv is what Marx calls the *surplus value*, or the *profit*, which is one of the most important concepts of Marxian economics. The magnitude c is what Marx calls the *constant capital* and v what he calls the *variable capital*. The sum $C = (c + v)$ is the total capital used in the process of production. Marx here introduces some further technical terms. The ratio $\Delta v/v$ is the rate of *surplus value*, or the *rate of exploitation*, and $\Delta v/C$ is the *profit rate*. The ratio $c/(c + v)$ is a measure of the *organic composition* of the capital.

To simplify the presentation, I assumed in the above example that the means of production in which capital is initially invested are totally worn out in the production of g. If they are worn out through the production of, say, n times g, we should, in order to render Marx's thought faithfully, replace "c" in (iv) by "c/n". This replacement does not affect the magnitude of the surplus value Δv or its rate $\Delta v/v$. But what about the profit rate and the organic composition? On this question Marx's ideas appear slightly ambiguous. According to his often repeated, very explicit explanations, the profit rate is in this case $\Delta v/(c/n + v)$ or $n \cdot \Delta v/(c + n \cdot v)$ and the organic composition is $(c/n)/(c/n + v)$ or $c/(c + n \cdot v)$. But in his reasonings he often understands the profit rate as the ratio of the profit to the total invested capital, $\Delta v/(c + v)$, and the organic composition as the ratio of constant capital to total investment, $(c/c + v)$. The two senses of the two concepts are, of course, enormously different. If buildings, machinery, etc. last for a long time, a high annual profit rate in the first sense may amount to a low one, in the latter sense.

A low organic composition in the former sense may, conversely, be high in the latter sense. The ambiguity is usually rendered innocuous by Marx's considering periods of time in which the total invested capital c is assumed to be entirely consumed just once.

If we assume that the temporary oscillation of market prices around the exchange values, or real values, can be ignored, we find that:

(v) The real values of v and of l are identical.

With regard to the relationship (v), Marx more than once stresses that the worker suffers no economic "wrong" when he sells l for v: he receives the full value of l. Still assuming that the oscillation may be ignored, we also find that:

(vi) The real values of g and of $c + v + \Delta v$ are identical.

The capitalist gets no "overprice" for his goods: he gets exactly what answers to their real value.

The process of production has thus led to an increase of the capital in the hands of the capitalist from $c + v$ to $c + v + \Delta v$. Since value is crystallized human labour, and since, it must be noted, on Marx's view, the only labour added consists in the use of the labour power l, the surplus value Δv derives entirely from this source. Thus we see:

(1) The labour power, when consumed in labour, creates a value $v + \Delta v$, which is greater than its own value v.

This is the secret of the capitalist mechanism which Marx thinks he has discovered:

(2) The increasing accumulation of capital by the capitalists is possible only because labour power creates more real value than it has and the capitalists appropriate the surplus value.

F. *The unpaid surplus labour*

The process (i)–(iv) which we considered in the previous section is analysed by Marx in greater detail as follows. The labour power l contributes to the production of g by being "consumed" in the form of labour. Let us designate the labour that is spent in the consumption of l as l'. Of g's value $c + v + \Delta v$, c derives, Marx says, from the means of production, whereas $v + \Delta v$ is created through l'. The value of the means of production is transferred to g in such a manner that the sum of the value remaining in the means and the value transferred to the product is always *equal to* c. At each moment during the process of production, this value c is thus in the hands of the capitalist. The value $v + \Delta v$, on the other hand, is being continuously formed during the process.

Let us now think of the labour, or the labour time, as divided into two parts, l'_1 during which v is created and l'_2 during which Δv is created. Presupposing that created value is proportional to labour time, Marx finds:

(3) l'_2/l'_1 = the rate of surplus value, or of exploitation, $\Delta v/v$.

On the same assumption, he finds also:

(4) l'_1 = the time it takes to create the labour power l and its value v.

Marx designates l'_1 as *necessary labour* (or necessary labour time). It is necessary, he says, from the point of view of the capitalist as well as that of the worker. For the worker l'_1 is necessary in view of (4). To continue living he must steadily recreate his own labour power and for that l'_1 is necessary. With doubtful realism Marx asserts that the worker must spend the same amount of labour irrespective of whether he works for a capitalist or on his own. For the same reason, l'_1 is also necessary for the capitalist: he cannot go on as entrepreneur without his workers staying alive.

The labour l'_2, on the other hand, Marx designates as *surplus labour* (or surplus labour time), and moreover he says:

(5) Surplus labour is unpaid labour.

This Thesis of the Unpaid Surplus Labour is obviously akin to Marx's assertion that the capitalist appropriates the surplus value and that the rate of surplus value is a measure of the exploitation.

Now, in what sense does Marx call the surplus labour "unpaid"?

First it must be remembered that labour on Marx's view has no value, either exchange value or real value, and that hence there can never be any commercial "payment" for labour. What has a value and can be sold, and bought, and paid for, in a commercial transaction, is only the labour power. Under the presuppositions of Marx's argument, the worker sells his power *l* at its full value. Without being grossly inconsistent, Marx cannot have intended to assert by (5) that the worker is not fully paid for the value of this labour power.

It might be thought that Marx is here invoking some general principle of justice which he takes the surplus labour to violate. Let us take a look at some principles that might possibly have been in his mind.

(a) A principle occurring in socialist thought is that of the right of the worker to the full value of the product of his labour. This, however, is a principle that Marx most emphatically rejected, e.g. in his critique (1875) of the so-called Gotha programme of the German social-democratic party. Neither does the Thesis of the Unpaid Surplus Labour include a demand that the worker should get the product's full value, $c + v + \Delta v$, but at most that he get $v + \Delta v$.

(b) Another principle that Marx could possibly have had in mind would be that the worker is entitled to the entire value that is bestowed upon the product through his labour, i.e. $v + \Delta v$. In his critique of the Gotha programme Marx rejects this principle; in a socialist society the worker must be prepared to give up part of the surplus value Δv for social purposes.

(c) A third conceivable moral principle that the Thesis of the Unpaid Surplus Labour could rest upon would be the principle that no individual person is entitled to make a profit through any commercial transaction with other persons. Strictly speaking, however, Marx wishes to abolish all commercial transactions: in the consummated socialist society no trade will occur at all, at least according to one of his thoughts. From this point of view, the Thesis of the Unpaid Surplus Labour appears as an understatement.

Considering Marx's ideas about the socialist society one finds that he condemns surplus labour as unpaid only in non-socialist societies. He has no objection in principle to the surplus labour that must also occur under socialism. What he objects to is in fact that the surplus value created by surplus labour comes into the possession of the individual capitalist, or of "capital", the capitalist class. Even according to Marx, however, the capitalist does not usually simply pocket the surplus value: the major part of it is usually reinvested in production. If pressed, and leaving details aside, Marx would probably say that the economy as a whole, production and consumption, is managed incomparably more justly and more efficiently for the well-being of the entire people in a socialist society than in a capitalist system. If something like this is what ultimately underlies his Thesis of the Unpaid Surplus Labour, the thesis is a singularly unfortunate expression of the thought. The mathematically formulated analysis of the model situation (i)–(iv) is, of course, no good reason for this political belief, whatever we may think of that mathematical analysis.

G. *The role of the theory of value in Marxism*

In his theory of capitalism Marx takes into account facts of social, economic, and technological history, facts of psychology, etc. Some of the assumptions he introduces have the form of propositions concerning the manner in which the magnitudes defined in his theory of value change, or "tend" to change, in the course of time. Some such assumptions are the following:

(a) The total capital in the possession of the capitalist class tends to increase and be concentrated in fewer hands.

(b) The organic composition of capital tends to increase; the capital invested in means of production becoming increasingly larger than that spent in wages.

(c) The profit rates in the various fields of production tend to converge.

(d) The average profit rate tends to decrease.

(e) The total profit tends to increase.

(f) The productivity of labour, i.e. the quantity of goods produced per time unit, tends to increase, and therewith the value and price of each individual commodity (i.e. $(c + v + \Delta v)$/number of items produced) tends to sink.

One might expect Marx to maintain that the exploitation rate tends to increase, but he does not seem to make any clear-cut general statement to this effect.

Many of Marx's assumptions of this kind may contain important truths; but when one attempts to sift out what is true, one must remember that, as they stand, the assumptions are very schematic, and also that the entire conceptual apparatus employed by Marx must be given more empirical import than it has on his definitions.

I think one is justified in saying that Marx's theory of the rise, evolution, and fall of capitalism is essentially independent of his theory of value. At the same time it is easy to understand that the theory of value must have contributed greatly to the ideological power of Marxism. That all real economic value has its source and its measure in labour, that the exploitation (the surplus value) is a fact that can be ascertained with mathematical exactitude, that the course of capitalism, so it may seem, can be predicted, on the basis of economic laws, with something of the same precision as the path of a cannon ball—all these ideas must have helped to give strength to the socialist labour movement.

43. THE FALL OF CAPITALISM AND THE COMING OF SOCIALISM

A. *The fall of capitalism*

Capitalism, according to Marx, is pregnant with its own death. Some of the factors in the capitalist system which in due time will necessarily bring about its collapse are the following:

(1) The competition from large capitalist industry forces more and more of those producers who work with pre-industrial methods to shut up their shops and sell their labour power to capital. Capitalism thus creates a gradually sharpening division of society into exploiting capitalists and exploited proletarians.

(2) The competition between the capitalists leads to ever greater enterprises. The big capitalists kill the small ones.

(3) In order to increase profit the capitalists are constantly forced to increase production. Increasing production demands a steadily growing market.

(4) The great mass of the proletarians obtain an inadequate purchasing power since a growing number become unemployed through the use of machinery ("the reserve army") and since also the capitalists constantly endeavour to lower wages.

(5) Periodically occurring crises when the entire economic system is brought to a standstill are a necessary feature of capitalism.

(6) The perfect organization within capitalist enterprises and the market's total lack of organization is an obvious absurdity.

(7) In their fight for markets the capitalist states are forced into devastating mutual wars and imperialist conquests.

(8) The diminishing number of the capitalists (or the capitalist enterprises) and the increasing number of the proletarians creates the conditions for the "expropriation of the expropriators".

On the question how the fall of capitalism will take place, Marx and Engels held hardly any settled opinions. They often envisaged a violent revolution, and again and again their hopes were roused by contemporary attempts at revolution (in France and Germany 1848, in France 1871). They sometimes said that "the dictatorship of the proletariat" would usher in the socialist era, yet without explaining what such a dictatorship would be like. They also admitted, however, that socialism might be introduced in a peaceful way in some countries.

B. *Socialism*

The critique that Marx and Engels levelled against the shortcomings of capitalism seems to license the inference that a socialist society as conceived by them would be free from these shortcomings. To the disappointment of the curious reader, however, Marx and Engels say very little about the character of the socialist society they hoped and worked for. Some of their ideas are these:

(1) The means of production (land, factories, etc.) will be public property. Sometimes they say that these means will be owned by "the state". But they also say that the expropriation of the means of production will be the last act of the state as the state, that the state will then wither away, and that the means of production will in the end become the property, not of the "state", but of "society". Engels even declares that the state as owner of the means of production would merely represent capitalist concentration and exploitation carried to its extreme.

How the withering away of the state is to be understood is none too clear. Marx and Engels sometimes seem inclined to define the state as an organization in the hands of the exploiting class for the protection of its interests. If this definition is assumed, the conclusion is obvious that, if there is no exploiting class then there is no state. Possibly, the death of the state is nothing but the disappearance of exploitation. Engels also borrows Saint-Simon's technocratic formula that the government over men will be replaced by the administration of things, by the steering of the process of production.

(2) Production will be organized with regard to social utility: the time devoted to production of various goods will be apportioned according to their "degree of social utility".

(3) Trade in a free market will no longer exist. According to one statement, money, in our accustomed sense, will not exist, only "non-circulating paper cheques" which entitle the productive worker to his share of the social product. At least in an early stage of socialism this share will be in proportion to his labour time. When the socialist society has been brought to perfection, the distribution will follow the maxim: "From each according to his ability to each according to his needs." Understood quite naïvely, this formula envisages a society that is an omniscient providence for its citizens.

In the *Communist Manifesto* a programme is stated whose realization will mark the beginning of socialism:

1. Abolition of property in land and application of all rents of land to public purposes.

2. A heavy progressive or graduated income tax.

3. Abolition of all right of inheritance.

4. Confiscation of the property of all emigrants and rebels.

5. Centralization of credit in the hands of the state, by means of a national bank with state capital and an exclusive monopoly.

6. Centralization of the means of communication and transport in the hands of the state.

7. Extension of factories and means of production owned by the state; the bringing into cultivation of waste lands, and the improvement of the soil generally in accordance with a common plan.

8. Equal liability of all to labour. Establishment of industrial armies, especially for agriculture.

9. Combination of agriculture with manufacturing industries; gradual abolition of the distinction between town and country, by a more equitable distribution of the population over the country.

10. Free education for all children in state schools. Abolition of children's factory labour in its present form. Combination of education with industrial production, etc.

Something that cannot fail to strike a reader of this programme—several items of which have been implemented today in many countries, "capitalist" as well as "socialist" and those with a "mixed economy"—is that the question of political democracy and the entire problem of the political power structure is not touched upon. Of the parliamentary democracies of their own time Marx and Engels entertained a very low opinion, and they were never seriously tempted to let their imagination play with the possibilities of developing democracy. The "freedom" that socialism itself implied, on their view, probably made the "freedom" that political democracy may give appear less important.

The nineteenth century was a century of belief in evolution and of utopias and dreams for the future. When reading the prophecies of Marx and Engels, and other nineteenth-century socialists, one is easily led to think of Jules Verne, who predicted submarines, aeroplanes, and space rockets—but also a voyage to the centre of the earth.

C. *Prophecy and valuation*

In his book *Utopian and Scientific Socialism* (1880) Engels classifies all non-Marxist socialist theories as utopian, while he gives Marxism alone the title of scientific socialism. Some of the features that in the eyes of Marx and Engels distinguish the two kinds of socialism are these:

Utopian socialism	*Scientific socialism*
Regards socialism as a moral ideal	Predicts, on a scientific basis, the fall of capitalism and the coming of socialism
Bases the socialist programme on moral principles of supposedly universal validity	Denies universally valid moral principles
Believes that socialism can be realized by an appeal to the altruistic feelings of the ruling classes	Considers the evolution of society to be determined by economic factors and economic interests: the proletariat is therefore the class that must realize socialism.

It is beyond doubt that Marx and Engels were deeply convinced of the injustice of the capitalist system and that they saw a juster system in socialism. They also thought that capitalism hinders the individual's development as an all-round free personality, while believing that socialism would open the road to this development. At the same time, their critique of so-called utopian socialism involves a tendency to dismiss moral evaluations as subjective and sentimental nonsense, to take up an attitude of "I do not evaluate, I only describe, analyse, and predict". This double attitude is likely to have increased the ideological power of Marxism: it has appeared to speak in the name of justice and at the same time with the impersonal authority of objective science. This attitude is no doubt in part inherited from Hegel. When Hegel describes the history of mankind as the evolution of Spirit or the Idea, he makes no distinction between statements of value and statements of fact. In part the attitude may also have been the solution of a personal dilemma: Marx and Engels were passionately convinced of the rottenness of capitalism and the blessings of socialism, and, at the same time, outside their political activity, they wanted to be cool-headed scientists.

Index